Our Country's
PRESIDENTS

OUR COUNTRY'S

PRESIDENTS

By FRANK FREIDEL
Bullitt Professor of American History
University of Washington

Foreword by MELVILLE BELL GROSVENOR
Editor Emeritus, 1977-1982
NATIONAL GEOGRAPHIC MAGAZINE

Prepared by
National Geographic Special Publications Division

NATIONAL GEOGRAPHIC SOCIETY
Washington, D. C.

OUR COUNTRY'S PRESIDENTS

By Frank Freidel
  Bullitt Professor of American History,
  University of Washington

Published by
  The National Geographic Society,
  Washington, D. C.
  GILBERT M. GROSVENOR, *President*
  MELVIN M. PAYNE, *Chairman of the Board*
  OWEN R. ANDERSON, *Executive Vice President*
  ROBERT L. BREEDEN, *Vice President, Publications*
  and Educational Media

Prepared by
  The Special Publications Division
  DONALD J. CRUMP, *Editor*
  PHILIP B. SILCOTT, *Associate Editor*
  WILLIAM L. ALLEN, WILLIAM R. GRAY, *Senior Editors*

Editorial Staff
  BRUCE BRANDER, DAVID R. BRIDGE, JOHANNA G.
  FARREN, RONALD M. FISHER, MARY ANN HARRELL,
  GERALDINE LINDER, MARGARET C. DEAN
  DORTHY M. CORSON, *Index*

Staff for Ninth Edition
  PAUL D. MARTIN, *Managing Editor*
  ALISON WILBUR, *Picture Editor*
  SUEZ B. KEHL, MARIANNE R. KOSZORUS, *Designers*
  JANE H. BUXTON, *Project Coordinator*
  BETSY BLAIR, ELIZABETH W. FISHER, *Researchers*
  D. RANDY YOUNG, *Design Assistant*
  LOUIS DE LA HABA, *Picture Legends*

Production and Printing
  ROBERT W. MESSER, *Manager*
  GEORGE V. WHITE, *Production Manager*
  RICHARD A. McCLURE, *Production Project Manager*
  MARK R. DUNLEVY, RAJA D. MURSHED, CHRISTINE
  A. ROBERTS, DAVID V. SHOWERS, GREGORY STORER,
  Assistant Production Managers; KATE DONOHUE,
  Production Staff Assistant
NANCY F. BERRY, PAMELA A. BLACK, BARBARA
  BRICKS, NETTIE BURKE, CLAIRE M. DOIG, JANET
  DYER, ROSAMUND GARNER, VICTORIA D. GARRETT,
  SUZANNE J. JACOBSON, VIRGINIA A. McCOY, CLEO
  PETROFF, TAMMY PRESLEY, CAROL A. ROCHELEAU,
  JENNY TAKACS, *Staff Assistants*
JOLENE M. BLOZIS, *Index*

ISBN 87044-024-1
Ninth Edition, Library of Congress Catalog Card No. 81-48067
Second Printing 1983

Tulips and grape hyacinths ring the fountain directly in front of the North Portico entrance of the
White House, where the President often greets official visitors. *Pages 2-3:* Washington takes the
oath of office in New York City, 1789. (Illustration
courtesy of the New York Historical Society.)

JAMES P. BLAIR, NATIONAL GEOGRAPHIC PHOTOGRAPHER

CONTENTS

FOREWORD

A FEW DECADES AGO, it was easy for any Washington resident to meet the President and First Lady. Until the early thirties the White House was always open on New Year's Day, and anyone who cared to stand in a long line could shake the Presidential hand.

Because I lived in Washington, and because my father was a distant cousin of William Howard Taft, I went to the White House as a boy of eight and got a chance to ride the President's private elevator. I ascended to the roof and there helped a guard haul up the United States Flag. For an eight-year-old, that elevator ride was as great a thrill as meeting President Taft himself, a big, jolly, and brilliant figure—and one of thirteen U. S. Presidents I have had the good fortune to meet.

I remember Theodore Roosevelt as an ex-President, weakened by fevers from his expedition to the South American River of Doubt. He reported on his explorations at a National Geographic Society lecture on a stiflingly hot afternoon in 1914, and he gave me an autographed picture that still hangs on my office wall. As a newly commissioned U. S. Navy ensign I marched in President Harding's funeral procession on a sweltering August day in 1923. At a Coolidge reception I saw Mrs. Coolidge in the same red dress pictured on page 181. I recall Franklin D. Roosevelt, with his big infectious smile, putting his guests instantly at ease. Once I watched him talk to a crusty political critic—and turn an adversary into an admirer with his famous charm.

The person of the President—any President—is touched with magic. The office illuminates the man. And as we meet the country's leader, in person or by reading a good biography, we shake hands with history.

In 1964, as a public service, the National Geographic Society produced a booklet on the Presidents for the White House Historical Association. One-page profiles by Frank Freidel, then professor of history at Harvard, accompanied each Presidential portrait.

Professor Freidel greatly amplified and enriched these sketches in the five-part series on the Presidents that appeared in NATIONAL GEOGRAPHIC. Members of the Society all over the world wrote letters asking that the series, with its exceptional collection of illustrations, be printed in book form. The Society responded with this volume. "The biographies of our Presidents are the stories of fallible men doing the best they can," President Lyndon B. Johnson wrote. "These are stories of human growth."

In this book we also see the growth of a Nation and of Presidential responsibilities. John Adams did the national business from his simple stand-up desk. Today President Ronald Reagan's chores are multiplied by the needs of more than 225 million Americans and the policies of more than 160 independent countries.

Said President Johnson as he dedicated the Society's new headquarters on January 18, 1964: "You have broadened the horizons and narrowed the misunderstandings of many generations; and you have helped us all to be better citizens of the world and better citizens of our time."

Ever mindful of this responsibility—and the need for knowledge of the past as perspective for wise judgments in the future—the National Geographic Society offers *Our Country's Presidents*.

Melville Bell Grosvenor

1 THE PRESIDENCY

ENGRAVING BY H. S. SADD FROM A PAINTING BY T. H. MATTESON

First President of the United States, George Washington gives his Inaugural Address in New York City, April 30, 1789. So nervous that his voice was often inaudible, he apologized for being

AND HOW IT GREW

George Washington through John Quincy Adams

"unpracticed in...civil administration" and announced that he would accept no salary.

O N THAT APRIL DAY in 1789 when President George Washington, hands trembling with emotion, delivered his first Inaugural Address to the First Congress, he was well aware of the momentous nature of the enterprise upon which he and the fledgling United States of America were embarked.

"The preservation of the sacred fire of liberty, and the destiny of the Republican model of Government," he pointed out, "are justly considered as *deeply,* perhaps as *finally* staked, on the experiment entrusted to the hands of the American people."

At the heart of that experiment was the Presidency. Washington was well aware that he must carry a large part of the responsibility for the success or failure of the new Government. The framers of the Constitution had provided in outline for a strong Chief Executive but had filled in few of the details. Washington had presided over their deliberations; they had envisaged him as the first President, and were ready to rely upon his judgment and discretion. Generations of Americans have relied similarly upon his successors, as slowly the modern Presidency has evolved with the modern Nation.

After eight years, Washington turned over to John Adams the office he had so effectively established. Adams in turn further molded the Presidency, as indeed have all the Presidents of the United States. Each has accepted the office as a solemn responsibility; each has brought to it the best of his talents.

No change has been more spectacular over the years—now nearly two centuries—than the sheer increase in the scope of the office. The Nation of four million agricultural people, which began as a hazardous experiment in the age of Enlightenment, now has a population that surpasses 225 million; moreover, it has become the prime bulwark of democracy throughout the world.

9

President John Adams, more than a century and a half ago, thought the demands of the office were serious enough. "A peck of troubles in a large bundle of papers, often in a handwriting almost illegible, comes every day," he complained to his wife, Abigail.

Yet even during the quasi war with France, Adams spent long summer months at his farm in Massachusetts. To be sure, even George Washington criticized President Adams for doing so, but the volume of business was so slight that Adams could conduct it from a single stand-up desk in which he allotted a pigeonhole to each department.

As the administrative branch of the Federal Government has grown, Presidents have been forced to slough off many of their earlier routine duties; they no longer sign a fraction of the documents that confronted John Adams, or even Woodrow Wilson. They have been forced to acquire large staffs to deal with many of the lesser problems that confronted their predecessors. Their increasing burdens made them curtail what earlier citizens had regarded as an American's prerogative—the right to call at the White House and meet the Chief Executive in person.

Some Presidents regarded their years in the White House as an exciting adventure; some found the office onerous. Years before he himself became President, Franklin D. Roosevelt liked to recount how, as a child, he had been ushered in to see Grover Cleveland, who solemnly expressed the hope that the boy would avoid the fate of growing up to be President.

With few exceptions the Presidents have felt themselves peculiarly representative of all the American people, regardless of party or sectional differences.

"In a government like ours," Thomas Jefferson wrote in a private letter in 1810, "it is the duty of the Chief Magistrate . . . to endeavor, by all honorable means, to unite in himself the confidence of the whole people. This alone, in any case where the energy of the nation is required, can produce a union of the powers of the whole, and point them in a single direction, as if all constituted but one body and one mind. . . ."

How vigorously the President should assert his powers in behalf of the people was a subject of debate through much of the 19th century and into the 20th.

When Andrew Jackson began to make extensive use of the Presidential veto to thwart his opponents in Congress, and through asserting his party leadership tried to shape Congressional actions, he came under vehement attack. His enemies dubbed him King Andrew I. Seeking an analogy with British Parliaments which had fought against royal usurpations, they labeled themselves "Whigs."

Several 19th-century Presidents, most notably William Henry Harrison, accepted the Whig view that they should not tamper with the policy-making prerogatives of Congress. Abraham Lincoln as an Illinois Congressman in 1848 concurred, but later as President in 1861 he stretched the powers of the Presidency to the utmost.

His successor, Andrew Johnson, vetoed the Civil Rights Act of 1866 and Reconstruction legislation, but Congress repeatedly overrode his vetoes, and, through impeachment, almost removed him from office.

Most Presidents after Johnson were more amenable to Congress, but James A. Garfield, during a dispute over patronage, wrote privately: "It better be known, in the outset, whether the President is the head of the Government, or the registering clerk of the Senate."

STRONG PRESIDENTS came into the ascendancy with the advent in 1901 of Theodore Roosevelt, who assumed energetic command in shaping both domestic programs and foreign policies. He too had to face a recalcitrant Congress. In 1936 the second Roosevelt recalled seeing his distant cousin clench his fist and exclaim, "Sometimes I wish I could be President and Congress too." Franklin D. Roosevelt added, "Well, I suppose if the truth were told, he is not the only President that has had that idea."

Like Washington, succeeding Presidents have felt an overwhelming sense of responsibility. Harry S. Truman jauntily displayed a sign on his desk, "The buck stops here," and confessed in his memoirs: "To be President of the United States is to be lonely, very lonely, at times of great decisions."

Since the day that Washington took his oath of office, the American Presidency has inspired awe both in its incumbent and in beholders, combining as it does effective power with enlightened responsibility. The Presidency, in combination and interaction with the Congress and the Supreme Court, repeatedly gives fresh manifestation that in the American Republic a free people can govern themselves with competence and vigor without sacrificing their traditional rights.

The "sacred fire of liberty" to which Washington dedicated his first administration glows on with undiminished brilliance, a beacon to all mankind.

Lincoln's Cabinet hears the Emancipation Proclamation. He expanded the powers of the Presidency.

Cleveland tells 5-year-old Franklin D. Roosevelt: ". . . I wish for you that you may never be President. . . ."

Theodore Roosevelt, a cousin of F. D. R., said of the Presidency: "Ripping, simply ripping!"

Happy to be rid of the burdens of the White House, Taft smiles at Wilson's Inauguration.

F. D. R. in Galveston, 1937, meets a young Texan he will support for Congress: Lyndon B. Johnson, who became the 36th President.

Serious steps at Camp David, Maryland. Kennedy (left) seeks Eisenhower's advice after the Bay of Pigs invasion of Cuba in 1961.

GEORGE WASHINGTON, as generations of school children have been taught, was the Father of his Country, and, in the words of Henry Lee, "first in war, first in peace, and first in the hearts of his countrymen." Olympian among Presidents, Washington even in his own lifetime was almost obscured as a person by the awe-inspiring legend enveloping him. But behind the legend stands an impressive human being who, foremost among that gifted coterie of Founding Fathers, wrought a new United States and guided it through its first years.

Decades of training prepared Washington for his leadership in the Revolution and the establishment of the new Republic. Born in 1732 into a planter family in Virginia, Washington received from his parents and half brothers schooling in the morals, manners, and body of knowledge requisite for an 18th-century Virginia gentleman. His birthplace at Wakefield is commemorated with a reconstructed brick mansion on the original plantation site in Westmoreland County. It is now a national monument.

In his youth, Washington pursued two intertwined interests that gave direction to much of his life—military arts and western expansion. War was almost a normal condition of affairs in those days, as the rivalry between England and France erupted intermittently into lengthy conflict. Washington's half brother Lawrence served in an expedition against Cartagena in Colombia, one of the possessions of the French ally, Spain, and named his estate on the Potomac in honor of the commander, Adm. Edward Vernon. In time, Washington acquired the property and retained the name, Mount Vernon.

At 16 Washington helped survey Shenandoah lands for Thomas, Lord Fairfax. Thereafter he spent much of his life in the saddle, surveying or soldiering in the wilderness.

In 1753, when French soldiers trespassed on lands claimed by Virginia in the Ohio country, Governor Robert Dinwiddie sent the 21-year-old Washington to warn them away. The following year, commissioned a lieutenant colonel, he fought the first skirmishes in what grew into the French and Indian War. The French defeated Washington and his force of about 300 men, and in 1755 surrounded and routed the British regulars under Gen. Edward Braddock. Washington, who served as an aide to Braddock, escaped injury, although four bullets ripped his coat and two horses were shot from under him.

Young Washington holds a surveying instrument while his companion pays out chain to fix distance. At 14 Washington surveyed his neighbors' fields. At 16 he plotted Lord Fairfax's lands, sleeping under "one thread Bear blanket with double its Weight of Vermin. . . ." His boyhood home, Ferry Farm, near Fredericksburg, Virginia, is open to the public. Wakefield, the farm on which Washington was born in 1732, is now a national monument.

Giant of his time, Washington stood six feet two and weighed 200 pounds. Gilbert Stuart's portrait is the only object in the White House that has been there since its occupancy in 1800. Dolley Madison in 1814 delayed her flight from the invading British until she safeguarded the canvas.

ENGRAVING BY G. R. HALL FROM A PAINTING
BY F. O. C. DARLEY, LIBRARY OF CONGRESS

Painting by Gilbert Stuart, White House Collection

For several years thereafter, as a colonel commanding a force of only 300 Virginians, he undertook the difficult task of defending a 350-mile frontier against Indian raids.

From 1759 to the outbreak of the American Revolution, Washington enjoyed a placid life, managing his lands around Mount Vernon and serving in the Virginia House of Burgesses. Married to a widow, Martha Dandridge Custis, he devoted himself to a busy but happy round of life among his stepchildren and friends, enlivened by fox hunts and much entertaining. He played hard, but he worked hard also. Supervising his estates called for managerial skill.

Like his fellow planters, Washington felt himself exploited by British merchants and hampered by British Government regulations. His experiences both as a planter and as a military leader made him increasingly dissatisfied with the Crown.

As the quarrel between the colonists and the mother country grew increasingly acute, Washington moderately but firmly voiced his resistance to British restrictions. He warned, "... more blood will be spilt ... if the ministry are determined to push matters to extremity, than history has ever yet furnished instances of in the annals of North America."

Washington and his fellow Virginians were of no temper to stand by while British troops stifled liberty in the colonies. He was elected

Rebuilt stockade and storehouse revive Fort Necessity near Union (now Uniontown), Pennsylvania. Washington built the fort in 1754 while leading an expedition against the French. His march out to surprise a French detachment touched off the French and Indian War. When he returned to Fort Necessity, a 900-man French force attacked. After a day's fighting in a driving rainstorm, he surrendered and returned to Virginia with his disarmed men. The defeat—Washington's only formal surrender—induced Great Britain to send an expedition to Virginia under Gen. Edward Braddock. Washington joined him as an aide.

Washington reads the burial service over General Braddock. Ignorant of frontier warfare, Braddock rejected the idea of fighting French and Indians with their own guerrilla tactics. As he advanced on Fort Duquesne (Pittsburgh) in 1755, he and half his men fell in battle. Retreating wagons ran over Braddock's grave to obliterate all signs lest Indians dig up the body for its scalp.

a delegate to the Second Continental Congress. By the time it assembled in Philadelphia in May, 1775, the battles at Lexington and Concord had taken place. Now a southerner was needed to command the minutemen assembled at Cambridge. Such a leader would bring the backing of all the colonies to the struggle thus far confined to New England. Of all the delegates to the Continental Congress, Washington was most imposing in his chosen blue uniform as a Virginia militia commander, and Congress elected him commander in chief.

On July 3, 1775, at Cambridge, Massachusetts, Washington assumed command of the ill-trained army and embarked upon a war that was to last six grueling years. The unwillingness of the British Government to grant concessions soon made apparent to Washington that this must be a war for independence—a viewpoint Congress confirmed on July 4, 1776.

Washington faced discouraging obstacles. The new state governments were usually lukewarm in their support, and Congress, often suspicious of Washington's military power, seldom gave him the men and supplies he needed. Washington, far from assuming dictatorial powers, was compliant with the orders of Congress, even, at times, when they went against his military judgment.

Working such long hours that biographers

First First Lady. Martha Washington paid $28 to Charles Willson Peale to paint this miniature in 1776, when she was 45. Later she described herself as an "old-fashioned Virginia house-keeper, steady as a clock, busy as a bee, and cheerful as a cricket."

Mount Vernon yearly receives more than a million visitors, who respond to Washington's own invitation: "I have no objection to any sober or orderly person's gratifying their curiosity in viewing the buildings, Gardens, &ca. about Mount Vernon." He felt "No estate in United America is more pleasantly situated" than his Potomac-side home.

have wondered when he found time to sleep, he somehow managed to build and maintain an army. He realized early that the best strategy for his weak, inexperienced troops was to harass the British rather than risk an all-out assault. He reported to Congress that "we should on all Occasions avoid a general Action, or put anything to the Risque, unless compelled by a necessity, into which we ought never to be drawn."

In ensuing years, from time to time he fell back slowly before superior British forces, then struck unexpectedly. It was sound strategy, and while Washington has seldom been ranked among the most skillful generals, he was an able commander.

Above all, he demonstrated his singular organizing talents and his unparalleled fortitude in the face of adversity. It was this fortitude that carried him through the bleak winter of 1777-78 at Valley Forge, where the State of Pennsylvania has restored his camp with its log huts and one-room hospital. The same steadfastness also carried him through later discouragements, even after—with the aid of French allies—he had forced Cornwallis to surrender in 1781 at Yorktown, where earthworks still bristle with cannon.

Yorktown ended the active fighting, but the Continental Army remained unpaid and restless. To Washington's acute dismay, one of the colonels proposed making him king.

NATIONAL GEOGRAPHIC PHOTOGRAPHER THOMAS NEBBIA

But, like his Roman model Cincinnatus, he wished upon the conclusion of peace in 1783 to retire to his fields.

As Washington, back at Mount Vernon, soon came to realize, the American Nation under its Confederation Government was not functioning very well. Powers were inadequate to maintain respect for American shippers and merchants overseas, to protect the frontier against incursions by British fur traders and marauding Indians, or to restrain the states from engaging in economic reprisals against each other.

"Internal dissentions, and jarrings with our Neighbours," wrote Washington, "are not only productive of mischievous consequences, as it respects ourselves, but has a tendency to lessen our national character, and importance in the eyes of European powers."

The news that Massachusetts farmers had taken up arms against heavy taxation led Washington to lament, "We are fast verging to anarchy and confusion!" Hence he became an influential mover in the steps leading to the Constitutional Convention at Philadelphia in the summer of 1787. Washington, presiding over the Convention, took little part in the debates, but lent his great conciliatory talents and his prestige to the framing of a stronger government.

As everyone had expected, as soon as the Constitution had been ratified and the new

17

SILVER EAGLE *adorned a cockade on Washington's hat. The accessories below served the Father of his Country through the years of the Revolutionary War. Mount Vernon displays the mementos.*

BONE-INLAID KNIFE *and fork went with the general on his campaigns.*

SILVER SPURS *from his own boots were given by Washington to Lt. Thomas Lamb, with orders to bring supplies to Valley Forge.*

AT VALLEY FORGE, *Washington and young Lafayette share their soldiers' hardships in the bitter winter of 1777-78. The general's indomitable will sustained the Continental Army of 11,000 men. Many died at that camp, few deserted him.*

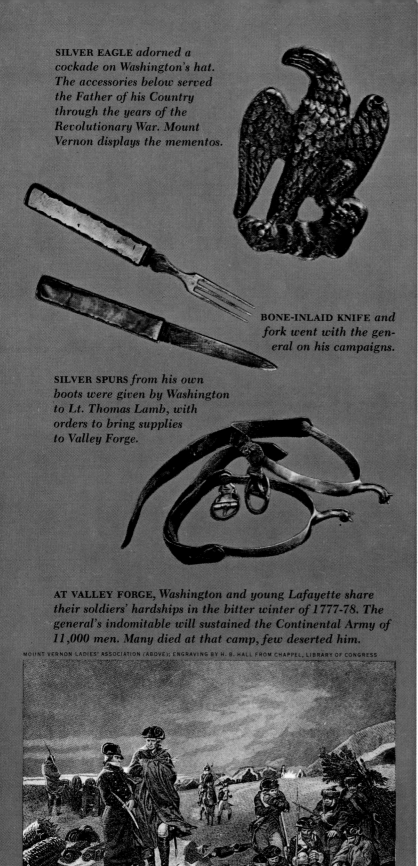

Lord Cornwallis's army marches out of Yorktown in surrender on October 19, 1781 —last great conflict of the Revolution. Victory marked the end of six years in which Washington fought the British in the field and withstood cabals aimed at undermining his authority. Declining salary, he paid his own expenses; Congress reimbursed him after the war. Tardy enlistments and discouraging desertions never eroded his devotion to the cause of liberty.

In John Trumbull's oil painting, displayed in the U. S. Capitol, Washington sits on a brown charger. His deputy, Maj. Gen. Benjamin Lincoln, on the white horse, conducts the British file to stack their arms. Washington delegated the honor because Cornwallis refused to appear.

UNITED STATES CAPITOL HISTORICAL SOCIETY

machinery of government began to operate, the electoral college unanimously cast its ballots for Washington for President. With considerable misgivings, Washington accepted.

On April 30, 1789, Washington, standing on the balcony of Federal Hall on Wall Street in New York, took his oath of office as the first President of the United States. When he entered the Senate chamber to deliver his Inaugural Address before the assembled Congress, his face was grave. His voice was low and the words almost inaudible.

The challenge facing President Washington and the fledgling Government gave him full reason to be grave. The United States was a weak agricultural republic in a world dominated by large unfriendly monarchies. Its population in 1790 was only 4,000,000, of whom 700,000 were slaves; its treasury was empty; it possessed no army or navy worthy of the name. The Constitution was no more than a framework, silent on many details.

"As the first of every thing, *in our situation* will serve to establish a Precedent," Washington wrote James Madison, "it is devoutly wished on my part, that these precedents may be fixed on true principles."

"Washington's Presidency was nothing if not painfully constitutional," Clinton Rossiter has written; Washington "did the new republic a mighty service by proving that power can ennoble as well as corrupt...."

Washington was of no disposition to infringe upon the policy-making powers that he felt the Constitution bestowed upon the Congress, and, except for exploring questions of constitutionality, did not question measures it enacted. On the other hand, the determination of foreign policy became preponderantly a Presidential concern.

When Washington, accepting literally the constitutional proviso that he should negotiate treaties with the advice and consent of the Senate, appeared before that body in person with a list of queries, the Senators, jealous of their prerogatives, refused to give him instant

19

answers. "This defeats every purpose of my coming here," Washington fumed. Thereafter he negotiated treaties as he judged best and sent them to the Senate to ratify or reject.

Again, while the Senate, according to the Constitution, had to give its consent to Presidential appointees, Washington insisted he could remove them without permission.

As Chief Executive, Washington gave considerable authority to his department heads, and gradually came to depend upon them for advice, at first through written opinions, then as a Cabinet. At these meetings, unlike most of his successors, he ordinarily did not set forth his own opinion, and unless the Cabinet was evenly divided, followed the recommendation of its majority.

This reluctance to wield executive authority singlehandedly has led many later historians to feel that Washington was eclipsed by his subordinates. It is easy to overlook the fact that Washington, while slow and deliberate, was also thorough in his analysis of problems,

and that he was more balanced in judgment than his subordinates. There was never any question at the time but that Washington was President, and that national policies had to have his approval. And Thomas Jefferson in 1796 admitted, "One man outweighs them all in influence over the people."

Jefferson spoke from firsthand knowledge, since clearly, during the years when Jefferson served as Secretary of State (and thereafter also), Washington's was the controlling hand in foreign affairs. Even before he became President, he felt strongly that it would be disastrous for the new Nation to become embroiled in the quarrels of the European titans. He wrote in 1788, "I hope the United States of America will be able to keep disengaged from the labyrinth of European politics and Wars.... It should be the policy of United America to administer to their wants, without being engaged in their quarrels."

When the French Revolution led to a major war between France and Britain, Jefferson,

"G. Washington" in the map title shows the autograph of the 19-year-old surveyor. Four decades later, full of years and honors, the President introduced more flourishes but still clung basically to the firm signature of his youth.

Victorious after long years of war, Washington resigns command of the Continental Army to resume the life of a Virginia squire, December 23, 1783. Edwin White's canvas hangs in the Annapolis State House, where Washington laid down his military power.

TRAVELS OF G. Washington

National Geographic Map by Lisa Biganzoli and John Garst after Aaron Arrowsmith's map of 1796 © N.G.S.

Washington's Secretary of State, was ardently pro-French, and Alexander Hamilton, his Secretary of the Treasury, equally pro-British. Washington would not be swayed by either; he insisted upon following a middle, neutral course until the United States could become stronger. Given twenty years of tranquillity, he believed, the American Nation could become sufficiently powerful to "bid defiance in a just cause to any power whatever." Thanks to the course that Washington firmly set, the United States gained those twenty years.

In one respect, Washington failed to envisage the direction the American Commonwealth would take. Like many of his contemporaries, he found the idea of political parties repugnant. He expected to be "President of all the people" and was disappointed when by the end of his first administration two parties began to develop. He tried to keep both the contending leaders, Hamilton and Jefferson, within his Cabinet. But if he had been forced to choose, his would have been more nearly the Hamiltonian position. At the end of 1793 Jefferson resigned, and by 1795 Washington was appointing to office only men of known Federalist views.

In creating respect for the United States, Washington felt he must comport himself with as much formality and ceremony as though he were a republican monarch. The firm insistence upon ceremonial had its advantages. When Washington visited Massachusetts at the end of his first year in office,

Master oarsmen row the Father of his Country up the East River. New York City tumultuously welcomes the hero, arriving from Mount Vernon for his first Inaugural. Washington recorded himself both pleased and pained by "the display of boats ... the roar of cannon, and the loud acclamations of the people as I passed along." He took his oath of office as the first President of the United States, April 30, 1789, and spectators gave three cheers.

President Washington (right), impressive in his dignity as in his stature, consults the four senior officers of the new executive branch: (from left) Edmund Randolph, Attorney General; Henry Knox, Secretary of War; Thomas Jefferson, Secretary of State; Alexander Hamilton, Secretary of the Treasury. In conferences like this, he weighed their advice but reserved major decisions for himself, aware that he was setting precedents for the Nation. From such small beginnings came the Cabinet of today.

ENGRAVING BY J. ROGERS FROM J. McNEVIN · PAINTING BY E. P. OTTENDORFF, COURTESY CONTINENTAL INSURANCE COMPANY

Governor John Hancock tried to force the President to pay the first call, and, failing, gave way. The President, thereafter, would take precedence over governors. But Washington found ceremonies a burden; privately he expressed his longing for Mount Vernon.

Wearied of politics, feeling old and tired, he determined to retire at the end of his second term. In September, 1796, as his political testament, he published a Farewell Address in which he urged his countrymen to form a union of hearts and minds, forswearing excessive party spirit and geographical distinctions. In foreign affairs, he warned against long-term alliances. The United States should demonstrate to Europe that "we act for *ourselves,* and not for *others.*"

Washington enjoyed less than three years of retirement at Mount Vernon, for he died of a throat infection December 14, 1799. The four-poster in which he lay still stands in his room looking down on the Potomac.

For months the entire Nation mourned him. Orators and preachers paid tribute with flowery hyperbole, but said less than Abigail, the wife of President John Adams, who commented to her sister: "He never grew giddy, but ever maintained a modest diffidence of his own talents.... Possessed of power, possessed of an extensive influence, he never used it but for the benefit of his country.... If we look through the whole tenor of his life, history will not produce to us a parallel."

John Adams

SECOND PRESIDENT 1797-1801

JOHN ADAMS is known as the President who saved the United States from fighting a needless war. He once suggested for his epitaph, "Here lies John Adams, who took upon himself the responsibility of the peace with France, in the year 1800."

This was Adams's crowning achievement, but he was also one of the leading patriots in the long struggle for colonial rights, a prime mover for the Declaration of Independence, a valued diplomat, the first Vice President, and the second President.

Adams was a learned and thoughtful man, master of the classics and the law, and more remarkable as a political philosopher than as a politician. "People and nations are forged in the fires of adversity," he once asserted, doubtless thinking of his own as well as the American experience.

For several generations his forebears had farmed stony fields at Braintree in Massachusetts Bay Colony. There, in 1735, Adams was born. The house still stands, the oldest original Presidential birthplace. It and the smaller house next door, where his son John Quincy was born, are preserved as historic sites in what is now Quincy.

Though early identified with the patriot cause, John Adams, a Harvard-educated lawyer, undertook the unpopular task of defending the British officer who he felt was unjustly charged with responsibility for the Boston Massacre. The officer was acquitted.

Adams was distrustful of mobs, yet considered the Boston Tea Party, which dumped cargoes of taxed tea into the harbor, "the grandest event which has ever yet happened since the controversy with Britain opened."

He became one of the most vigorous delegates to the First and Second Continental Congresses. By the summer of 1776 he was a leader in the movement for independence.

Adams spent most of the remainder of the Revolutionary War on diplomatic missions, serving in France and Holland and helping negotiate the Treaty of Peace. From 1785 to 1788 he was Minister to the Court of St. James's, returning in time to be elected Vice President under George Washington. Adams's two terms as Vice President were frustrating experiences for a man of his vigor, intellect, and vanity. When he suggested an elaborate title for the President, his reward was to be himself mocked as "His Rotundity."

Like Washington, Adams seldom tried to act as a party leader; he left the organization of the Federalists to Hamilton. In his political thinking, Adams was more moderate than

Wife of one President, mother of another, Abigail Adams managed the Adams farm in Massachusetts during the Revolution. Experience in Paris and London as a diplomat's wife made her an astute First Lady. Adams usually sought her advice on public problems, relying on her good sense. First mistress of the White House, she hung washing in the unfinished East Room to dry.

Burning with patriotic fire, strong-minded John Adams put oratory and law training to good use in the Revolutionary struggle. In the Continental Congress he led the floor fight for the Declaration of Independence.

24

PAINTING BY GILBERT STUART, NATIONAL GALLERY OF ART, GIFT OF MRS. ROBERT HOMANS

Painting by Edgar Parker, White House Collection

Hamilton. Both men were afraid of the volatile masses and feared that a government responsive to them might bring on excesses like the French Reign of Terror. But Adams, unlike Hamilton, regarded government by the well-born and rich as equally distasteful. To him the British political institutions, "purged of their corruptions," seemed ideal.

Adams's stubborn moderation was badly needed as he took over the administration from Washington. The war between the French and British was causing great difficulties for the United States on the high seas and intense partisanship among contending factions at home. As Washington was leaving office, Jefferson wrote, "The President is fortunate to get off just as the bubble is bursting, leaving others to hold the bag."

Although Adams delivered a mild Inaugural Address, promising that he would continue Washington's policies, the Hamiltonians considered him too conciliatory toward the Jeffersonians. And the party of Jefferson became increasingly hostile.

(By 1792 Jefferson's followers called themselves "Republicans," but the Republican Party of today had its beginnings in the 1850's.)

The focus of the new administration was upon France, where the Directory, the ruling group, had refused to receive the American envoy and had suspended commercial relations. Adams, calling Congress into special session, announced what in effect was a war crisis. He recommended the arming of merchant ships, the speedy building of a navy, and if necessary the recruiting of a larger

Spectacles and quill pen rest atop a stained diary in the John Adams House at Quincy, Massachusetts, as if the writer had merely paused to rub tired eyes. Adams in 1775 began a collection of family diaries and papers that by 1889 had mounted to 400,000 pieces and is now being published.

Wisteria climbs the Old House in Quincy, which John Adams bought in 1787. Four generations of Adamses brought furnishings from missions abroad.

Birthplaces of two Presidents began as farmhouses. Preserved as national historic sites, they look much the same as in this 1852 woodcut, but now the town of Quincy surrounds them. John Adams was born in the wooden salt box on the right, built about 1681. His son John Quincy was born in the other cottage, dating from 1716.

army. Republicans in Congress whittled the recommendations to authorization of three frigates, the calling out of 80,000 militiamen if needed, and the arming of only those merchantmen in the East Indies or Mediterranean trade.

Adams sent three commissioners to France, but in the spring of 1798 word arrived that the French Foreign Minister Talleyrand and the Directory had refused to negotiate with them unless they would first pay a substantial bribe. Adams reported the insult to Congress, and the Senate printed and distributed the correspondence, in which the Frenchmen were referred to only as "X, Y, and Z."

The Nation broke out into what Jefferson called "the X. Y. Z. fever," increased in intensity by Adams's exhortations. He stated that there was "no alternative between war and submission to the Executive of France." The populace cheered itself hoarse wherever the President appeared. Never had the Federalists been so popular. Congress appropriated money to complete the three new frigates and build additional ships, and authorized the raising of a provisional army.

President Adams did not call for a declaration of war, but hostilities began on the seas. At first, American shipping was almost defenseless against French privateers. But by 1800, armed merchantmen and U. S. warships were clearing the sea lanes. The most famous of that fleet survives today.

The *Constitution*—"Her deck, once red with heroes' blood" —is on exhibition at the Boston Navy Yard. No mere museum, "Old Ironsides" still ranks as a commissioned ship of the United States Navy.

Despite several brilliant naval victories, Adams saw the war fever gradually subside. Accompanying its defense measures, the Federalist administration had passed the Alien and Sedition Acts, intended to frighten foreign agents out of the country

Undeclared war against France stirred national pride, and President Adams called for ships like the U. S. frigate *Constellation* that captured *L'Insurgente* in 1799. A contemporary engraving records her success: crossing the Frenchman's bow, she attacks with a broadside.

Defying critics in his own party, Adams negotiated a settlement when he thought peace would serve his country best.

Diplomats of victory prepare to sign the treaty ending the Revolutionary War in 1783, at Paris. Adams, Benjamin Franklin, and secretary Temple Franklin sit; John Jay (left) and Henry Laurens stand. A British delegate died, and artist Benjamin West left this painting unfinished.

and to stifle the attacks of Republican editors. Harsh prosecution transformed several of these editors into martyrs and unified the Republican Party. Moreover, the French crisis was costly, almost doubling the Federal budget between 1796 and 1800 and necessitating heavy and unpopular taxes.

Soon President Adams had second thoughts about the wisdom of a war and returned to his customary moderation. Word came that France also had no stomach for war and would receive a new envoy with respect. Long negotiations ended the quasi war.

The sending of the peace mission launched against Adams the full fury of Hamilton and his devotees. In the campaign of 1800 the Republicans were united and effective; the Federalists were badly divided. Nevertheless, Adams polled only eight fewer electoral votes than Jefferson, who became President.

Just before the election—on November 1, 1800—Adams arrived in the new capital city to take up his residence in the White House. On his second evening in its damp, unfinished rooms, he wrote his wife, "Before I end my letter, I pray Heaven to bestow the best of Blessings on this House and all that shall hereafter inhabit it. May none but honest and wise men ever rule under this roof."

Adams retired to his farm in Quincy, living many years in the mansion known as the Old House, now a national historic site. From that spacious home—where succeeding generations of Adamses have added to the family archives—he penned his elaborate letters to Thomas Jefferson.

In this house, on July 4, 1826, he whispered his last words: "Thomas Jefferson survives." But Jefferson had died at Monticello a few hours earlier.

The American people were awestruck that they had lost two of their greatest Founding Fathers on the same day—the 50th anniversary of the Declaration of Independence.

THOMAS JEFFERSON, taking his oath of office in March, 1801, for the first time shifted the administration from the control of one political party to another. He came into office in the wake of years of the bitterest party strife and amidst the dire predictions of the High Federalists, who feared he would destroy the political and economic institutions so carefully erected in the previous 12 years. Quite the reverse proved true. In his Inaugural Address he proclaimed policies of moderation and tolerance:

"... every difference of opinion is not a difference of principle.... If there be any among us who would wish to dissolve this Union or to change its republican form, let them stand undisturbed as monuments of the safety with which error of opinion may be tolerated where reason is left free to combat it."

During Jefferson's eight years in office, despite the titanic conflict in Europe between Napoleon and his foes, the United States continued to grow in population, doubled in area, and during most of the time prospered. Jefferson was an agrarian and highly popular as the spokesman for an overwhelmingly agrarian country.

Less a states' rights advocate than an ardent believer in the future of the American Republic and indeed of all mankind, Jefferson's noble dream, as Julian Boyd, the editor of his papers, has pointed out, was an "empire of liberty."

This powerful advocate of liberty was born in 1743 in Albemarle County, Virginia, at that time on the outer fringe of the British empire in America. He inherited from his father, a planter and surveyor, some 5,000 acres of land, and from his mother, a Randolph, high social standing. He studied at the College of William and Mary, then prepared himself as a lawyer; he also developed the rich sweep of interests that so distinguished him as a man.

In 1772 he married Martha Wayles Skelton and took her to live in his partly constructed mountaintop home, Monticello, with its

Deliberately informal, Thomas Jefferson wore his hair without powder and gave parties without protocol. A noted scholar, he owned so many books that when the British burned the Library of Congress in 1814, he sold it some 6,000 of his volumes.

As committee chairman, Jefferson hears his colleagues' comments on the Declaration of Independence he has composed for the Continental Congress meeting in Philadelphia's Independence Hall. Committee members Benjamin Franklin (left), Jefferson, John Adams, Robert R. Livingston, and Roger Sherman altered it slightly. Congress revised and proclaimed it July 4, 1776.

ENGRAVING FROM A PAINTING BY ALONZO CHAPPEL FROM "LIFE AND TIMES OF WASHINGTON," BY J. F. SCHROEDER, LIBRARY OF CONGRESS

Painting by Rembrandt Peale, White House Collection

sweeping view across the valleys and ridges. He practiced law successfully and managed his large estates.

Young Thomas Jefferson, freckled and sandy-haired, rather tall and awkward, was charming among his friends and eloquent as a correspondent, but he was no public speaker. In contrast to Patrick Henry, whom he admired, Jefferson, both in the Virginia House of Burgesses and the Continental Congress, contributed his pen rather than his voice to the patriot cause.

As the "silent member" of the Congress with the "reputation of a masterly pen," Jefferson, aged 33, drafted the Declaration of Independence. It was distinguished, like his other works, less by its originality than the felicity with which it set forth the grievances of the revolutionaries and asserted their natural rights.

In the next several years Jefferson labored to make its words a reality in Virginia. Most notably, he drafted a bill establishing religious freedom, enacted in 1786. It declared that, because "Almighty God hath created the mind free," a man has the right to think as he pleases without interference from the government, and that he should possess "the comfortable liberty of giving his contributions to the particular pastor whose morals he would make his pattern."

JEFFERSON, in the Confederation Congress, made another remarkable contribution with his reports on the government of western territory, out of which came the Northwest Ordinance of 1784. It provided that western territories when sufficiently populous should enter the Union as states coequal with the original thirteen.

In 1785 Jefferson succeeded Benjamin Franklin as Minister to France. Like his predecessor, he was respected as a scientist and man of wide learning, and like Franklin he was a hardheaded diplomat. He was intimate with the moderates who were in control in the early stages of the French Revolution, and despite later excesses, which he deplored, remained basically sympathetic toward the Revolution. This sympathy led him into conflict with Hamilton, when Jefferson served as Secretary of State in President Washington's Cabinet. At the end of 1793 he resigned.

During these years sharp political conflict developed, and two separate parties, the Federalists and the Republicans, began to take shape. Madison was at first the guiding force within the Republican group, focusing attention upon his friend Jefferson and his principles. During the sharp struggle between the new parties, Jefferson gradually assumed leadership, never through making speeches and seldom through pamphleteering, but for the most part through suggestions in letters to friends. When he drafted the forceful states' rights resolutions for the Kentucky legislature, attacking the Alien and Sedition Acts, he kept his authorship secret.

He championed the rights of the states "in behalf of human rights," as his biographer, Dumas Malone, has said.

As a reluctant candidate for President in 1796, Jefferson came within three votes of election. Through a flaw in the Constitution, which had no provision for political parties, Jefferson became Vice President, although an opponent of President Adams. In 1800 the defect took a more serious turn. Republican electors eliminated President Adams and, attempting to name both a President and a Vice President from their own party, cast a tie vote between Thomas Jefferson and Aaron Burr. The tie was broken by a vote in the House of Representatives.

Wounded sailor interposes his body to save fallen Lt. Stephen Decatur from a Barbary pirate's scimitar. Halting appeasement, Jefferson had sent naval forces to quell the pirates and protect American shipping.

ENGRAVING FROM A PAINTING BY ALONZO CHAPPEL FROM "OUR COUNTRY," BY B. J. LOSSING, VOL. II, LIBRARY OF CONGRESS

PAINTING BY THURE DE THULESTRUP, LOUISIANA HISTORICAL SOCIETY

Fifteen-star Old Glory rises over New Orleans as the French Tricolor descends on December 20, 1803. A musket salute echoes across the Place d'Armes, now Jackson Square. The Louisiana Purchase, outstanding event of Jefferson's administration, added 830,000 square miles to the United States, almost doubling its size. For $15,000,000 Napoleon parted with all French lands from the Mississippi Delta to modern Montana. 33

Concealed beside a fireplace at Monticello, dumbwaiters returned an empty wine bottle each time a full flask came up. Jefferson also designed a revolving chair, a portable writing desk, a letter-copying device, and a cannonball-weighted clock that told the day of the week.

"All my wishes end," wrote Jefferson, "where I hope my days will end, at Monticello." He designed his dream house, and during 25 years he built it, near Charlottesville, Virginia. Jefferson did end his days there, observing the construction of the University of Virginia, four miles away, through a telescope. But hordes of visitors proved his undoing. His steward groaned, "I have often sent a wagon-load of hay up to the stable and the next morning there would not be enough to make a bird's nest. I have killed a fine beef and it would all be eaten in a day or two." After Jefferson's death, his daughter had to sell Monticello to pay his debts.

Stone, brick, lumber, and nails used in the house came from the estate itself.

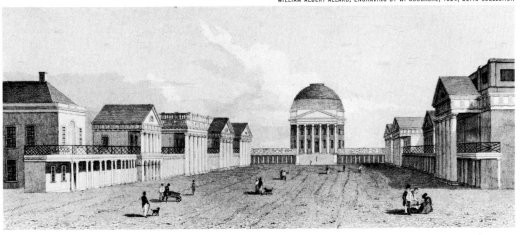

Thus did the University of Virginia look in 1824, when Jefferson was supervising its construction in Charlottesville. Rotunda and other buildings face the central Lawn. Student riots in 1825 led two professors to resign; Jefferson helped to restore order. He died in 1826 on the fiftieth anniversary of the Declaration of Independence.

The House still had a Federalist majority. Hamilton, disliking both Jefferson and Burr, nevertheless urged his friends to vote for Jefferson. "To my mind," wrote Hamilton, "a true estimate of Mr. Jefferson's character warrants the expectation of a temporizing rather than a violent system." After days of suspense, the House elected Jefferson on the 36th ballot; and by 1804 the Twelfth Amendment provided that electors should vote separately for President and Vice President.

Upon assuming office, Jefferson was as temporizing as Hamilton predicted. The crises in France had passed, so that he was able to slash expenditures for the Army and Navy, cut the budget, eliminate the tax on whiskey so unpopular in the West, and still make substantial payments to reduce the national debt by a third.

Several weeks after he took office he sent a naval squadron to fight the Barbary pirates, who were harassing American commerce in the Mediterranean. Further, although the Constitution made no provision for the acquisition of new land, Jefferson suppressed his qualms when he had the opportunity to acquire the Louisiana Territory from Napoleon in 1803.

Running for re-election, Jefferson carried every state but two. During his second term, he was increasingly preoccupied with keeping the Nation from involvement in the Napoleonic wars, while both Britain and France interfered with the neutral rights of American merchantmen. But his effort at a solution, an embargo upon American shipping, worked badly and was unpopular.

With relief Jefferson retired to his fields, his books, his architectural plans, and his inventions. In Monticello, he built his own memorial. Painstakingly preserved, the historic site dazzles tourists today no less than a French nobleman who observed that Jefferson had placed his house and his mind "on an elevated situation, from which he might contemplate the universe."

At the pivot-top desk and the swivel chair in his study, he pondered such projects as his grand designs for the University of Virginia in Charlottesville. There on the campus, Jefferson, in bronze, watches over the students, heirs to his masterpiece.

He is most often remembered as sage rather than President. But there was a strongly relevant interconnection between his political career and his intellectual life. In the thick of the party conflict in 1800, he wrote in a private letter the famous words inscribed on the Thomas Jefferson National Memorial in Washington, D. C.: "I have sworn upon the altar of God eternal hostility against every form of tyranny over the mind of man."

Jefferson stands today on a Liberty Bell in front of the Rotunda (above). He surveyed the sites with pegs and twine, calculated the brick and lumber needed, hired bricklayers and carpenters, and sent a scholar to Britain to scout for professors. "Mr. Jefferson," as the university community still affectionately calls him, loved domes, and the Rotunda was his favorite. Modeled after the Pantheon in Rome, it was completed in 1826.

James Madison [signature]

FOURTH PRESIDENT 1809-1817

JAMES MADISON, the fourth President of the United States, is less renowned for his eight years in the White House than for his remarkable services at the Constitutional Convention. As a political philosopher and practical politician, he was the peer of Jefferson, and in some respects was a more original thinker. But he was always overshadowed by his older, more personable friend.

Born in 1751, Madison was brought up in Orange County, Virginia, a few miles northeast of Jefferson's home. At Princeton (then called the College of New Jersey) the study of history and government especially interested him. Some years later he read law so as to have a profession in which he would "depend as little as possible on the labour of slaves." He participated in the framing of the Virginia Constitution in 1776, served in the Continental Congress, and was leader in the Virginia Assembly.

Fearing for the welfare of both Virginia and the American Nation under the ineffective government created by the Articles of Confederation, he took part in a series of conferences out of which he hoped would come a stronger national commercial policy. The result of these was the calling of the Constitutional Convention at Philadelphia, where he served as a member of the Virginia delegation. In preparation, he wrote a number of recommendations which helped shape the Virginia plan that Edmund Randolph presented to the Convention.

When the delegates assembled at Philadelphia, the 36-year-old Madison took frequent and emphatic part in the debates. His meticulous notes have provided later generations with the fullest account of the sessions. One delegate wrote:

"...every Person seems to acknowledge his greatness. He blends together the profound politician, with the Scholar. In the management of every great question he evidently took the lead in the Convention, and tho' he

cannot be called an Orator, he is a most agreeable, eloquent, and convincing Speaker.... The affairs of the United States, he perhaps, has the most correct knowledge of, of any Man in the Union."

In later years, when he was referred to as the "Father of the Constitution," Madison protested that the Constitution was not "the off-spring of a single brain," but "the work of many heads and many hands."

Madison made a major contribution to the ratification of the Constitution by writing a series of essays together with Alexander Hamilton and John Jay. They first appeared in New York newspapers, and were published in book form in 1788 as *The Federalist*. In the Virginia ratifying convention, Madison's quiet, realistic arguments overcame the flamboyant oratory of the anti-Federalist leader, Patrick Henry.

Madison, as a Member of the House of Representatives, helped enact the first revenue legislation and to frame the Bill of Rights. Soon he became critical of Hamilton's financial proposals, which he felt would unduly bestow wealth and power upon northern financiers. Out of his leadership in opposition to Hamilton slowly came the development of the Republican, or Jeffersonian, Party.

When Jefferson became President in 1801, he elevated his friend Madison to be Secretary of State. Madison was also Jefferson's chief adviser. Thus it was that Madison, previously inexperienced in diplomacy, wrestled with the difficult problems facing the United States as a neutral during the long war between France and Britain. Madison protested to the belligerents against their seizure of American ships, contrary to the international law of neutrality. The effect of his activities, as John Randolph commented at the time, was that of "a shilling pamphlet hurled against eight hundred ships of war."

The administration tried to coerce the warring nations into respecting its neutral

"**A small man, quiet, somewhat precise in manner,** pleasant, fond of conversation," ran Henry Adams's description of James Madison. Standing only five-feet-six and weighing 100 pounds, Madison had a frail body and an almost inaudible voice. But his scholarship, intelligence, and cool judgment at the Constitutional Convention earned him an honor he modestly declined—"Father of the United States Constitution."

Flagship Disabled, Oliver Hazard Perry Transfers His Colors to *Niagara*

During the unpopular War of 1812, scornfully dubbed "Mr. Madison's War," Master Commandant Perry went to Erie, Pennsylvania, to organize a fleet that could challenge British control of Lake Erie. On September 10, 1813, his nine vessels engaged the enemy. After a two-hour clash, Perry had to abandon his battered flagship, the *Lawrence,* ironically named for James Lawrence, the dying naval officer who had said, "Don't give up the ship." Aboard *Niagara,* Perry boldly attacked the British ships, raking them with such fire that the squadron surrendered. Perry then sent to Maj. Gen. William Henry Harrison his famous dispatch, "We have met the enemy and they are ours." The battle gave the United States control of Lake Erie and enabled Perry and Harrison to drive British troops from Detroit.

Half-burned White House still stands after pillage by the British. A storm on the night of August 24, 1814, put out the flames, but roof and interior were lost. Only the walls remained. In the 1948-52 renovation, workmen found fire-blackened stones in place just as James Hoban, the original architect, left them when he rebuilt the mansion.

The Madisons, who reached safety before the British arrived, never returned to the President's House. During the looting, a soldier carried off a walnut medicine chest. A Canadian descendant gave it back to the White House in 1939 as a goodwill gesture.

rights through the Embargo Act of 1807, intended to keep all American shipping at home and deprive the belligerents of the foodstuffs they needed. Despite the unpopularity of the embargo, Madison was elected President in 1808; three days before he took office the Embargo Act was repealed.

At his Inauguration, President Madison, a small, wizened man who had never been impressive looking, appeared old and worn; Washington Irving described him as "but a withered little apple-John."

A frustrating and difficult eight years lay ahead of him, in which much went wrong with the United States. Later generations tended to lay the troubles at the White House doorstep and to regard Madison as a weak administrator.

Irving Brant, his biographer, has amassed

evidence to prove that Madison dominated foreign policy during his Presidency, making the best of what was a hopeless impasse abroad and at home. He was a fairly strong President. Whatever his deficiencies in charm, his buxom wife Dolley compensated for them with her warmth and gaiety; she was the toast of Washington.

During the first year of Madison's administration, the United States prohibited trade with both Britain and France; then in May, 1810, Congress authorized trade with both, but directed the President, if either would accept America's view of neutral rights, to forbid trade with the other nation.

Napoleon saw a chance to stir up trouble between the United States and Britain; he pretended to comply with American policy. In response, late in 1810, Madison proclaimed

non-intercourse with Great Britain. Thereafter American relations with Britain gradually grew worse, while in Congress a young group including Henry Clay and John C. Calhoun, the "War Hawks," harassed the President with demands for a more militant policy to protect the frontiers and sweep the British from the seas.

Impelled primarily by the maritime issues —the British impressment of American seamen and the seizure of cargoes—Madison gave in and on June 1, 1812, asked Congress for a declaration of war. Had there been rapid communication, the war would have been avoided, for two days before Congress voted, the British suspended their policy of seizures.

The American Nation was in no way ready to fight, and the rapid conquest of Canada that the frontier Congressmen had predicted did not take place. Long afterward Madison told George Bancroft, the historian, that "he knew the unprepared state of the country, but he esteemed it necessary to throw forward the flag of the country, sure that the people would press forward and defend it."

"**Mrs. Madison** is a fine, portly, buxom dame, who has a smile and a pleasant word for everybody," reported Washington Irving. Dolley married Madison even though he was an inch shorter, 17 years older, and at least one other lady had turned him down. She loved to wear bejeweled turbans, use snuff, play cards for money, and entertain 15 or 20 people at dinner.

Dolley's charm made her one of the most popular First Ladies in American history. "Everybody loves Mrs. Madison," Henry Clay said to her. She gaily replied, "Mrs. Madison loves everybody."

Montpelier, Madison's home in Orange County, Virginia, was built about 1760 by James Madison, father of the President. Beginning in 1798, Dolley helped her husband modernize the house. They added the stately portico, following a suggestion by Thomas Jefferson. From France, Jefferson shipped a mantelpiece; James Monroe sent linens and furniture, bought at bargain prices from impoverished noblemen. Today privately owned, Montpelier is known for its fine racing horses. Both the President and his First Lady are buried on the grounds.

For many months little happened, and men like Richard Rush were only amused at Madison's attempts to organize the armed forces.

"He visited in person—a thing never known before—all the offices of the departments of war and navy," Rush reported two days after war was declared, "stimulating everything in a manner worthy of a little commander-in-chief, with his little round hat and huge cockade."

On land and at sea, American forces took a trouncing, the nadir being reached when the British entered Washington and set fire to the White House and Capitol. But the attack on Baltimore a month later met galling salvos from Fort McHenry. Its guns still loom on the barbettes of the national historic shrine. Its tattered banner, which the hostage Francis Scott Key saw "gallantly streaming" after 25 hours' bombardment, now occupies a place of honor in the Smithsonian Institution's National Museum of American History.

A few notable military and naval victories were climaxed by Gen. Andrew Jackson's epic triumph at New Orleans, thus convincing Americans that the war had been gloriously successful. The War of 1812, so ill-fought by a Nation so badly divided, resulted in an upsurge of nationalism.

The New England Federalists who had opposed the war—and who had even talked secession—were so thoroughly repudiated that Federalism disappeared as a national political party.

In 1816 Madison signed a series of bills establishing a national program for the American people, including a tariff to protect American "infant industries," chartering of a new Bank of the United States, and strengthening of the regular Army and Navy.

In retirement at his Orange County, Virginia, estate Montpelier—now privately owned —Madison spoke out against the disruptive states' rights influences that by the 1830's threatened to shatter the Federal Union. A note entitled "Advice to my Country," opened after his death in 1836, stated in conclusion:

"The advice nearest to my heart and deepest in my convictions is that the Union of the States be cherished and perpetuated."

James Monroe

FIFTH PRESIDENT 1817-1825

J AMES MONROE was the last of the Virginia dynasty of Presidents and the last of the great Revolutionary generation to occupy the White House. Lacking the intellectual fire of his predecessors, as Chief Executive he nevertheless demonstrated solid common sense and administrative qualities.

"His understanding was very much underrated," Madison declared; "his judgment was particularly good...."

In so many respects representing the last of the old, Monroe still wore knee breeches as young America rushed toward the age of the common man. He was President during the exciting years when the Nation was fast filling in the fertile valleys beyond the Appalachian Mountains and first faced responsibilities throughout the Western Hemisphere.

He could not cope successfully with the sharp quarrel over slavery, but he did bequeath to the United States and its sister republics to the south the basic policy that the Americas were not open to exploitation from outside—the Monroe Doctrine.

As President Monroe stood near the door of the White House on New Year's Day, 1825, at the last of his annual receptions, he made a pleasing impression upon a Virginia lady:

"He is tall and well formed.... His manner was quiet and dignified. From the frank, honest expression of his eye, which is said to be 'the window of the soul,' I think he well deserves the encomium passed upon him by the great Jefferson, who said, 'Monroe was so honest that if you turned his soul inside out there would not be a spot on it.'"

Last of Revolutionary War Presidents, James Monroe clung to colonial-style knee breeches after most men had taken to long trousers. Contemporaries smiled at his old-fashioned ways but hailed his "Era of Good Feelings." Monroe purchased the Floridas from Spain, neutralized the Canadian border, and signed the Missouri Compromise.

Belle of New York, Elizabeth Kortright Monroe met her husband when he went to the Continental Congress. In this portrait by Benjamin West, she wears turban and velvet dress. Ermine tails spot her scarf.

Born in Westmoreland County, Virginia, in 1758, Monroe attended the College of William and Mary, fought with distinction in the Continental Army—he was wounded at Trenton —and practiced law in Fredericksburg, Virginia. His law office, filled with memorabilia, is now a museum with an adjacent library.

As a youthful politician, he arrayed himself with the anti-Federalists in the Virginia convention which ratified the Constitution, and in 1790 was elected to the United States Senate, where he ardently pursued Jeffersonian policies. As Minister to France in 1794-1796, he displayed strong sympathies for the French cause; later, President Jefferson again sent him to France, where, together with Minister Robert R. Livingston, he helped negotiate the Louisiana Purchase.

Friend and mentor Jefferson designed a house, Oak Hill in Loudoun County, Virginia, where Monroe worked on state papers in a calm atmosphere.

President Madison appointed him Secretary of State in 1811, and for some months during the War of 1812 he served as Secretary of War as well. His ambition and energy, together with the backing of the President,

Painting by Samuel F. B. Morse, White House Collection

Oak Hill, Monroe's home in Loudoun County, Virginia, owes its design to Jefferson and its execution to White House architect James Hoban. Monroe sometimes rode here from Washington, 35 miles away, to study state papers in peace. Here he pondered the ideas embodied in the Monroe Doctrine. He so neglected private affairs during public service that he had to sell another estate, now called Ash Lawn, near Jefferson's Monticello. After his wife's death in 1830, he lived with his daughter and son-in-law in New York City.

Secret compartment lies under the three books between the small drawers of his Louis XVI desk, which Monroe purchased in 1794 to furnish the United States Legation in Paris. The compartment went undiscovered until 1906, when Laurence Gouverneur Hoes, a descendant then six years of age, damaged the desk. Taken to a cabinetmaker, the board under the books fell out, revealing trays containing letters from Jefferson, Madison, John Marshall, and Lafayette. One recorded Jefferson's now famous words: "How little do my countrymen know what precious blessings they are in possession of, and which no other people on earth enjoy." Treasured at Monroe's law office in Fredericksburg, Virginia, the desk remains just as Monroe knew it, with his inkstand, sander, eyeglasses, and clock.

made him the choice of the Republican Congressional caucus for the Presidency in 1816. He won with little opposition from the Federalists, and in 1820 was re-elected with only a single electoral vote cast against him.

As President, Monroe put behind him the sectional bias that had marked his earlier career. In appointing new secretaries, he made unusually strong choices, especially in

naming a southerner, John C. Calhoun, as Secretary of War, and a northerner, John Quincy Adams, as Secretary of State. Only the refusal of Henry Clay kept him from adding to the Cabinet an outstanding westerner.

To demonstrate further the national nature of his administration, Monroe undertook at its outset a goodwill tour of the North and West, going as far as Portland and Detroit. At Boston, the Federalist *Columbian Centinel* hailed his visit there as signaling an "Era of Good Feelings." The phrase, catching the popular fancy, in time became synonymous with Monroe's Presidency.

Unfortunately the "good feelings" did not endure, although Monroe, his popularity undiminished, continued to follow nationalist policies. Suppressing his distaste for broadly

47

construing the Constitution, he signed several measures to provide Federal funds for internal improvements such as national roads.

But behind the façade of nationalism, ugly sectional cracks began to appear, intensified by a painful economic depression precipitated by the panic of 1819. The depression undoubtedly increased the dismay of the people of Missouri Territory in 1819 when Congress rejected their application for admission to the Union as a slave state. A New York Representative amended the bill to provide for the gradual elimination of slavery in Missouri, thus setting off two years of bitter debate in Congress and alerting the Nation to the menacing sectional issue, which Jefferson likened to "a fire bell in the night."

Monroe sided with the South, but, true to his view of the Presidency, made no effort to influence Congress. When Clay resolved the struggle through the Missouri Compromise, pairing Missouri as a slave state with Maine, a free state, and providing that territory north and west of the southern boundary of Missouri should enter the Union as free states, Monroe signed the measure.

Monroe's great contribution as President was in the realm of foreign affairs, where he proclaimed the fundamental policy that bears his name. He enunciated the Monroe Doctrine primarily in response to the threat that the more conservative governments in Europe might try to aid Spain in winning back her former colonies, the newly established Latin American republics.

From the outset American sympathies had been with the revolutionaries to the south, but Monroe did not begin formally to recog-

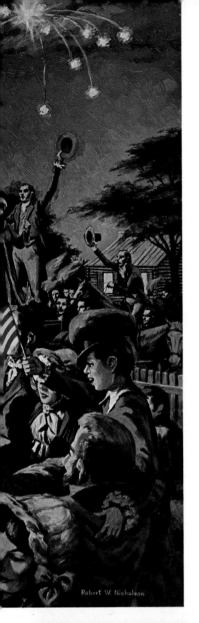

nize the sister republics until 1822, and then only after ascertaining that Congress would vote appropriations for diplomatic missions. He and Secretary of State John Quincy Adams wished to avoid trouble with Spain until it had relinquished the Floridas, as Spain did in 1821.

By 1823 Great Britain, with its powerful navy, was also opposed to the reconquest of Latin America and suggested that the United States join in proclaiming "hands off." Both ex-Presidents Jefferson and Madison counseled Monroe to accept the offer, but Secretary Adams advised, "It would be more candid, as well as more dignified, to avow our principles explicitly to Russia and France, than to come in as a cock-boat in the wake of the British man-of-war."

Monroe accepted Adams's advice. In his Annual Message to Congress of December, 1823, he warned not only that Latin America must be left alone but also that Russia must not encroach southward on the Pacific Coast.

"...the American continents, by the free...condition which they have assumed and maintain, are henceforth not to be considered as subjects for future colonization by any European Power," the President stated. This basic tenet became known some thirty years later as the Monroe Doctrine.

In 1831, Monroe died in New York—on Independence Day.

Fireworks light the sky as Detroit salutes Monroe in 1817. Hand lifted, the President stands outside a high stockade surrounding the city. GEOGRAPHIC artist Robert W. Nicholson re-created the scene from details in contemporary newspaper accounts, even to the slogans on the pole-borne lamps.

Monroe and his advisers debate the hands-off-America policy that became known as the Monroe Doctrine. Left to right: Secretary of State John Quincy Adams, Secretary of the Treasury William H. Crawford, Attorney General William Wirt, President Monroe (at globe), Secretary of War John C. Calhoun, Secretary of the Navy Samuel L. Southard, and Postmaster General John McLean. Crawford, erroneously shown by the artist, was critically ill during the debate.

PAINTING BY CLYDE O. DELAND, COURTESY THE BOARD OF PUBLIC EDUCATION, PHILADELPHIA, PA.

John Quincy Adams

SIXTH PRESIDENT 1825-1829

JOHN QUINCY ADAMS served his Nation with selfless, intelligent devotion from the age of 14, when he went to Russia as secretary to the United States Minister, until nearly 80, when he was fatally stricken in the House of Representatives. His four years as President were, ironically, less distinguished than his long career in foreign affairs before he went to the White House and the 17 years he spent thereafter in Congress as a defender of civil liberties.

Adams was the only President who was the son of a President, and in many respects his career as well as his temperament and viewpoints paralleled those of his famous father.

Born in Braintree, Massachusetts, in 1767, he witnessed, with his mother, Abigail Adams, the Battle of Bunker Hill from the top of Penn's Hill above the family farm. A stone cairn marks the spot today.

With his father in Europe, he became an accomplished linguist and assiduous diarist, and served as secretary not only at the St. Petersburg Legation but also at the Paris

peace negotiations in 1783—all before he entered Harvard College.

After graduation he became a lawyer. His essays defending Washington's neutrality policy so favorably impressed the first President that he was appointed, aged 26, as Minister to The Hague. As President, John Adams promoted his talented son to the Berlin Legation.

In 1802 John Quincy Adams was elected to the United States Senate, and for several years served simultaneously as Boylston Professor of Rhetorick and Oratory at Harvard. In both positions he encountered hostility because he would not act as an orthodox New England Federalist. In 1808 Massachusetts Federalists forced him out of the Senate, but within the following year the Republican President, James Madison, appointed him as Minister to Russia.

But Adams would not follow strict Republican positions either. Rather, like his father, he demonstrated a lifelong disdain for fixed party ideology and refused to practice the arts of the politician. For some years this disdain was little handicap as he served on the commission to negotiate an end to the War of 1812, became Minister to Great Britain, and, beginning in 1817, served as Secretary of State under President Monroe. He was one of America's great Secretaries of State, arranging with England for the joint occupation of the Oregon Territory, obtaining from Spain the cession of the Floridas, and, with the

Charming Louisa Adams, born in London to an American merchant, married John Quincy Adams when she was 22. After four years in Europe as a diplomat's wife, she saw the United States for the first time.

"Old Man Eloquent," John Quincy Adams alone of Presidents' sons occupied the White House in his own right. Reserved and conscientious, he won his Presidency by vote of the House of Representatives over Andrew Jackson, who gathered a plurality of electoral votes but not a majority. The austere and plain-minded Adams took early morning swims in the Potomac. One day a startled servant had to dash back to the White House to get a carriage for the dripping President, whose boat had swamped.

Painting by George P. A. Healy, White House Collection

PAINTING BY SIR AMÉDÉE FORESTIER, SMITHSONIAN INSTITUTION

President, formulating the Monroe Doctrine.

In the political tradition of the early 19th century, Adams as Secretary of State was thought the political heir to the Presidency. But the old ways of choosing a President were giving way in 1824 before the clamor for a popular choice.

Within the one and only party, the Republicans, sectionalism and factionalism were developing, and each section put up, by a variety of means, its own candidates for the Presidency. Adams, the candidate of the North, fell behind Gen. Andrew Jackson in both popular and electoral votes, but received more votes than William H. Crawford and Henry Clay. Since no candidate had a majority of the electoral votes, the election was decided among the top three by the House of Representatives. Clay, who favored a program similar to that of Adams, threw his crucial support in the House to the New Englander.

Upon becoming President, Adams appointed Clay as Secretary of State. Jackson and his angry followers charged that a corrupt bargain had taken place and immediately began their campaign to wrest the Presidency from Adams in 1828. Against the angry op-

position of the Jacksonians, President John Quincy Adams tried to run his administration as though politics did not exist. He not only kept several of his political enemies in the Cabinet, but would even have liked to appoint Jackson as Secretary of War.

Well aware that he would face hostility in Congress, he nevertheless proclaimed in his first Annual Message a spectacular national program. He proposed that the Federal Government bring the sections together with a network of highways and canals, and that it develop and conserve the public domain, using funds from the sale of public lands. He also urged the United States to take a lead in the development of the arts and sciences by establishing a national university, financing scientific expeditions, and building an observatory. In Europe, he pointed out, there were more than 130 observatories—"these light-houses of the skies"—and in the American hemisphere not one.

"The spirit of improvement is abroad upon the earth," he reminded Congress. "While foreign nations less blessed . . . than ourselves are advancing with gigantic strides in the career of public improvement, were we to slumber . . . would it not be to cast away the

Inconclusive War of 1812 ends at Ghent on Christmas Eve, 1814. For the British, Lord Gambier (left) exchanges a handclasp with John Quincy Adams, chief American commissioner. The treaty, imposingly sealed, virtually restored the status quo at the outbreak of hostilities and left for future settlement all the issues over which the war had been fought.

Fatal Stroke Fells Congressman Adams at His Desk

In some ways Adams was a failure in the White House, but in the Congress he found himself. Told that membership in the House might demean a former President, he replied that no man was degraded by serving the people. A small bronze plate marks the spot where Adams collapsed. By coincidence, it is the "whisper spot," the place in today's Statuary Hall where one can hear a whisper spoken across the room, though it is inaudible close by.

THE YOUTHS' HISTORY OF THE UNITED STATES, BY EDWARD S. ELLIS, LIBRARY OF CONGRESS

bounties of Providence and doom ourselves to perpetual inferiority?"

Adams, behind his times as a political leader, was ahead of them in tasks he wished to set for the Government. Political foes expressed horror at his proposals which they said far transcended constitutional limits. The press ridiculed him. But he did enjoy one moment of popular acclaim in 1828, when he turned the first spadeful of earth for the 185-mile C & O Canal—now partly restored by the National Park Service.

Aggrieved and frustrated, Adams arose every morning at four to pour his hurt feelings into long entries in his diary. As part of his Spartan regimen he sometimes also took early morning swims in the Potomac. Once when his boat sprang a leak and swamped, he lost most of his clothes and had to return to the White House in embarrassment.

The campaign of 1828, in which his Jacksonian opponents charged him with corruption, was an ordeal he did not easily bear. Adams, the short, bald, reserved intellectual, cut an unimpressive public figure compared with the hero of New Orleans.

After his defeat, he returned to Massachusetts, expecting to spend the remainder of his life enjoying his farm and his books. Unexpectedly, in 1830, the Plymouth district elected him to the House of Representatives, and there for the remainder of his life he served as a powerful leader. When an English bequest came to the United States to establish an institution for the "increase and diffusion of knowledge," it was Adams who fought for years against proposed dissipations of the fund until it could be used to found a scientific agency, the Smithsonian Institution.

Above all, he fought against a circumscription of civil liberties that grew out of the heightened controversy over slavery. In 1836 southerners in the House passed a "gag rule" providing that petitions against slavery would be automatically tabled. Adams, taking the view that the rights of his constituents were violated, fought with vigor until finally, in 1844, he obtained repeal of the rule.

In 1848, he collapsed on the floor of the House from a stroke and was carried to the Speaker's room, where two days later he died. He was buried—as were his father, mother, and wife—at First Parish Church in Quincy, a historic landmark. To the very end, "Old Man Eloquent" had fought for what he considered right.

2 A RESTLESS

FROM ANDREW JACKSON through James Buchanan, a generation of Presidents faced westward. In this age of "manifest destiny," ambitious settlers surged beyond the old frontiers. Presidents sought to push the national boundaries to the Pacific—a dream finally realized by James K. Polk.

Presidents of this era also faced the hopeless task of mediating the bitter quarrel between South and North over whether western areas should become slave states or free.

Jackson was the first westerner in the White House; Harrison, Polk, and Taylor also came from the West. Their nicknames suggest western informality: "Old Hickory," "Old Tippecanoe," "Young Hickory," and "Old Rough and Ready." Three won their first renown as Indian fighters; the fourth, Polk, gained election by advocating sweeping expansion.

During these years, even Presidents from

NATION MOVES WEST

Andrew Jackson through James Buchanan

the seaboard wrestled constantly with western problems: Martin Van Buren and John Tyler with the question of Texas; Millard Fillmore with the territorial quarrels following the Mexican War; and Franklin Pierce and James Buchanan with "bleeding Kansas." The fact that during this 32-year span only Jackson won re-election indicates to some degree the difficult nature of these problems.

The spirit of westward expansion cannot

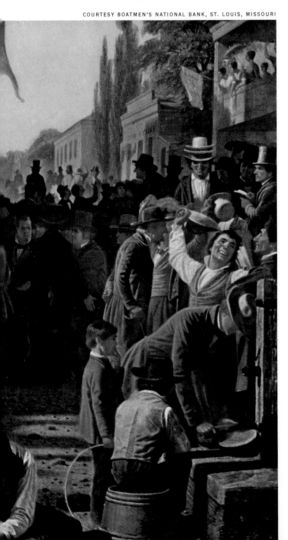

be dismissed as merely one of selfish aggrandizement. It included a sense of mission, a desire to see the inhabitants of areas outside the boundary of the United States join the great democratic experiment of their own free will. Ex-President Jackson, advocating the annexation of Texas, wrote in 1843 of "extending the area of freedom." At the close of the Mexican War, Albert Gallatin, who had served as Secretary of the Treasury under Jefferson, exhorted Americans: "Your mission is to improve the state of the world, to be the 'model republic,' to show that men are capable of governing themselves...."

Inevitably, the wave of settlers forced back the Indians, who fell victim to a great tragedy of American history. Jackson, like most frontier figures, felt scant sympathy for them; as President, he authorized a long-planned removal policy, transferring them beyond the thrust of settlement onto the western plains.

In 1843 when a group of Wyandots, the last Indians to be removed from their traditional lands in Ohio, journeyed by steamer down the Ohio River, they stood in silent respect as they passed the tomb of President Harrison, under whose command a number of them had fought. Their chief proclaimed, "Farewell, Ohio, and her brave."

Soon the Indians were gone, the hunting grounds of their fathers transformed into plantations and farms. The "star of empire" unswervingly continued its move westward.

From the courthouse steps, an official proclaims election results. By 1855, when Missouri artist George Caleb Bingham painted "Verdict of the People," property qualifications for voting had vanished; citizens trooped to the polls. A young democracy was building strength for greatness and for crisis—already the question of slavery posed a threat to the Union.

SEVENTH PRESIDENT 1829-1837

ANDREW JACKSON's Inauguration in March, 1829, celebrated the coming into political power of a new America. Farms and plantations were spreading rapidly westward beyond the Mississippi River; newborn cities were revolutionizing commerce and manufacturing.

Countryside and cities alike stirred with ambitious men striving to improve their lot, impatient to overthrow older, more aristocratic political and economic institutions. In President Jackson they found their hero and their spokesman. Jackson, in his rise from a Carolina log cabin to the Hermitage, a gracious plantation home in Tennessee, typified their aspirations; in his insistence that Americans should enjoy equality of opportunity, he voiced their credo.

More nearly than any of his predecessors, Jackson was elected by popular vote, and as President he acted as the direct representative of the common man. During his years in the White House, the people felt a larger sense of participation in their government, whether or not they were actually gaining more democratic rights.

Jackson was born in the Waxhaws, a backwoods settlement on the border between North and South Carolina, in 1767, two years after his Scotch-Irish parents had migrated from northern Ireland. His father died shortly before he was born. Jackson received scant education, but liked to recall with pride that as a 9-year-old he had read a newly arrived copy of the Declaration of Independence to a group of illiterate frontiersmen.

At 13 he served as a messenger with American troops, surviving several skirmishes; captured, he refused to polish a British officer's boots and received a saber blow on his head that scarred him for life. His mother died when he was 14. In his late teens, he read law for about two years, but was more interested in cockfighting, horse racing, and wrestling. Jackson and a friend joined the first party to traverse a new wagon road to the settlement of Nashville in the fall of 1788. Remarkable for his physical courage and audacity rather than for his legal knowledge, Jackson commanded respect on the frontier. He rapidly established himself as one of Tennessee's outstanding young lawyers.

In many respects Jackson epitomized the frontier ideal—fiercely jealous of his honor, he engaged in brawls, and, in one duel, killed a man who had cast an unjustified slur on his beloved wife, Rachel.

He speculated in land and assorted business ventures, losing money to banks and eastern financial interests in time of panic, but prospering sufficiently to buy slaves, plant cotton, and build a splendid mansion. He was the first man elected from his state to the House of Representatives, served briefly in the Senate, and became a judge notable for his practical approach to the law. In 1801, he was elected to be major general in the Tennessee Militia by the field officers.

Taking to the field despite a wounded arm, he punished the Creek Indians for their massacre of frontiersmen and in 1814 gained a commission as major general in the United States Army. Imposing an iron discipline on mutinous regiments from the southwestern frontier, he beat back seasoned British troops that had earlier won victories under Wellington in Europe. Jackson's final triumph in the Battle of New Orleans, January 8, 1815, established him as the hero of a generation of Americans.

In the chaotic politics of the 1820's, as national party lines and issues were obliterated by sectional tensions, the increasing number of voters led to the building of new-style parties and factions in state after state. Already in 1824 some of these rallied around Jackson; by 1828 still more raised his standard.

By proclaiming their allegiance to "Old Hickory," who had committed himself on scarcely any of the troublesome issues of

Tempestuous Andrew Jackson, whose frontier reputation horrified the genteel, won the hearts of the people. John Quincy Adams remonstrated when Harvard conferred a doctorate of laws on a "barbarian who could ... hardly spell his own name." Jackson killed one man in a duel and was shot while threatening to horsewhip another. He often clashed with Congress, fought anything smacking of special privilege, and by the force of his personality strengthened the office of the Presidency.

the day, these factions lured to the polls in 1828 more than three times as many voters as four years previously, and thus won numerous state elections and control of the Federal administration in Washington.

Jackson's Inauguration was "a proud day for the people," a Kentucky follower, Amos Kendall, reported in his newspaper. "General Jackson is *their own* president." But Justice Joseph Story of the Supreme Court, distressed by the jam of people that nearly wrecked the White House, lamented, "The reign of King 'Mob' seemed triumphant."

Although such scenes bracketed his terms of office—another boisterous throng hacked a 1,400-pound cheese to pieces at Jackson's last public reception in 1837—Old Hickory continued the sophisticated tradition of the White House. More than $50,000 went into renovations and furniture. Excellent foods and fine wine graced his table; one guest said it boasted "every good and glittering thing French skill could devise."

President Jackson saw his election as a mandate for greater democracy, especially in holding Federal jobs. Already state machines

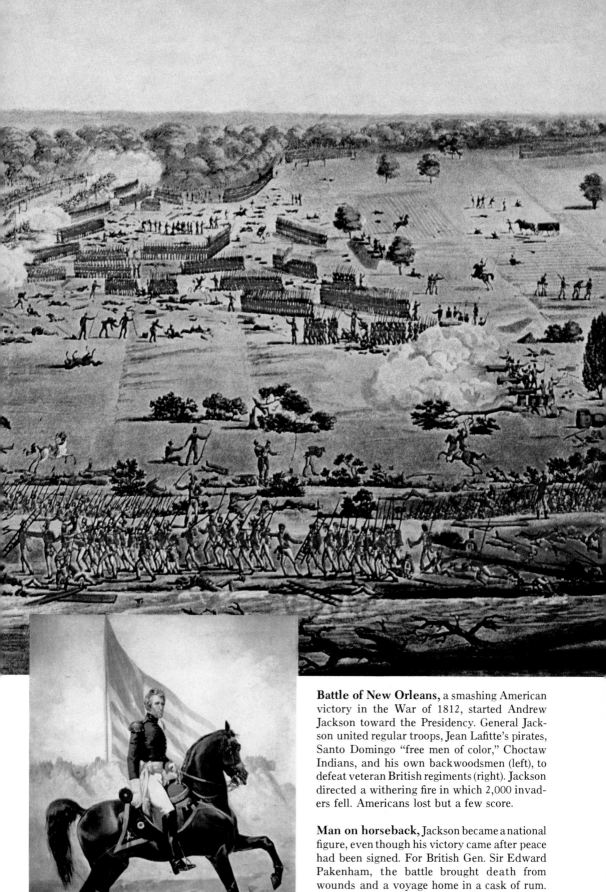

Battle of New Orleans, a smashing American victory in the War of 1812, started Andrew Jackson toward the Presidency. General Jackson united regular troops, Jean Lafitte's pirates, Santo Domingo "free men of color," Choctaw Indians, and his own backwoodsmen (left), to defeat veteran British regiments (right). Jackson directed a withering fire in which 2,000 invaders fell. Americans lost but a few score.

Man on horseback, Jackson became a national figure, even though his victory came after peace had been signed. For British Gen. Sir Edward Pakenham, the battle brought death from wounds and a voyage home in a cask of rum.

PAINTING BY ALONZO CHAPPEL, CHICAGO HISTORICAL SOCIETY

depended on patronage; Senator William L. Marcy declared that American politicians "see nothing wrong in the rule, that to the victor belong the spoils of the enemy."

Jackson took a milder view than the term "spoils system" would suggest. Decrying indifferent or corrupt officeholders who seemed to enjoy life tenure, he complained: "Office is considered as a species of property, and government rather as a means of promoting individual interests than as an instrument created solely for the service of the people." He thought official duties could be made "so plain and simple that men of intelligence may readily qualify themselves for their performance." Opponents charged Jackson with a "general proscription" of officeholders, yet he removed only about one-fifth during his two terms, and some of these for sound reasons.

A complete turnover of Federal offices when a new party came into power did not begin until 1841. By that time much of the apparatus of the new politics had been developed: national organizations, nurtured through patronage and spreading their views through a party press; nominating conventions

Celebrators storm the White House after Jackson's Inauguration in 1829. Inside, muddy boots climbed silk chairs, fists flew, china crashed, and ladies fainted in the crush to greet the President. Jackson retreated out a back door; tubs of punch placed on the lawn lured the crowd outside. British caricaturist Robert Cruikshank recorded the tumult in "The President's Levee, or all Creation going to the White House."

Jackson escapes death at the Capitol—the first assassination attempt on a President, January 30, 1835. A tall stranger aimed a pistol at Jackson (shown carrying a walking stick), but the weapon misfired. Before the officer at left could seize him, the gunman raised a second pistol, which also misfired. Reacting fast, Jackson went for the assailant with his stick. The attacker later was committed to an insane asylum.

to choose candidates, draft platforms, and proclaim slogans. As national politics polarized around President Jackson and his opposition, two parties emerged—the Democratic Republicans, or Democrats, adhering to Jackson, and the National Republicans, or Whigs, opposing him.

Henry Clay, Daniel Webster, and other Whig leaders in the Senate compared themselves to the English Whigs in Parliament who sought to limit the powers of the King. They proclaimed themselves defenders of popular liberties against the usurpation of President Jackson. Hostile cartoonists portrayed Jackson as King Andrew I.

Behind the Whig accusations lay the indisputable fact that President Jackson, unlike his immediate predecessors, did not defer to Congress but used his veto power and his party leadership to assume command. Much of his policy making seemed intertwined with personal prejudices, but the American people saw their own prejudices reflected in his.

In his contests with the master politicians in the Senate, Jackson proved himself the shrewdest politician of all. Thus Jackson vetoed Clay's Maysville Turnpike bill, which proposed national funds for a road entirely in Kentucky, on the ground that Federal funds should go only to internal improvements that transcended state lines.

Jackson's greatest political battle centered around the Second Bank of the United States, a private corporation with a near monopoly on the currency. Despite its considerable merits, the Bank was viewed with abhorrence in the West, where, during the depression of the 1820's, it had engaged in widespread foreclosures. Because of its size and wealth, it had considerable power and, when Jackson appeared hostile, the Bank threw its influence against the President.

Clay and Webster, who had acted as attorneys for the Bank, fought for its recharter in

Congress, confident that Jackson's veto of the recharter would result in his defeat in 1832.

"The Bank," Jackson told Van Buren, "is trying to kill me, *but I will kill it!*" The President, in vetoing the bill, raised questions of constitutionality but, more than this, charged the Bank with undue economic privilege.

"There are no necessary evils in government," he declared in his Veto Message: "Its evils exist only in its abuses. If it would confine itself to equal protection, and, as Heaven does its rains, shower its favors alike on the high and the low, the rich and the poor, it would be an unqualified blessing." Jackson's views were in touch with the spirit of the American electorate; in 1832 he received more than 56 percent of the popular vote and almost five times as many electoral votes as Clay.

As a nationalist, Jackson was equally forthright in meeting the challenge of John C. Calhoun. Formerly a nationalist himself, Calhoun had become the spokesman of South Carolina forces which proposed nullification by the states to rid themselves of a high protective tariff they disliked. They hoped to win Jackson to their views, but at a Jefferson Day banquet he gave them a dramatic warning.

Knowing he would be expected to speak, he had written out his words and underscored several of them. After 24 toasts supporting states' rights, Jackson rose, looked sternly at Calhoun, and proposed a toast of his own: "Our *Federal* Union—*It must be preserved.*" An eye-witness reported that "an order to arrest Calhoun where he sat could not have come with more blinding, staggering force."

When South Carolina undertook to nullify the tariff, Jackson issued a proclamation declaring: "... our present happy Constitution was formed... in vain if this fatal doctrine prevails." He ordered armed forces to Charleston and privately threatened to hang Calhoun. For several months violence seemed imminent, but Clay negotiated a compromise which resulted in a lowering of tariffs and a dropping of nullification.

In January, 1832, a visitor was waiting in the White House to meet the President, who was dining with friends. "It was not long before the doors were thrown open," the man wrote later, "and General Jackson entered at the head of his company, talking and laughing with much animation.... I was absorbed for some minutes scanning the face and mien of this remarkable man. In person he was tall, slim, and straight.... His head was long, but narrow, and covered with thick gray hair that stood erect, as though impregnated with his defiant spirit; his brow was deeply furrowed, and his eye, even in his present mood, was one 'to threaten and command.'... His mouth displayed firmness. The whole conveyed an impression of energy and daring."

Before the young man could be introduced, someone came to whisper to the President that the Senate had rejected the nomination of Martin Van Buren as Minister to Great Britain. Jackson jumped to his feet and exclaimed, "By the Eternal! I'll smash them!" So Jackson did. Van Buren became Vice President, and gained the Presidency when Old Hickory retired to the Hermitage.

There Jackson remained, a hero of legendary proportions and a force in the Democratic Party, until his death in 1845.

Majestic portico of the Hermitage near Nashville, Tennessee, reflects Jackson's success as a cotton planter. Now his home is a national historic landmark; he and his wife lie buried in a corner of this garden.

Rachel Jackson suffered over the years from gossip and slander: She married Jackson in the mistaken belief that her first husband had divorced her. The campaign of 1828 revived old, and unjust, slurs that hurt her deeply; her health failed; she died on December 22, less than three months before Jackson entered the White House. He wore next to his heart an ivory miniature painted when she was in her 40's; this heirloom apparently represents a copy made for one of her many devoted relatives.

MARTIN VAN BUREN, the "Little Magician," inherited more of the troubles than the glory of Jacksonian Democracy. Loyal to President Jackson, he continued faithfully the policies of his predecessor but reaped a painful economic depression. For good measure, the Whigs defeated him for re-election in 1840 by turning against him the same political techniques with which he and his fellow Jacksonians had engineered their earlier victories.

Van Buren, born in 1782, was of Dutch descent, the son of a tavernkeeper and farmer in Kinderhook, New York. At 14 he became a law clerk, soon distinguishing himself for his cleverness in debate. As a young lawyer, he upheld Jeffersonian principles with zeal, becoming deeply involved in New York politics.

A sound administrator, Van Buren once wrote, would bring to the support of "the governmental standard the good the virtuous & the capable." However, as leader of an effective New York political organization, the Albany Regency, he shrewdly dispensed public offices and bounty in a fashion calculated to bring votes, and in 1821 was elected to the United States Senate.

There he came to oppose Federal subsidies for internal improvements, a position pleasing to his constituents, who were afraid the money would help construct routes rivaling the Erie Canal. By 1827 he had emerged as the principal northern leader for Jackson.

President Jackson rewarded Van Buren by bringing him into the Cabinet as Secretary of State. As those members of the Cabinet appointed at Calhoun's recommendation began to demonstrate that they held only secondary loyalty to Jackson, Van Buren emerged as the President's most trusted confidential adviser. Jackson referred to him as *a true man* with no guile."

The rift in the Cabinet became serious because of Jackson's differences with Calhoun, a Presidential aspirant; but on the surface it developed over the coldness of Cabinet wives toward the wife of the Secretary of War, Peggy O'Neale Eaton, the object of unsavory rumors. Jackson, remembering the injustices that had afflicted his own wife, defended Mrs. Eaton, and Van Buren, also a widower, gallantly befriended her.

The stubborn Cabinet became unacceptable to Jackson. Van Buren suggested a way out of the impasse; he and then Eaton resigned, causing the Calhoun men also to resign. Jackson appointed a new and loyal Cabinet and sought to reward Van Buren by appointing him Minister to the Court of St. James's. Vice President Calhoun, as President of the Senate, cast the deciding vote against the appointment—and made a martyr of Van Buren in the eyes of western Jacksonians, who until then had scarcely known of his existence.

Blue eyes twinkling and muttonchop whiskers flanking a cherubic mouth, sunny-tempered Martin Van Buren exchanged jokes with his deadliest political foes. Washington Irving called him "one of the gentlest ... men I have ever met with." He spoke softly and sometimes changed his mind. Enemies accused him of expediency, but Van Buren argued: "To yield to necessity is the real triumph of reason." He was the first President born under the U. S. flag.

Democratic handbill of 1840 shows Van Buren producing Liberty and Equal Rights with a magic lantern. His political success earned him the nickname "Little Magician." Mint in background suggests his hard-money policy in the face of wild issuance of paper currency by private banks. The 1837 panic defeated his bid for re-election.

DEMOCRATIC TICKET.

FOR PRESIDENT,
MARTIN VAN BUREN.
FOR VICE PRESIDENT,
RICHARD M. JOHNSON.

OHIO ELECTORS.
John M. Goodenow,
Othniel Looker,
Jacob Felter,
James B. Cameron;
David S. Davis

Painting by G. P. A. Healy, White House Collection

65

He was elected Vice President on the Jacksonian ticket in 1832, and nominated for the Presidency in 1835.

The Whigs tried to defeat Van Buren by running several candidates, each strong in his own section of the country, but Van Buren won 170 electoral votes compared with 124 for his four opponents combined. One of the Whig leaders, William H. Seward, explained Van Buren's triumph. "The people are for him," Seward pointed out. "Not so much for him as for the principle they suppose he represents. That principle is Democracy."

PROUDLY, in his Inaugural Address, Van Buren mentioned that he was the first President born under the American flag. He held up the American experiment as an example to the rest of the world. At that particular moment the experiment seemed highly successful, for the Nation was enjoying unprecedented prosperity and serenity. But less than three months later the panic of 1837 punctured the economic bubble.

The 19th-century cyclical economy of "boom-and-bust" was merely following its regular pattern, but Jackson's financial measures contributed to the crash. His destruction of the Second Bank of the United States had removed restrictions upon the reckless and inflationary practices of some state banks; wild speculation in lands, based on easy bank credit, had swept the West. To put an end to this speculation, Jackson in 1836 had taken a deflationary step; he issued a Specie Circular requiring that lands be purchased with hard money—gold or silver.

In 1837 hundreds of banks and businesses failed. Unemployment became serious in towns and cities. Thousands of speculators lost their lands. Railroad and canal construction almost halted, and several states temporarily repudiated their debts. For some five years the United States was wracked by the worst depression of its young history.

It did not occur to President Van Buren or his advisers that the Government should try to alleviate the crisis. "All communities are apt to look to Government for far too much," he told Congress. "Even in our own country ... we are prone to do so, especially at periods of ... distress. But this ought not to be." So he followed the policies that President Jackson had initiated. If these had any effect at all upon the depression, it was to deepen and prolong it.

Declaring that the panic was due to recklessness in business and overexpansion of credit, Van Buren devoted himself to maintaining the solvency of the Government. He wished the "money power" to be cut off completely from access to Federal funds, and opposed not only creation of a new Bank of the United States but also the placing of Government funds in state banks. He fought for an independent treasury system to handle Government receipts and disbursements. He cut Federal expenditures so deeply that the Government even sold the tools it had used on public works.

Despite his humble background, Van Buren had developed a taste for elegance. He was only about 5 feet 6 inches tall, but trim and erect, and he dressed fastidiously. An observer, seeing him attired for church one Sunday in 1828, described him in these words: "He wore an elegant snuff-colored broadcloth coat with a velvet collar; his cravat was orange with modest lace tips; his vest was of a pearl hue; his trousers were white duck; his shoes were morocco; his neatly fitting gloves were yellow kid; his long-furred beaver hat with a broad brim was of a Quaker color."

As President, Van Buren rode in an olive-green carriage attended by liveried footmen and pulled by fine horses with silver-mounted harness. These touches of luxury, belying Van Buren's amiable accessibility, made him an easy target for the Whigs in 1840.

"We'll beat little Van, Van, Van," sang the Whig glee clubs; "Van is a used-up man."

Out of office, Van Buren inclined more and more to oppose the expansion of slavery. Indeed, as President, he had blocked the annexation of Texas because it might bring war with Mexico and assuredly would add to slave territory. In 1848 he ran unsuccessfully for President on the Free Soil ticket, and by the time of his death in 1862 had placed his faith in Abraham Lincoln. The House of History in Kinderhook has preserved mementos of Van Buren the man and the President.

Ninety-nine-step tower of Van Buren's Lindenwald estate at Kinderhook, New York, overlooks the valley of the Hudson River. The former President, born nearby, bought this farmhouse, turned it into a mansion, and added the Italianate tower. He hoped—in vain—that his home would become another Monticello. It survived in private ownership. In 1974 the National Park Service took title, to restore it as a historic site. "Old Kinderhook," abbreviated to "O.K.," became a Democratic catchword in the 1840 campaign.

DAVID S. BOYER, NATIONAL GEOGRAPHIC STAFF

W H Harrison

NINTH PRESIDENT 1841

WILLIAM HENRY HARRISON, known only as a military hero, served perfectly the purposes of the divided Whig Party. Casting Harrison as another General Jackson, Whigs rallied the Nation around his standard in 1840 and won victory. Then, ironically, he died, leaving a hostile successor who vetoed their measures.

Harrison, a scion of Virginia aristocracy and son of a signer of the Declaration of Independence, was born in 1773 at Berkeley on the James River. The plantation house, some six miles from Charles City, still stands and is open daily to the public. Harrison studied classics and history, for which he had a life-long affection, at Hampden-Sidney College, then began the study of medicine in Richmond, and continued it in Philadelphia under the renowned Dr. Benjamin Rush.

Abruptly, in 1791, young Harrison obtained a commission as ensign in the First Infantry Regiment of the Regular Army and headed to the Northwest Territory—the frontier region between the Ohio and Mississippi Rivers. In 1795 he married Anna T. Symmes.

Harrison served as aide-de-camp to Gen. "Mad Anthony" Wayne at the Battle of Fallen Timbers, which opened most of the Ohio area to settlement. Resigning from the Army in 1798, he became Secretary of the Northwest Territory and, in 1799, its first delegate to Congress. There he helped obtain legislation that split the Indiana Territory from the Northwest. When only 28 he became Gover-

nor of the Indiana Territory; his 12 years in that office won him a national reputation.

When the Indians attacked Indiana's frontier settlements, upon Harrison fell the responsibility of defense. The problem came to a head in 1809 when an eloquent and energetic chieftain, Tecumseh, together with his brother, the Prophet, began to rally the tribes.

Harrison received permission in 1811 to attack. He marched with about a thousand

Short-lived President, William Henry Harrison was first to die in office. A ruddy-faced outdoorsman, he refused to wear hat or coat in a chilly March wind while giving the longest Inaugural Address on record: one hour and forty minutes. Three weeks later he went walking in slush, caught cold, and died. While in the White House, he liked to do his own marketing before breakfast.

Silk mourning ribbon commemorates the death of Harrison. First buried in the Congressional Cemetery in Washington, his body was later moved to a tomb—now a state memorial—overlooking the Ohio River at North Bend, Ohio.

IN MEMORY OF DEPARTED WORTH.

1841.

WILLIAM HENRY HARRISON,
Late President of the United States
Born at Berkley, Charles City Co. Va. Feb. 9, 1773.
DIED at Washington City, D. C. April 4, 1841.
Aged 68 Years.

"Sir,—I wish you to understand the true principles of the Government. I wish them carried out. I ask nothing more."
(Dying words of Harrison)

Painting by E. F. Andrews, White House Collection

men toward the Prophet's town. Suddenly, before dawn on November 7, while his small army lay encamped on the Tippecanoe River, the Indians attacked. After heavy fighting, Harrison succeeded in repulsing them, but lost 190 dead and wounded in "2 hours and 20 minuts of a Continewel firing," as one soldier described it in his journal. Harrison went on to destroy the Prophet's settlement.

Scarcely a notable triumph, this was the Battle of Tippecanoe upon which Harrison's future fame was to rest. It disrupted Tecumseh's confederation but failed to diminish the Indian raids, which, by the spring of 1812— under British encouragement—terrorized the frontier. In the War of 1812, Harrison won more substantial military laurels when, after American forces had been trounced, he took command of the Army in the Northwest with the rank of brigadier general. At the Battle of the Thames, north of Lake Erie, on October 5, 1813, he defeated the combined British and Indian forces. With Tecumseh dead, the Indians scattered and never again offered serious resistance in the Northwest.

Thereafter Harrison served briefly in Congress and later as Minister to Colombia, but primarily devoted himself to management of his Ohio farm. He lived in an impressive house but debts plagued him. In the 1830's he served as clerk of a county court in order to augment his slender income.

Attack by Indians shatters the dawn of November 7, 1811, beside the Tippecanoe River in Indiana Territory. Harrison, leading a thousand soldiers into the wilderness to smash a gathering of tribes, beats off repeated assaults, burns a village nearby, and becomes a hero. Years later, the victory swept him into the Presidency on the slogan, "Tippecanoe and Tyler Too."

LITHOGRAPH BY KURZ AND ALLISON, LIBRARY OF CONGRESS

Still, people remembered Tippecanoe. Harrison was a national hero, and the Whigs needed one. Clay and Webster, their famous leaders in Congress, held well-known views that were not acceptable to all of the country.

As the Whig candidate for President in the Northwest, Harrison ran well in 1836; hence, in 1839, he received the national nomination.

A Democratic newspaper correspondent foolishly gibed, "Give him a barrel of hard cider and settle a pension of two thousand a year on him, and my word for it, he will sit the remainder of his days in his log cabin by the side of a 'sea coal' fire, and study moral philosophy." The Whigs, eagerly seizing upon this misstep, utilized all the new paraphernalia of politics to present their candidate as a simple, straightforward man of the frontier, an Indian fighter living in a log cabin and drinking hard cider. They accused the "aristocratic" Van Buren of lolling in splendor at the "President's Palace," dabbing himself with eau de cologne and sipping champagne poured into an imported glass from a silver cooler.

One of the campaign stunts of the Whigs was to roll a huge paper ball through the countryside, shouting slogans like "Keep the ball rolling on to Washington." By means of such excitement, they brought out a popular vote more than double that of 1836; about 78 percent of those eligible went to the polls. Harrison won by a majority of fewer than 150,000, but swept the Electoral College, 234 to 60.

When Harrison arrived in Washington in February, 1841, he let Webster edit his Inaugural Address, ornate with classical allusions. Webster succeeded in obtaining some deletions, boasting in a jolly fashion that he had killed "seventeen Roman proconsuls as dead as smelts, every one of them."

Webster had reason to be exuberant, for Harrison emphasized in his Inaugural that he would be obedient to the will of the people as expressed through Congress.

He said of the Constitution: "I can not conceive that by fair construction any or either of its provisions would be found to constitute the President a part of the legislative power. . . . And it is preposterous to suppose that a thought could for a moment have been entertained that the President, placed at the capital . . . could better understand the wants and wishes of the people than their own immediate representatives, who spend a part of every year among them . . . and [are] bound to them by the triple tie of interest, duty, and affection."

Whigs in Congress were confident that the President would accept their policies; he called Congress to meet in special session on May 31. But when he had been in office only three weeks, he caught a cold that developed into pneumonia. On April 4, 1841, he died—the first President to do so in office—and with him died the Whig program.

71

John Tyler

TENTH PRESIDENT 1841-1845

JOHN TYLER was the first Vice President to be elevated to the Presidency by the death of his predecessor. His detractors, claiming that he should function only as acting President, dubbed him "His Accidency."

Tyler refused to accept a mere regency and set a momentous precedent by insisting that he had succeeded to the full powers of his office. He pursued the states' rights course in which he believed, even though he soon found himself a President without a party.

Born in Virginia in 1790, the son of one of Jefferson's friends and adherents, he was reared believing that the constitutional powers granted to the Federal Government must be strictly, or narrowly, construed. He never wavered from this conviction.

Tyler attended the College of William and Mary and later studied law. Serving in the House of Representatives from 1816 to 1821, he voted against most of the nationalist legislation of the time. After leaving the House, he served twice as Governor of Virginia. Later, as a Senator, he reluctantly supported Jackson for President as a choice of evils, but regarded many of his actions and measures as unconstitutional.

Tyler soon became one of the states' rights southerners in Congress who banded with Clay, Webster, and the newly formed Whig Party in opposing President Jackson. He resigned as Senator in 1836 rather than follow the instructions of the Virginia Legislature that he vote to expunge a Senate resolution censuring Jackson. In Virginia politics, he was nominally a Whig, and even though he disapproved of Clay's nationalistic program, he remained a personal friend of Clay.

Thus the Whigs nominated Tyler for Vice President in 1840, hoping that his name would bring to the polls southern states' righters who could not stomach Jacksonian Democracy. The slogan "Tippecanoe and Tyler Too" implied flag-waving nationalism plus a dash of southern sectionalism.

Clay, intending to keep party leadership, minimized his own views during the campaign; Webster proclaimed himself "a Jeffersonian Democrat." With the election won, both discarded these habiliments and tried to dominate the President-elect. "Old Tippecanoe" was a bit disturbed, but appointed Webster as Secretary of State and put four of Clay's supporters into the Cabinet.

PERLEY'S REMINISCENCES

Man without a party, John Tyler clutches a copy of the *National Intelligencer.* The paper printed the first rumors of his secret moves to annex Texas, the brightest achievement in a troubled tenure. His veto of a bank bill caused all but one member of his Cabinet to resign, and his party spurned him.

Jagged metal rakes deck of the frigate *Princeton* as the Navy's largest gun explodes during a Potomac cruise. Tyler, going topside to see the firing, paused on a ladder, and by that margin escaped the blast. Eight dead included the father of Julia Gardiner, 24, who became Tyler's second wife.

Painting by G. P. A. Healy, White House Collection

Whale-shaped Independence Rock rises above the Oregon Trail, heavily traveled during Tyler's Presidency. Beside the Sweetwater River, the rock marked the only safe water for 50 miles west from Casper, Wyoming. Spirits refreshed, pioneers camp near the trail and exchange news. Wagons form protective rings in case of Indian attack.

Suddenly President Harrison was dead and "Tyler Too" in the White House. He insisted upon assuming the full powers and privileges of a President rather than narrowly interpreting the constitutional provision to "act as President." He even delivered an Inaugural Address, full of good Whig doctrine.

Further, Tyler retained Harrison's Cabinet. Tyler's applications of states' rights dogma in the past had led him to oppose many of Jackson's executive actions, including removal of the deposits from the Bank of the United States; Whigs were optimistic that Tyler would consequently accept their program. They soon were disillusioned.

At the first Cabinet meeting, on the day after Harrison's death, Webster asked the President (as Tyler's son later recounted) whether he intended to continue Harrison's procedures. When Tyler nodded slightly, Webster told him that Harrison had agreed that at Cabinet meetings questions were "to be decided by the majority [of votes], each member of the Cabinet and the President having but one vote." Rising to his feet, Tyler retorted, "...I can never consent to being dictated to....I, as President, shall be responsible for my administration."

When Senator Clay brought forward the national program that had been obscured during the campaign, Tyler felt that Clay was acting in bad faith. Tyler was ready to compromise on the banking question, but Clay would not budge. He controlled a majority in Congress, but the President had the veto. Clay would not accept Tyler's "exchequer system," and Tyler vetoed Clay's bill to establish a national bank with branches in several states. A second bank bill, similar to the first, passed Congress. "I will drive him before me," Clay vowed. But again the President vetoed it.

In retaliation, the Whigs expelled Tyler from their party. All of the Cabinet resigned but Webster, who suspected Clay's hand in the dissolution of the Cabinet and distrusted the Senator's ambitions for power. Webster, therefore, stayed on as Secretary of State and Tyler, who had no intention of abandoning his office, replaced his Cabinet immediately. A

year later, when Tyler vetoed a tariff bill, an impeachment resolution against a President was introduced in the House of Representatives for the first time in American history. A committee headed by Representative John Quincy Adams reported that the President had misused the veto power, but the resolution failed.

Despite their differences, President Tyler and the Whig Congress enacted considerable positive legislation. To the delight of westerners, the President in 1841 signed the "Log-Cabin bill," which enabled a settler to claim 160 acres of land before it was offered publicly for sale, and later pay $1.25 an acre for it. In foreign affairs, the Webster-Ashburton Treaty ended a dispute between the United States and Great Britain over the Canadian

PAINTING BY WILLIAM HENRY JACKSON, COURTESY MRS. HOWARD R. DRIGGS, BAYSIDE, LONG ISLAND, NEW YORK

boundary, and, at the end of the administration, Texas was annexed.

To his friends, President Tyler was an attractive figure: "In his official intercourse with all men, high or low, he was ... approachable, courteous, always willing to do a kindly action. ... He was above the middle height, somewhat slender, clean-shaven, with light hair. His light blue eyes were penetrating, and had a humorous twinkle. ..."

The over-all effect of the administration of this states' righter was to strengthen the Presidential office. It also increased the sectional cleavage that led toward the Civil War.

Five Whigs resigned from the Cabinet in 1841. Thereafter Tyler sought the counsel of southern conservatives, former Democrats like himself. In 1844 Calhoun became his Secretary of State. Later, all these men rejoined the Democratic Party. With like-minded southerners, they directed it toward preservation of states' rights, planter interests, and the institution of slavery, while the Whigs became more representative of northern business and farming interests.

When the first southern states seceded from the Union in 1861, Tyler led a compromise movement; failing, he participated in creation of the Southern Confederacy. He died in 1862 after winning election to the Confederate House of Representatives.

At the time, the Government in Washington took no official notice of his death, but in 1915 Congress erected a monument to Tyler at his final resting place, Hollywood Cemetery in Richmond, Virginia.

75

IF JUDGED BY HIS SUCCESS in fulfilling campaign promises, James K. Polk was one of the most notable of Presidents. He ran in 1844 on a spread-eagle expansionist platform; by the time he left the White House in 1849, the Stars and Stripes flew from San Diego Bay to Puget Sound.

Polk, often referred to as the first "dark-horse" President, was scarcely as unknown as his Whig opponents wished voters to think, since he had served four years as Speaker of the House of Representatives. Last of the Jacksonians to sit in the White House, and the last strong President until Lincoln, he became the first to conduct a war in all its phases—fulfilling to the constitutional limits his role as Commander in Chief.

Polk was born in Mecklenburg County, North Carolina, in 1795, the son of a Scotch-Irish farmer. A stone pyramid marks the site of his birthplace, near Pineville. The family moved to Tennessee in 1806. Studious and industrious, but too frail for farm work, Polk graduated in 1818 with top honors from the University of North Carolina.

As a young lawyer he entered politics, and through serving in the Tennessee Legislature became a friend of Jackson. In the House of Representatives, Polk aided Old Hickory in his Bank war, and, as Speaker between 1835 and 1839, endured the heckling of Davy Crockett and other anti-Jacksonians. He left Congress to become Governor of Tennessee.

Until circumstances raised Polk's ambitions, he was a leading contender for the Democratic nomination for Vice President in 1844. Both Van Buren, who had been expected to win the Democratic nomination, and Clay, who was to be the Whig nominee, tried to mute the expansionist issue by declaring themselves opposed to the annexation of Texas. Polk, in contrast, publicly asserted that Texas should be "re-annexed" and all of Oregon "reoccupied."

Jackson correctly sensed that the electorate approved of territorial expansion, and he regarded it as vital to the national security: "Political matters out of the question, Texas [is] the key to our future safety," he wrote. Calling political friends to a conference at the Hermitage, he urged them to choose a candidate committed to the Nation's "manifest destiny." At the Democratic Convention, when more prominent candidates deadlocked, Polk was nominated on the ninth ballot.

"Who is James K. Polk?" jeered the Whigs. Jackson answered in a widely published letter: "His capacity for business [is] great... and to extraordinary powers of labor, both mental and physical, he unites that tact and judgment which are requisite to the successful direction of such an office."

What finally elected Polk was the fact that he stood for expansion, linking the Texas issue, popular in the South, with the Oregon question, attractive in the North.

"There are four great measures which are to be the measures of my administration," President Polk told George Bancroft, the historian, shortly after his Inauguration: "one, a reduction of the tariff; another, the independent treasury; a third, the settlement of the Oregon boundary question; and, lastly, the acquisition of California."

Taking firm command of both his Cabinet and the Democrats in Congress, by the end of his administration he attained all four goals. The first two, the Walker Tariff Act and the Independent Treasury Act, passed Congress and became law in 1846.

The other two, however, absorbed Polk's years as President. Before he took office, Congress passed a joint resolution offering annexation to Texas, thus bequeathing Polk the probability of war with Mexico.

In his strong stand on Oregon, the President seemed to be risking war with Great

First "dark-horse" President, James Knox Polk defeated famed Henry Clay by forthrightly declaring himself for Texas annexation. Not only Texas, but lands westward to the Pacific and northward to Puget Sound came under the U. S. flag during his administration, increasing the Nation's size by two-thirds. Congressmen like Abraham Lincoln charged that Polk "unnecessarily and unconstitutionally" started the Mexican War, but other Americans hungered for new lands in the West. Polk extended the frontiers of the mind as well: On August 10, 1846, he signed the bill creating the Smithsonian Institution, "for the increase and diffusion of knowledge among men."

Painting by G. P. A. Healy, White House Collection

Frenzied forty-niners scramble for gold: a contemporary engraving. Heavy metal settles through

Britain also. The migration of thousands of American settlers, traveling by covered wagon over the Oregon Trail to the rich farmlands of the Willamette Valley, had brought pressure for an end of the joint Anglo-American occupation of the Oregon country.

Although almost all the Americans had settled south of the Columbia River, the Democrats in their 1844 platform laid claim to the entire Oregon area, stretching from the California boundary northward to a latitude of 54° 40′, the southern boundary of the Russian territory that became present-day Alaska.

Extremists proclaimed "54° 40′ or fight," but Polk, aware of diplomatic realities, knew that only war could obtain all of Oregon. Happily, neither he nor the British wanted to fight. He offered to settle by extending the Ca-

nadian boundary, which ran along the 49th parallel, from the Rockies to the Pacific.

When the British Minister in Washington declined, Polk withdrew his offer and reasserted the American claim to the entire area. To a worried Congressman he remarked that the only way to treat John Bull was "to look him straight in the eye." And indeed the British did settle for the 49th parallel, except for the southern tip of Vancouver Island. The treaty was signed in 1846.

Acquisition of California proved more difficult. Polk, hoping to purchase the sparsely populated but potentially valuable area, sent an envoy to offer Mexico as much as $20,000,000, plus the settlement of damage claims owed to Americans, in return for California and New Mexico. Since no Mexican leader could cede

sand and water to bottom of pan and cradle.

Sailing card helped fan gold fever. Despite the card's claim of a 94-day passage, history records *Witchcraft*'s best time as 98 days from New York to San Francisco. In 1849 alone, almost 100,000 treasure seekers reached California.

half his country and hope to remain in power, Polk's envoy received no audience. The President, in a bold application of pressure, sent Gen. Zachary Taylor to the disputed area on the Rio Grande. To the Mexicans, this represented a clear act of aggression.

Polk and his Cabinet were discussing the possibility of war when word arrived that Mexican troops had already attacked Taylor's forces. Polk drafted a war message. "Mexico has passed the boundary of the United States," he informed Congress on May 11, 1846, "has invaded our territory, and shed American blood on American soil."

Congress promptly declared war and, despite considerable northern opposition, supported the military operations. American forces won repeated victories and even occu-

pied Mexico City, but the Mexicans rejected treaty offers. Finally, in 1848, Polk's envoy, Nicholas P. Trist, negotiated an agreement by which Mexico ceded New Mexico and California in return for $15,000,000 and American assumption of damage claims.

Polk added a vast area to the United States, but the Presidents who followed him had to face the possibility of civil war, as the North and South quarreled bitterly over whether the new territories should be free or slave.

Polk, leaving office with his health undermined from hard work, died in June, 1849. Bancroft eulogized him as "one of the very best and most honest and most successful Presidents the country ever had." With his wife Sarah, Polk lies entombed on the grounds of the State Capitol in Nashville, Tennessee.

Z. Taylor

TWELFTH PRESIDENT 1849-1850

ZACHARY TAYLOR, acclaimed for his military victories in the Mexican War, was elevated to the White House in 1849, and as President had to grapple with the acute political problems these victories had helped create.

Northerners and southerners disputed sharply whether the vast lands wrested from Mexico should be opened to slavery, and some southerners even threatened secession. Standing firm, "Old Rough and Ready" was prepared to hold the Union together by armed force rather than promote a compromise of which he disapproved. In the summer of 1850, as he faced this issue, he suddenly died.

From his background, Taylor would have seemed likely to become a southern sympathizer. Born in Virginia in 1784, he was taken as an infant to Kentucky and raised on a plantation; James Madison was one of his many cousins, Robert E. Lee another. He was a career officer in the Army, but his talk was most often of cotton raising. His home was in Baton Rouge, Louisiana, and he owned a plantation in Mississippi.

Being a slaveholder did not make Taylor a defender of slavery or of southern sectionalism; rather, his forty years in the Army imbued him with a strong nationalist spirit. He received a commission in the Regular Army in 1808 and spent decades policing the frontiers against Indians, during the War of 1812, in the Indiana Territory during the Black Hawk War, and in Florida during the long struggle against the Seminole Indians and escaped Negro slaves. In the Mexican War, using much the same direct offensive tactics he had employed against the Indians, he won victories at Monterrey and Buena Vista.

President Polk, disturbed by Taylor's informal habits of command (and perhaps by his Whiggery as well), regarded him as a "narrow-minded bigotted partisan, without resources, and wholly unqualified."

Restricting Taylor to northern Mexico, Polk sent an expedition under Gen. Winfield Scott (also a Whig) to capture Mexico City. Taylor, incensed, thought that his victory in "the battle of Buena Vista [had] opened the road to the city of Mexico and the halls of Montezuma, that others might revel in them."

While not a remarkable general, Taylor did possess very solid merits that U. S. Grant, who served under him, pointed out years later: "No soldier could face either danger or responsibility more calmly than he. These are qualities more rarely found than genius or physical courage . . . General Taylor never

ROUGH AND READY.

Battered straw hat helped give Zachary Taylor his nickname: "Old Rough and Ready." His sloppy dress increased with rank; as a general in the Mexican War, he wore old farm clothes. Taylor treated bullets as trifles and never lost a battle. He had legs so short that an orderly had to assist him in mounting his horse.

First professional soldier in the White House, tobacco-chewing Taylor had never voted and lacked political experience. The question of slavery expansion threatened the Union which Taylor, a southerner, staunchly upheld. He fell ill and died, a bitter man. "My motives have been misconstrued," he said, "and my feelings grossly betrayed."

Painting by Joseph H. Bush, White House Collection

wore uniform, but dressed himself entirely for comfort. He moved about the field in which he was operating to see through his own eyes the situation.... He was very much given to sit his horse side-ways—with both feet on one side—particularly on the battlefield."

Taylor's homespun idiosyncrasies were political assets. Americans preferred a general who wore a straw hat and gingham coat as he led his men into battle to a punctilious military man like his rival, Winfield Scott, nicknamed "Old Fuss and Feathers."

While Taylor's long military record would appeal to northerners, his experience as a planter and his ownership of a hundred slaves would lure southern votes. He had never held any civil office, by appointment or election—in fact, he had never bothered to vote—and this apolitical background meant he had not committed himself on troublesome issues. Hence the Whigs nominated Taylor to run

against the Democratic candidate, Lewis Cass of Michigan, who favored letting the residents of territories decide for themselves whether or not they wanted slavery.

Both the major parties tried to play down the slavery question. In protest against Taylor the slaveholder and Cass the advocate of "squatter sovereignty," northerners who wanted no extension whatever of slavery formed a Free Soil Party that nominated Van Buren. It was a close election in which the Free Soilers pulled enough votes away from Cass, especially in New York, to elect Taylor.

Although Taylor had subscribed suitably to Whig principles of legislative leadership, he soon demonstrated no inclination to be a puppet of Whig leaders in Congress. To their distress, he acted at times as if he were above parties and politics. His inexperience and lack of knowledge of the office of President led him to too heavy a reliance at first upon the advice of others, and later, to too great

Mexicans attack through their Sierra Madre pass in the Battle of Buena Vista, February 23, 1847. Gen. Antonio de Santa Anna's 15,000 troops, advancing along the base of the mountains, hoped to crush Taylor's 4,700 inexperienced invaders. But the Americans (foreground), matching long-range mountain howitzers against less efficient Mexican artillery, won the victory, making Taylor a national hero.

members of both Houses of Congress were also dismayed, since they felt the President was encroaching upon their policy-making prerogatives. In addition, Taylor's solution ignored several acute side issues: the northern dislike of the slave market operating in the District of Columbia, which was Federal territory, and the southern demands for a more stringent fugitive slave law to prevent northerners from harboring runaways.

Three of the great statesmen of the previous generation—Webster, Clay, and Calhoun—still sat in the 31st Congress. Many zealous young men destined for fame in coming years were also there, eager to make their marks. Debate, reaching fever pitch, threatened to rend the Union. Clay's proposals for compromise made little headway, in part because they were embodied in one great bill few members of Congress would accept in totality, and in part because President Taylor still stubbornly persisted in his demand that first California and New Mexico should be admitted as states.

In February, 1850, President Taylor held a stormy private conference with several southern leaders who threatened secession. Taylor told the southerners that to enforce the laws he would lead the Army in person, and if they were "taken in rebellion against the Union, he would hang them with less reluctance than he had hanged deserters and spies in Mexico." In a public address, he urged his fellow southerners to *"preserve the Union at all hazards."* He never wavered.

Then events took an unexpected and tragic turn. After participating in ceremonies at the Washington Monument on the sweltering afternoon of July 4, Taylor fell ill; five days later he was dead. After his death, the forces of compromise triumphed, but the war Taylor had been willing to face came 11 years later. Ironically, his only son Richard served as a general in the Confederate Army.

Taylor lies buried in a cemetery named for him—Zachary Taylor National Cemetery—not far from Louisville, Kentucky.

a faith in his own judgment, regardless of political complications.

As disheveled as always, garbed in a black broadcloth suit purposely cut too large, Taylor tried to run his administration in the same rule-of-thumb fashion that he had used in fighting Indians.

He accepted a simple formula for ending the dispute over the new possessions, ignoring the fact that it appealed to the North rather than the South. He reasoned that the easy way to decide whether the new areas were to be free or slave was to encourage their organization into states, since, traditionally, the citizens could decide the question for themselves when they drew up a state constitution. Therefore, he urged settlers in New Mexico and in California—flooded with nearly 100,000 gold-seeking forty-niners—to draft constitutions and apply for statehood.

Southerners were furious, since neither state constitution was likely to permit slavery;

Millard Fillmore

THIRTEENTH PRESIDENT 1850-1853

UNEXPECTEDLY taking office in July, 1850, at a time of acute sectional crisis, Millard Fillmore lent his political skills and the prestige of the Presidency to the enactment of the Compromise of 1850. This attempt to satisfy both slavery and anti-slavery forces temporarily abated the crisis, but brought down upon Fillmore the wrath of some northern Whigs who deplored his moderation. He was the last Whig President.

In his rise from a log cabin to wealth and the White House, Fillmore demonstrated that an uninspiring man, through industry and competence, could make the American dream come true. He was born in the Finger Lakes section of New York in 1800, and in his youth endured the privations of frontier life. The log cabin of his birth no longer exists; a reproduction, however, stands in Fillmore Glen State Park, near Moravia.

Young Fillmore worked on his father's farm, and at 15 was apprenticed to a wool carder. When he could, he attended a one-room school, and in 1818 fell in love with his red-haired teacher, Abigail Powers, whom he later married. She tutored him so efficiently that he was able to teach school as a means of financing his study of law.

Admitted to the bar in 1823, he moved his law practice to Buffalo in 1830. As an associate of the Whig politician, Thurlow Weed, Fillmore served in the House of Representatives. In 1848, while Comptroller of New York, he was elected Vice President.

In this office, Fillmore presided over the Senate during the months of nerve-wracking debate over the Compromise of 1850. Fillmore looked more the part of a President than Taylor, a diarist commented, as the tall, handsome, impeccably groomed, good-natured man labored to maintain an atmosphere of fairness in the Senate Chamber. He made no public comment on the merits of the compro-

mise proposals, but a few days before Taylor's death intimated to the President that if there should be a tie vote on Clay's bill in the Senate, he would vote in favor of it.

Thus the sudden accession of Fillmore to the Presidency brought an abrupt political shift in the administration. Taylor's Cabinet resigned, and President Fillmore at once appointed Webster as Secretary of State, thus proclaiming his alliance with the moderate Whigs, who favored the compromise.

On the last day of July, Clay's compromise bill was defeated except for a provision giving Utah territorial status. A separate bill for California statehood, then introduced by Sen. Stephen A. Douglas of Illinois, brought forth once again all the violent arguments for and against the extension of slavery, without any progress toward settling the major issues. Clay, exhausted, left Washington to recuperate, throwing leadership upon Douglas.

At this critical juncture, President Fillmore aligned the full weight of his administrative and party leadership in favor of compromise. On August 6, 1850, he sent a message to Congress recommending that Texas be paid a substantial sum to abandon her claims to part of New Mexico. Significantly he asserted near the end of the message:

"I think no event would be hailed with more gratification by the people of the United States than the amicable adjustment of questions of difficulty which have now for a long time agitated the country and occupied, to the exclusion of other subjects, the time and attention of Congress."

Fillmore's message, coming at a time when public opinion throughout the Nation was increasingly favoring conciliation, helped influence a critical number of northern Whigs in Congress away from their adamant insistence upon the Wilmot Proviso—the stipulation that all the territory gained as a result of the

Erect, impeccably dressed Millard Fillmore, a dramatic opposite in appearance to squat, unkempt Zachary Taylor, carried the contrast into politics as well. Old-soldier Taylor, though a Virginian by birth, warned secessionists he would hang them as traitors. Succeeding him as Chief Executive, New Yorker Fillmore favored conciliation and endorsed the Compromise of 1850 to settle the angry dispute between North and South. The Fugitive Slave Act, one provision of the Compromise, so outraged many northerners that it ended Fillmore's career. His Presidency foreshadowed the end of the Whig Party.

LITHOGRAPH FROM PAINTING BY WILLIAM HEINE, COURTESY MRS. MARY CRAIG OWENS, CHARLOTTESVILLE, VIRGINIA

war with Mexico must be closed to slavery.

Representative Horace Mann of Massachusetts wrote: "Here are twenty, perhaps thirty, men from the North in this House, who, before General Taylor's death, would have sworn, like St. Paul, not to eat or drink until they had voted the proviso, who now, in the face of the world, turn about, defy the instruction of their States, take back their own declarations, a thousand times uttered, and vote against it."

Senator Salmon P. Chase of Ohio, reporting that the President had changed the votes of six New England Senators, lamented, "The Texas Surrender Bill was passed by the influence of the new administration which is Hunker & Compromise all over. The Message of Fillmore asserting the right of the United States and declaring his purpose to support it *and then* begging Congress to relieve him from the necessity of doing so by a compromise—that message did the work."

Douglas's strategy in Congress combined

with Fillmore's pressure from the White House to give impetus to the compromise movement. Breaking up Clay's single legislative package, Douglas presented five separate bills to the Senate, each of which obtained a reluctant majority. These bills (1) admitted California as a free state; (2) provided for settlement of the Texas boundary; (3) granted territorial status to New Mexico; (4) placed Federal officers at the disposal of slaveholders seeking fugitives; (5) abolished the slave trade in the District of Columbia.

By September 20, President Fillmore had signed all these measures. Collectively, history knows them as the Compromise of 1850. Webster wrote, "I can now sleep of nights." In December, Fillmore announced that the "difficulties felt and the dangers apprehended . . . seem now happily overcome . . ." He congratulated "Congress and the country."

Some militant northern Whigs, refusing to forgive Fillmore for having signed the Fugitive Slave Act, helped deprive him of the

Presidential nomination in 1852. Many southerners likewise viewed the Compromise of 1850 with serious misgivings. The next few years proved that although the Compromise was intended to settle permanently the controversy over slavery, it merely served as an uneasy sectional truce.

After his return to Buffalo, Fillmore continued for the remainder of his life to favor moderation and conciliation. As the Whig Party disintegrated in the 1850's, he refused to join the Republican Party, but instead, in 1856, accepted the nomination for President of the Know Nothing, or American, Party. Throughout the Civil War he opposed President Lincoln, and during Reconstruction he supported President Johnson. He died in 1874.

Japan receives Commodore Matthew C. Perry, who lands near Tokyo, March 8, 1854. Sent out by Fillmore to seek relations with the feudal island nation, Perry had called the previous year to present his request. Now he returns for a reply, flanked by U. S. Marines and backed by a fleet including steam frigates. Japan's answer: Yes.

Fugitive slaves arrive at an Underground Railroad station—Levi Coffin's Newport, Indiana, home. Coffin stands in the wagon while his wife helps an elderly passenger. The cruel Fugitive Slave Act signed by Fillmore moved many citizens to defy the law and help runaways find haven in Canada.

PAINTING BY CHARLES T. WEBBER, CINCINNATI ART MUSEUM

FOURTEENTH PRESIDENT 1853-1857

FRANKLIN PIERCE became President at a time of apparent tranquillity. The United States, by virtue of the Compromise of 1850, seemed to have weathered its sectional storm. By pursuing the recommendations of southern advisers, Pierce—a New Englander—hoped to prevent still another outbreak of that storm. But his policies, far from preserving calm, hastened the disruption of the Union.

Too much blame should not be assessed against Pierce, even though his amiability was more striking than his judgment. It is doubtful if even the wisest and strongest of Presidents could greatly have altered the course of events had he taken office as did Pierce, in the deceptively peaceful eye of a great national hurricane.

Born at Hillsboro, New Hampshire, in 1804, Pierce was a member of the class of 1824 at Bowdoin College, where he became a friend of Nathaniel Hawthorne. After graduation he studied law and entered politics. When his father became governor for the second time, Pierce was elected to the New Hampshire General Court—the state legislature—at the age of 24; two years later, he became Speaker. During the 1830's he went to Washington, first as a Representative, then as a Senator. He was notable only for his un-swerving devotion to Jacksonian Democracy and his dislike for the disruptive effects of abolitionist agitation. Since his ailing wife, Jane Appleton Pierce, detested Washington, and he needed a larger income to support his family, he resigned in 1842 to practice law in Concord, New Hampshire.

During the Mexican War, President Polk commissioned Pierce a colonel, then a brigadier general; his only qualification for either rank was the fact that he was a Democrat. Nevertheless, some of his New Hampshire friends decided to promote him for the Presidential nomination in 1852.

At the convention, the delegates agreed easily enough upon a platform pledging undeviating support of the Compromise of 1850 and hostility to efforts of any "shape or color" to agitate the question of slavery. But they balloted 48 times and eliminated all the well-known candidates before nominating Pierce, a true "dark horse."

Probably because the Democrats stood more firmly for the Compromise than the

Thin and careworn, Franklin Pierce suffered from malaria during summers in the White House. Persistent gloom choked the mansion during his Presidency. Two months before Inauguration, a train wreck killed his son; Mrs. Pierce, grief-stricken and hating politics, bided the term in seclusion. An inept leader, Pierce struggled with minor details, bungling major issues. He opened Kansas to slavery by endorsing the repeal of the Missouri Compromise. A costly blunder, the repeal fostered feelings that led to civil war.

Campaign poster helped answer the question, "Who is Frank Pierce?" A "dark horse," Pierce put his picture on brass medals, handkerchiefs, and posters like this one. Pierce's running mate, William R. King, died before he could serve in office.

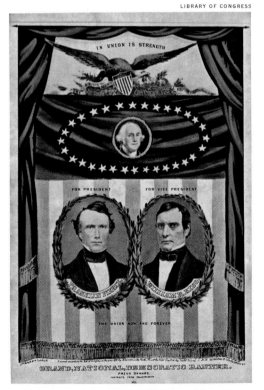

Painting by G. P. A. Healy, White House Collection

89

Whigs, and because the Whig candidate, Gen. Winfield Scott, was suspect in the South, Pierce won. With a narrow margin of popular votes, he swept the electoral college, 254 to 42. Thus this handsome, well-meaning, but indecisive and inexperienced man found himself President at a time when the challenge of the office far exceeded his modest abilities— borne, he said, "to a position so suitable for others rather than desirable for myself."

TWO MONTHS before he took office, a railroad train in which he and his wife were riding was wrecked, and their only remaining child out of three, an 11-year-old boy, was killed before his eyes. He entered the Presidency grief-stricken and nervously exhausted.

In his Inaugural, Pierce proclaimed an era of peace and prosperity at home and vigor in relations with other nations. The United States might have to acquire additional possessions for the sake of its own security, he pointed out, and would not be deterred by "any timid forebodings of evil."

Pierce had only to make gestures toward expansion to excite the wrath of northerners, who accused him of acting as a cat's-paw of southerners eager for areas into which to extend slavery. Thus there was apprehension when he pressured Great Britain to relinquish its special interests along part of the coast of Central America, and even more when he tried to persuade Spain to sell Cuba.

Pierce was successful only in friendlier directions. He continued efforts to open Japan. President Fillmore had sent Commodore Matthew C. Perry, who, acting with skill and firmness, had delivered a message in 1853; returning to Japan the next year, Perry brought back to Pierce a treaty opening two relatively inaccessible ports.

Pierce was also successful in negotiating a reciprocity treaty with Great Britain in 1854. It won concessions off Canadian shores for American fishermen in return for opening the United States to more Canadian products.

At home, almost every measure Pierce favored worked out badly, in considerable part because the conflict between the North and South colored almost all domestic matters. Favoring the South at nearly every point, Pierce signed a lower tariff measure

and vetoed an internal improvements bill; southern votes in Congress blocked a homestead bill. Each of these aggrieved northerners. He angered them even more by blaming sectional tensions on northerners' "pernicious agitation" against slavery, and saying their efforts had "for twenty years produced nothing save unmitigated evil, North and South."

But the most violent renewal of the storm stemmed from the Kansas-Nebraska Act of 1854. Pierce endorsed the bill, which repealed the Missouri Compromise, destroyed the truce of 1850, and reopened the question of slavery in the West.

This measure, the handiwork of Senator Stephen A. Douglas, grew in part out of his desire to promote a railroad from Chicago to California through Nebraska. Already Secretary of War Jefferson Davis, advocate of a southern transcontinental route, had persuaded Pierce to send James Gadsden to Mexico to purchase lands along the Gila River through which a southern railroad might best run. Gadsden, for $10,000,000, purchased the area now comprising southern Arizona and part of southern New Mexico.

Douglas's proposal, to organize western territories through which a railroad might run, caused extreme trouble. A proponent of "popular sovereignty," Douglas provided in his bills that the residents of the new territories could decide the slavery question for themselves. As a result, northerners and southerners rushed into Kansas, vying for control of the territorial government. The North sent in more settlers, but Pierce tended to throw his influence toward the South. Shooting broke out in "bleeding Kansas." As Pierce said, it became a "battlefield . . . of the conflicting passions of the whole people." It was a prelude to the Civil War.

By the end of his administration, Pierce could claim "a peaceful condition of things in Kansas." But, to his disappointment, the Democratic Party in 1856 refused to renominate him, turning to the less controversial Buchanan. Pierce returned to New Hampshire, leaving his successor to face the rising fury of the sectional whirlwind. Obscure and unpopular even at home, Pierce died in 1869.

New Hampshire maintains the family home near Hillsboro as a state historic site.

Lifelong friends, Pierce and writer Nathaniel Hawthorne stroll under the Arch of Titus in the ruins of the Roman Forum. Meeting Pierce in Rome shortly after the President had left office, Hawthorne noted "many a whitening hair" and a "something that seemed to have passed away out of him, without leaving any trace." Hawthorne, who attended Bowdoin College with Pierce, helped propel his friend toward the Presidency by writing his biography. PAINTING BY NATIONAL GEOGRAPHIC ARTIST IRVIN E. ALLEMAN

Irvin E. Alleman

James Buchanan

JAMES BUCHANAN presided over a Federal Union rushing recklessly toward disintegration. He seemed to think he could stem the course of events only by offering concession after concession to the South regardless of the anger he provoked in the North. When the actual breakup of the Union began, he expressed his disapproval but considered himself legally powerless to stem the course of secession.

Born in 1791 in Franklin County, Pennsylvania, Buchanan graduated from Dickinson College. His childhood home, moved from its original site, now stands—after careers as museum and antique shop—on the campus of Mercersburg Academy.

Learned in law and a gifted debater, Buchanan rose rapidly in politics. Only one incident marred his early life; his betrothed broke her engagement and shortly thereafter died. He was the only President who never married.

Although a Federalist of moderate views early in his career, Buchanan found it easy in the 1820's to shift his allegiance to Jackson. After five terms in the House of Representatives, he served as Minister to Russia, then for a decade in the Senate. He became Polk's Secretary of State and Pierce's Minister to Great Britain. His service abroad brought him the Democratic nomination in 1856 because it had exempted him from involvement in bitter domestic controversies.

In a calmer age, Buchanan might have been a successful President. But in the bitter 1850's he failed as abysmally as Pierce—not through inexperience, but because he grasped inadequately the political realities of the time. Tall, stately, stiffly formal in the high stock he wore around his jowls, he acted as if firm adherence to constitutional doctrines would somehow bridge the widening rift; Buchanan failed to understand that the North would not accept constitutional arguments which favored the South. Nor did he realize how sectionalism had realigned political parties.

This sectional cleavage, destroying the Whigs, had brought the rise of the Republicans. The Republican Party, formed in 1854 in protest against the Kansas-Nebraska Act, coalesced northerners and westerners irked with southern domination of the national administration—manufacturers seeking a protective tariff, farmers irritated because the South blocked a homestead bill, westerners wanting subsidies for internal improvements. A common commitment to fight the extension of slavery also united these diverse groups.

To militant southerners, the Republicans seemed an intolerable menace. The fledgling party ran John C. Frémont for President in 1856 and might have defeated Buchanan by polling a few additional votes in Pennsylvania and Illinois.

At the time of his Inauguration, Buchanan thought that the crisis would disappear if he maintained a sectional balance in his appointments and could persuade the people to accept constitutional law as the Supreme Court interpreted it. The Court was then considering the legality of restricting slavery in the territories, and two Justices hinted to Buchanan what the decision would be.

Thus, in his Inaugural the new President referred to the territorial question as "happily, a matter of but little practical importance" since the Supreme Court was about to settle it "speedily and finally."

Two days later Chief Justice Roger B. Taney delivered his opinion in the notorious Dred Scott case, asserting that Congress had no constitutional power to deprive persons of their property rights in slaves in the territories. Southerners were delighted, of course, but the decision created a furor in the North; Republicans promptly dedicated themselves to reversing it.

Buchanan decided to end the troubles in Kansas by admitting the territory as a slave state. Although he directed his Presidential authority to this goal, he succeeded only in

Confirmed bachelor James Buchanan delighted in lively White House parties and the latest Washington gossip, but threatening civil war clouded his Presidency. Stately black suit and white stock enhanced his blue eyes and silk-white hair. People often met him near sunrise or at dusk taking a solitary walk along Pennsylvania Avenue.

Painting by William M. Chase, White House Collection

PAINTING BY THOMAS PRICHARD ROSSITER, SMITHSONIAN INSTITUTION; (BELOW) FRANK LESLIE'S ILLUSTRATED NEWSPAPER

Prince and President stand before Washington's tomb at Mount Vernon. The young Prince of Wales, later Edward VII, gazes reverently at the crypt of the man who defeated troops of his great-grandfather, George III. Having been entertained at Windsor Castle while Minister to Great Britain, Buchanan reciprocated by inviting the Prince to visit the United States as his personal guest.

On this occasion the Prince planted a buckeye tree near the tomb. It died. In 1919 another Prince of Wales—the late Duke of Windsor—planted an English yew that survives nearby. At left in this painting, Harriet Lane, Buchanan's niece and White House hostess, holds a parasol.

Wounded John Brown lies outside the fire-engine house where he made his stand at Harpers Ferry. Marines sent by Buchanan subdued the abolitionist and his little band. Brown's bid to provoke slave insurrection enraged the South; his subsequent hanging inflamed antislavery forces in the North. Brown's martyrdom inspired four soldiers to write the words of the ballad, "John Brown's Body." Union troops sang the song as they marched to battle in the Civil War.

further angering the Republicans. By his rejection of popular sovereignty, he alienated Senator Douglas. Despite all the President's efforts, Kansas remained a territory.

When Republicans won a plurality in the House of Representatives in the congressional election of 1858, every significant bill they passed fell before southern votes in the Senate or a Presidential veto. The Federal Government had reached a stalemate.

Republicans waited hopefully for the 1860 election, expecting to win the Presidency. Southerners, already fearful, were even more alarmed by abolitionist John Brown's raid at Harpers Ferry in 1859; this, they warned one another, was a foretaste of the future.

Political strife reached such a fever stage in 1860 that the Democratic Party split into northern and southern wings, each nominating a candidate for the Presidency. Thus, it was a foregone conclusion that the Republican nominee, Abraham Lincoln, would be elected even though his name appeared on no southern ballot. When news of Lincoln's election reached South Carolina, southern "fire-eaters" forced secession. Other states in the deep South followed.

In Washington, President Buchanan, dismayed and hesitant, denied the legal right of states to secede but held that the Federal Government could not prevent them. He hoped to pave the way for conciliation, and directed his most stinging words against the abolitionists. But every proposed compromise, consisting entirely of concessions to the South, proved unacceptable to the Republicans. In any event, southern leaders of the secession movement did not want to compromise.

Then Buchanan took a militant tack. As several Cabinet members resigned, he appointed northerners in their places and sent the *Star of the West* to carry reinforcements to Fort Sumter. On January 9, 1861, shore batteries opened fire, driving the ship away.

Buchanan reverted to a policy of inactivity that continued until he relinquished his office. Basically, he believed in coercing the South, but had he acted more vigorously he would only have precipitated the war several months earlier. He retired to his Pennsylvania home in March, 1861, leaving it to his successor to resolve the frightful issue.

As Lincoln acted in April, 1861, Buchanan declared, "The present administration had no alternative but accept the war. . . . The North will sustain the administration almost to a man; and it ought to be sustained at all hazards." Buchanan died in 1868.

3 THE AMERICAN

GIANT COMES OF AGE

Abraham Lincoln through William McKinley

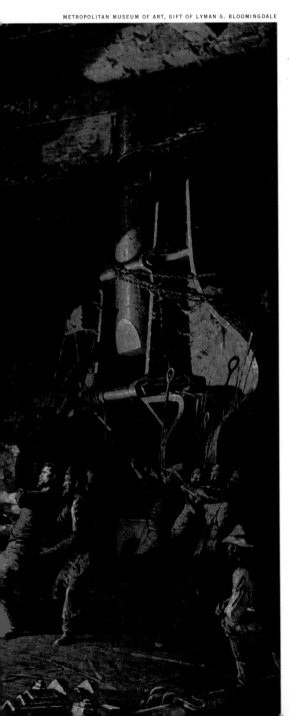

AMERICAN PRESIDENTS between 1861 and 1901 found themselves presiding over a Nation spectacularly transforming itself into an industrial giant. Scarcely deterred by the shattering four years of the Civil War, the Nation moved forward at an ever-accelerating tempo. Settlers poured into the West in such numbers that by 1890 frontier lines had to be erased from the maps.

These were decades of bonanza, and sometimes of bust, in the boom towns, on cattle ranges, and across ever-expanding wheat lands. These were the years when rail networks spread to knit the continent more tightly than men had dreamed possible.

Above all, this was the era when the United States advanced from fourth to first place among manufacturing nations. Inventors like Alexander Graham Bell and Thomas A. Edison helped revolutionize American life.

From farms and overseas, ambitious men and women moved to the growing cities. As the era began, only a sixth of the people lived in cities; as it closed, a third were urbanites.

Through the centennial years of the 1870's and 1880's, Presidents proudly emphasized the progress the Nation had made since its founding. Benjamin Harrison, taking office in 1889, a hundred years after George Washington, remarked that the center of population had moved westward from the vicinity of Baltimore to near Cincinnati.

"But our growth has not been limited to territory, population, and . . . wealth," he said.

With blast-furnace fury, America's industrial revolution exploded in the mid-1800's. As science reached new heights and immigrants new shores, the country emerged a colossus. In his painting "Forging the Shaft," artist John Ferguson Weir depicts the foundry at Cold Spring, New York, where Abraham Lincoln inspected guns produced for the Civil War.

"The masses of our people are better fed, clothed, and housed than their fathers were.... Not all of our people are happy and prosperous.... But on the whole the opportunities... to the individual to secure the comforts of life are better than are found elsewhere."

In part, Harrison was answering Grover Cleveland, who uttered stern warnings in his message to Congress of December, 1888:

"Our survival for one hundred years is not sufficient to assure us that we no longer have dangers to fear in the maintenance, with all its promised blessings, of a government founded upon the freedom of the people.... Upon more careful inspection we find the wealth and luxury of our cities mingled with poverty and.... discontent with agricultural pursuits.... Corporations, which should be the carefully restrained creatures of the law and the servants of the people, are fast becoming the people's masters."

In Harrison's optimism and Cleveland's pessimism are reflected the two faces of the age. Yet both men, like every President from Lincoln through McKinley, believed the Nation basically must solve its problems through a free working of economic laws. In theory, Presidents seemed to have little responsibility for the economy.

Nevertheless, Lincoln had brought to the Federal administration such dynamism that it fought and won a great war for survival. Nor did Lincoln hold so firm a view of the limitations of government. In 1854 he wrote: "The legitimate object of government is to do for the people what needs to be done, but which they can not, by individual effort, do at all, or do so well, for themselves."

From the 1870's into the 1890's, numerous dissatisfied people repeatedly sought Federal aid to help lift their economic burdens. They obtained considerable legislation—to increase money supply, regulate railroads, and dissolve monopolies. But not until the 20th century, with Theodore Roosevelt, were they to obtain a President who would wield in their behalf the positive strength of a Lincoln.

First Presidential phone call connects Rutherford B. Hayes with Alexander Graham Bell. In 1877, at Rocky Point, Rhode Island, Hayes (left) listens over a bobbinlike receiver-transmitter. From Providence, Mr. Bell speaks to the President through 13 miles of wire. A few months later, Hayes installed the first telephone in the White House. Not until the Hoover Administration in 1929, however, did the instrument sit on the desk of a Chief Executive.

Melting pot of the West, Chicago in 1870 reels from droves of immigrants, merchants, frontiersmen, and Indians who jam the station platforms. Only one year earlier, east and west coasts had been stapled together by a steel ribbon of track. As early as 1854, this booming metropolis had become the Nation's railway hub; more than 200 trains rumbled into the city each day.

Steam-snorting engines power threshing machines harvesting the wheat crop in the Dakota Territory during the late 1870's. Men bag the grain that pours out of the horseless thresher at a rate of some 600 bushels a day. Wagon in foreground hauls away the sacked bounty.

DRAWING BY LISA BIGANZOLI, NATIONAL GEOGRAPHIC STAFF

FRANK LESLIE'S ILLUSTRATED NEWSPAPER, 1878

Abraham Lincoln

SIXTEENTH PRESIDENT 1861-1865

ABRAHAM LINCOLN, inaugurated at a time of crisis when the Federal Union seemed irrevocably dissolved, pledged all his political skills and statecraft to the Union's preservation. He grew in office and achieved that rare greatness necessary to rally the North, to sustain it through a long and discouraging war, and ultimately to reunite the American Nation.

He also lifted from the land the stigma of slavery. And in words of unsurpassed eloquence, he set forth the humanitarian ideals that gave meaning to the conflict and inspiration to later generations.

The son of a Kentucky frontiersman, Lincoln in his youth had to struggle for a living and for learning. Five months before receiving the nomination for President, he sketched his early life:

"I was born Feb. 12, 1809, in Hardin County, Kentucky. My parents were both born in Virginia, of undistinguished families—second families, perhaps I should say. My mother, who died in my tenth year, was of a family of the name of Hanks.... My father ... removed from Kentucky to what is now Spencer county, Indiana, in my eighth year.... It was a wild region, with many bears and other wild animals still in the woods. There I grew up. There were some schools, so called; but no qualification was ever required of a teacher, beyond 'readin, writin, and cipherin,' to the Rule of Three.... Of course when I came of age I did not know much.... I could read, write, and cipher ... but that was all.... The little advance I now have upon this store of education, I have picked up from time to time under the pressure of necessity."

Of his physical appearance, Lincoln added, "I am, in height, six feet, four inches, nearly; lean in flesh, weighing, on an average, one hundred and eighty pounds; dark complexion, with coarse black hair, and grey eyes—no other marks or brands recollected."

Lincoln grew up with a keen desire for knowledge and made extraordinary efforts to attain it while working on a farm, splitting rails for fences, and keeping store in the log-cabin village of New Salem, Illinois, now reconstructed.

After his "bloody struggles with the musquetoes" as a captain in the Black Hawk War, he spent eight years in the Illinois Legislature. He became a licensed attorney, and moved to Springfield in 1837. For years he rode the circuit of courts, sharpening his skills and enjoying success as a prairie lawyer, talking politics and swapping jokes.

LIBRARY OF CONGRESS

Pipestem figure, angular 6-foot-4 Abe, tallest of the Presidents, often walked alone late at night near the White House, sometimes pausing to talk to strangers. His clothes "hung upon him as if on a rack to dry," said biographer Carl Sandburg. Charles W. Reed, a trumpeter of the 9th Massachusetts Battery, executed this rarely seen sketch.

"He can sit and think without food or rest longer than any man I ever saw," said his law partner of Abraham Lincoln, whose election triggered the Civil War but whose firm hand preserved the Union. He was the first President to be cut down by an assassin.

Painting by G. P. A. Healy, White House Collection

In 1842 he married Mary Todd, from Lexington, Kentucky, who had been staying with her sister in Springfield. Lincoln bought a large frame house at Eighth and Jackson Streets, now maintained as a state memorial. In his favorite rocker, one of the many original furnishings on display, he stretched out his long legs and watched his four boys, those "dear codgers," romp at his feet. Only one son, Robert Todd Lincoln, lived to maturity.

Elected to Congress in 1846 as a member of the minority Whig Party, Lincoln was able to win little national distinction and returned to his thriving law practice after a single term. But his law partner said of him, "His ambition was a little engine that knew no rest."

As a Whig politician, Lincoln rose less spectacularly than his Democratic rival Stephen A. Douglas, the "Little Giant." But the repeal of the Missouri Compromise aroused him, he said, "as he had never been before." By 1858 after he had joined the new Republican Party, he was recognized as the strongest man to oppose Douglas for Senator.

Lincoln opened that campaign with his portentous "House Divided" speech: "I believe this government cannot endure, permanently half *slave* and half *free*. I do not expect the Union to be *dissolved*—I do not expect the house to *fall*—but I do expect it will cease to be divided. It will become *all* one thing, or *all* the other."

He challenged Douglas's doctrine of popular sovereignty in a remarkable series of debates, calling it a "don't care" policy of indifference to a question of right and wrong. At Knox College in Galesburg, Illinois, Lincoln branded slavery "a moral, social and political evil," a threat to the liberty of the people and a danger to the Union.

Lincoln lost that election, but acquired a nationwide reputation that brought him the Republican nomination for President two years later, in 1860. Several months before the convention, he made headlines in the East for his speech at Cooper Union, a New York landmark which visitors find virtually unchanged from Lincoln's day. His audience stood up to cheer at his concluding words.

"Let us have faith that right makes might," Lincoln said, "and in that faith, let us, to the end, dare to do our duty as we understand it."

In the election, Lincoln received only a plurality of the popular vote over Democrat Douglas, Southern Democrat John C. Breckinridge, and Constitutional Union Party candidate John Bell; but he gained a majority of the electoral vote.

Rustic mill in New Salem, Illinois, overlooks the spot where Lincoln in 1831 ran aground with a flatboat full of squealing pigs. Later he lived in New Salem and became a state representative. The mill rises above a snow-covered field where the Sangamon River formerly flowed.

"May he yet guide the Ship of State," read the title of this 1860 campaign poster depicting Lincoln as a young man piloting a flatboat down the Mississippi to New Orleans. A line engraving tinted for posters, the picture lacks color around the flagstaff and Abe's chest.

There was little in Lincoln's background and appearance to inspire confidence that he could meet the challenge posed by the tier of states in the Deep South that had seceded to form the Confederacy. One reporter traveling eastward with the President-elect remembered how dismayed people were by Lincoln's high-pitched voice, and his "most unprepossessing features ... gawkiest figure, and ... most awkward manners." These superficialities were quickly overshadowed as Lincoln began to take action as President.

In his Inaugural Address, on March 4, 1861, Lincoln was conciliatory yet firm toward the South. "In *your* hands, my dissatisfied fellow countrymen, and not in *mine,* is the momentous issue of civil war," he warned them. "The government will not assail *you.* ... *You* have no oath registered in Heaven to destroy the government, while *I* shall have the most solemn one to 'preserve, protect, and defend' it."

Lincoln thought secession legally impossible. He was determined to enforce Federal laws—"to hold, occupy, and possess" Government property—in the South. The Nation turned its attention to Fort Sumter, Federal property in the harbor of secessionist Charleston, South Carolina. On April 6, the President announced he was sending supplies to the fort. Confederate batteries opened fire on

ILLINOIS BORN UNDER THE ORDINANCE OF '87.

"WESTWARD THE
THE GIRLS LINK
THEIR M

April 12 and forced its surrender. The Civil War had begun.

In the hectic early months of the war, which brought the Union rout at Manassas, or Bull Run, Lincoln pursued a careful political course in order to retain the sympathies of border states.

At the same time he boldly exercised to the utmost his wartime powers as Commander in Chief. He raised troops and conducted the war for several months before Congress met, at his summons, for a special session, convening on July 4.

Rail Splitter Lincoln drives a wedge with a maul in an 1860 campaign poster, an allusion to his hard-working youth. Down the river floats a flatboat, recalling his trips on the Mississippi. On the far bank looms a hazy image of the White House—a result of artistic license. The slogan "Rail Splitter" first became popular at a state convention when two rails were displayed from a lot of 3,000 he helped cleave. At 21, Abe paid for some trousers by splitting 400 rails for each yard of cloth.

Second of seven great debates: Lincoln talks to a crowd of 15,000 on a misty day at Freeport, Illinois, in 1858. Behind him, with hand jauntily on hip, stands Democrat Stephen A. Douglas, the "Little Giant." Running for the Senate, Lincoln challenged the incumbent Douglas to debate. The ensuing series of oratorical jousts made Lincoln a national figure. Douglas won the election, but he split his party with his affirmative stand on the question Lincoln here poses: "Can the people of a United States Territory exclude slavery . . . prior to the formation of a State Constitution?" Two years later the Democratic rift helped Lincoln defeat Douglas for the Presidency. In 1958, this scene from an old lantern slide decorated a 4-cent stamp commemorating the 100th anniversary of the Lincoln-Douglas Debates.

105

Proud and graceful, Mary Todd Lincoln wears a brooch portraying her husband. Ambitious for his career, she once remarked: "Doesn't he look as if he would make a magnificent President?" A polished hostess, she longed to entertain lavishly at the White House—her Inaugural gown in 1865 cost $2,000. But the strain of the war and the loss of "Little Willie," second of her sons to die, shattered her spirit. Nevertheless, the First Lady devoted much of her time to work among the wounded soldiers in hospitals, where she distributed fruit and wine.

Through shrewd dispensation of patronage, he built the Republican Party into a strong national organization. By his extraordinary arts of personal persuasion, he kept within the party politicians ranging in their views from the conservatism of northern Democrats and former Whigs, such as Secretary of State William H. Seward, to the radicalism of the abolitionists, such as Secretary of the Treasury Salmon P. Chase. Lincoln, a brilliant politician, emerged a great statesman.

Sensing public opinion as had no President since Andrew Jackson, he assumed leadership over popular attitudes through an occasional public statement or letter to the press. Thus, he maintained relative unity while charting a course in 1862 toward emancipation, even as the Union Army recoiled from shattering clashes in Virginia—the Seven Days' Battles on the peninsula, and the Valley Campaign— where Robert E. Lee and Stonewall Jackson repeatedly inflicted disconcerting blows.

Union heroism in September beside bloody Antietam Creek in Maryland gave President Lincoln the victory he needed to announce, on January 1, 1863, the Emancipation Proclamation, declaring slaves in Confederate territory "forever free."

Only home Lincoln ever owned, this venerable frame dwelling stands in Springfield, Illinois. Today a state memorial, it wears "Quaker brown," the original tan color. Lincoln lived here for 17 years before moving to the White House.

Trademarks of Lincoln, beaver, white kid gloves, and cane actually belonged to him. Stovepipe hat served as his "office"; he carried important papers in its crown. Lincoln disliked wearing gloves, though his wife dutifully outfitted him with them. He kept stuffing them into his coat until, upon one occasion, he discovered his pockets bulging with seven or eight pairs.

107

Appealing for volunteers, posters papered the North at the outbreak of the Civil War. Lincoln, assuming unprecedented powers, called for recruits without prior Congressional approval. An improvised guard force camped in the East Room of the White House (below) in April, 1861, when officials feared a Southern seizure of Washington.

PAINTING (ABOVE) BY EUGENIE DE LAND SAUGSTAD, LINCOLN MUSEUM; 1865 ENGRAVING FROM A PAINTING BY FRANCIS B. CARPENTER, LIBRARY OF CONGRESS

"Amid the whizzing bullets," wrote Lincoln biographers Nicolay and Hay, "the President... stood... with that grave and impassive countenance... until an officer fell mortally wounded within three feet of him...." Thus Lincoln in 1864 sees Union troops repel an attack on Fort Stevens, seven miles from the Capitol. Maj. Gen. Horatio Wright tugs at the arm of his Commander in Chief, who finally took cover. Lincoln saw only this one Civil War battle.

Addressing the Cabinet, Lincoln reads his Emancipation Proclamation for the first time. The edict freed slaves in Confederate territory, bolstered northern morale, and won sympathy abroad. The original painting hangs in the Capitol.

Final destruction of the institution of slavery came through the Thirteenth Amendment. By dint of Lincoln's persistent political pressure, the amendment received the necessary two-thirds vote in Congress in January, 1865, and was ratified before the end of the year.

Maj. Gen. George B. McClellan's failure at Antietam to pursue and destroy Lee's army rankled Lincoln, as did the blundering of Ambrose E. Burnside at Fredericksburg, Virginia, and the retreat of "Fighting Joe" Hooker from nearby Chancellorsville. "My God! My God!" moaned Lincoln, "What will the country say?" Not until July of 1863, when Ulysses S. Grant took Vicksburg and George G. Meade prevailed at Gettysburg (though he, too, irked Lincoln by his failure to pursue Lee), could the President see improved military leadership.

At Gettysburg, where batteries of mute cannon today brood over the national battlefield, President Lincoln addressed himself to the conscience and aspirations of the American people, and, indeed, the world.

In the David Wills home, which still faces the town square, the bedroom where Lincoln revised his "few appropriate remarks" remains much the same as when the President slept there. At the battlefield cemetery the next morning, he spoke for two minutes, ending the immortal Gettysburg Address with the resolve "that this nation, under God, shall have a new birth of freedom—and that government of the people, by the people, for the people, shall not perish from the earth."

In planning for peace, Lincoln was flexible and generous, wishing to persuade southerners to lay down their arms and join in reunion.

Black-plumed hearse drawn by 16 shrouded horses bears the body of the martyred President through New York City in a primitive painting.

On Good Friday, 1865, Lincoln fell at the hand of John Wilkes Booth. After lying in state at the White House and Capitol, his body began a 1,700-mile trip to Springfield, Illinois, for burial in Oak Ridge Cemetery. The train paused in many cities, reversing the route Lincoln followed to his first Inauguration. Here troops at present arms meet the bier at a railway station in New York. Black cloth drapes the building at left.

Every year, thousands of persons visit Lincoln's tomb in Springfield, which bears the inscription: "Now he belongs to the ages."

Official mourning ring with box honors Lincoln. Washington is the only other President known to have been so memorialized.

The generous terms of reconstruction he announced in December, 1863, failed to weaken resistance and provoked sharp criticism among Radical Republicans in Congress.

Lincoln thought in August, 1864, that he would probably not be re-elected. Then Maj. Gen. William Tecumseh Sherman took Atlanta and marched on through Georgia, cutting the Confederacy in two, while Grant besieged Lee's army, entrenched at Petersburg. With Andrew Johnson for his running mate, Lincoln defeated McClellan in November as the Civil War neared its end.

In the spring of 1865, facing serious challenge from the Radical Republicans, Lincoln offered no single detailed formula to return the "seceded States, so called" to their "proper practical relation" with the Union. The spirit that guided him, however, was clearly that of his Second Inaugural Address, seen today inscribed on a wall of the Lincoln Memorial in the Nation's Capital:

"With malice toward none; with charity for all; with firmness in the right, as God gives us to see the right, let us strive on to finish the work we are in; to bind up the nation's wounds."

On April 14, 1865, just five days after General Lee's surrender at Appomattox Court House, President Lincoln was assassinated. In Ford's Theatre in Washington, now restored by the National Park Service as the Lincoln Museum, the President was shot in the head by an actor, John Wilkes Booth, who somehow thought he was helping the South. Quite the opposite was the result, for with Lincoln's death the chance for peace with magnanimity died.

SEVENTEENTH PRESIDENT 1865-1869

ANDREW JOHNSON, thrust into the White House by the assassination of Abraham Lincoln, was an old-fashioned southern Jacksonian Democrat of pronounced states' rights views. He tried to reconstruct the Federal Union by giving speedy control of southern states to those who would take the oath of allegiance. Arrayed against him were the Radical Republicans in Congress, a loose coalition of men of varying views ranging from idealistic to mercenary, but brilliantly led and ruthless in their tactics.

Johnson, lacking Lincoln's statecraft and adroitness of political maneuver, was no match for them. Although courageous and stubborn, he was indecisive, putting off action until too late. Defeated in his policies, almost removed from office by the Senate, he was one of the most unfortunate of Presidents.

Born in Raleigh, North Carolina, in 1808, he grew up in poverty and without schooling. His father died while Andrew was very young, and the boy later was apprenticed to a tailor. He ran away from his master, and in a few years he opened a tailorshop of his own in Greeneville, Tennessee. There, when he was 19, he married Eliza McCardle, who taught him reading and writing. In later years he paid tribute to her, saying: "God's best gift to a man—a noble woman."

As the young tailor prospered—he boasted that he always "was punctual to my customers, and did good work"—he bought a comfortable home in Greeneville, which has now been restored as part of a national historic site. Johnson participated in local debating forums, developing a powerful though crude oratorical style.

Entering politics, he became an adept stump speaker, delivering withering retorts to hecklers, everlastingly championing the common man, and vilifying the plantation aristocracy. Elected alderman, then mayor, he advanced to the state legislature and on to the U. S. House of Representatives for ten years. He returned to Tennessee to serve as governor, and after two terms he won election to the U. S. Senate.

In Congress during the 1840's and '50's, Johnson tirelessly advocated a homestead bill to provide free farms to the landless. He was enraged when President Buchanan, heeding planter protests, vetoed one such bill.

During the secession crisis, Johnson made a firm stand in defense of the Union and Constitution. Remaining in his seat in the Senate even when Tennessee seceded, he became a hero in the North but a traitor in the eyes of most southerners. At the request of President Lincoln, in 1862 he went back to

FROM "A PICTURE OF THE DESOLATED STATES" BY J. T. TROWBRIDGE

Piercing eyes and grim mouth of Andrew Johnson reflect the bitter fight he waged with Congress over Reconstruction in the South. He favored leniency in permitting southern states to resume their constitutional functions, while the Radicals in Congress cried for a harsher course. When Johnson stood in their way, they impeached him—making him the only Chief Executive to face such a trial.

Crowds jeer Johnson in almost every city as he makes the "Swing around the Circle," a tour of East and Middle West in 1866. He failed to win support of the people in his battle with Congress over Reconstruction.

Painting by Eliphalet F. Andrews, White House Collection

EIGHTEENTH PRESIDENT 1869 1877

U LYSSES S. GRANT, who displayed such conspicuous and inspiring leadership as commander of the Union armies during the Civil War, was the logical Republican candidate for President in 1868. In accepting the nomination, he urged, "Let us have peace."

When he was elected, after a spirited campaign, the American people hoped for an end to the turmoil of the previous decade. But his initial ignorance of the functioning of the Government and of political machinery led him to look to Republican leaders. Though he served two terms and became adept in the routine of the Presidency, he seldom rose above the level of those who advised him.

Born in 1822, the son of a Point Pleasant, Ohio, tanner, Grant was a shy boy notable only for his skill in handling horses. He went to West Point rather against his will and graduated in the middle of his class.

Although he regarded the Mexican War "as one of the most unjust ever waged by a stronger against a weaker nation," he fought under Zachary Taylor, whom he admired and whose casual way of dress he adopted. After the war, Lieutenant Grant married Julia Dent, sister of one of his West Point roommates. In 1854, while doing dreary duty on the Pacific coast and lonely without his family, he resigned from the Army.

Discouraging and unsuccessful civilian years followed. He tried farming, and in 1856 built near St. Louis his log "Hardscrabble" house, now on public display. His next unsuccessful venture was in real estate.

At the outbreak of the Civil War he was working in his father's leather store in Galena, Illinois. A substantial home presented by Galena townspeople to the general after the war is now a state memorial; in it repose original furnishings, including Grant's favorite chair, his cuspidors, and cigars.

Grant did not promote himself vigorously for a command, but at 39 the quiet, diffident, stubby little man was appointed by the Governor of Illinois to be colonel of an unruly volunteer regiment. He quickly whipped it into a disciplined unit, and by September, 1861, he was a brigadier general in command

Civil War hero who attained the Presidency, Ulysses S. Grant ironically came to hate both warfare and politics. Rejected as nominee for a third term, penniless, and stricken with cancer, the general went to Mount McGregor, New York, in the Adirondacks. He died there in 1885, soon after finishing the memoirs that earned his family nearly half a million dollars. He lies buried in the world-famous tomb on Riverside Drive in New York City.

On the battlefield, Grant meets with members of his staff in 1864 during the siege of Petersburg, Virginia.

Painting by Henry Ulke, White House Collection

Tipping his top hat, President Grant with his wife greets Egyptian commissioners in Philadelphia at the opening of the Nation's Centennial in May, 1876.

A month later, Alexander Graham Bell gave the first public demonstration of the telephone in the east gallery of this building. Judges almost overlooked the exhibit, until a royal visitor and friend of Bell's, Dom Pedro, Emperor of Brazil, called their attention to the invention.

at Cairo, Illinois. Within three years after re-entering the Army he had become commander of all Union land forces; within eight years, President of the United States.

Grant's unusual aptitude was hard to analyze; perhaps Charles Francis Adams, Jr., took his measure in these words: "... he is cool and quiet... and in a crisis he is one against whom all around, whether few in number or a great army as here, would instinctively lean. He is a man of the most exquisite judgment and tact. See how he has handled this Army."

Grant recognized the importance of controlling the Mississippi Valley. In February, 1862, he started up the Tennessee River in pursuit of this objective, captured Fort Henry, and then attacked Fort Donelson on the Cumberland. When the Confederate commander asked for an armistice, Grant replied, "No terms except an unconditional and immediate surrender can be accepted." The Confederates capitulated, and Lincoln promoted "Unconditional Surrender" Grant to major general.

On April 6-7, at Shiloh, its somber woods now a national military park, Grant fought one of the bloodiest battles in the West and won a narrow victory. President Lincoln fended off demands for his removal by saying, "I can't spare this man—he fights."

Now the approaches to Vicksburg lay open. Grant maneuvered and fought with skill and ingenuity to win this city, key point on the Mississippi, and thus cut the Confederacy in two. On July 4, 1863, Vicksburg surrendered. In November, 1863, Grant's troops stormed up Lookout Mountain and Missionary Ridge, breaking the Confederate hold on Chattanooga and opening the way for a deep thrust into the South.

Lincoln recognized in Grant the talents required for supreme command, and in March, 1864, appointed him general in chief. Presenting the commission, the President said: "As the country herein trusts you, so, under God, it will sustain you."

Taking an overall view of the war, Grant directed William T. Sherman to drive through the South while he himself stayed with George G. Meade's Army of the Potomac as it pinned down Robert E. Lee's Army of Northern Virginia.

After a year of fighting in Virginia, Grant forced Lee's surrender. On April 9, 1865, at Appomattox Court House, Grant wrote out magnanimous terms of capitulation that would prevent treason trials.

When Grant became President, he ran the

Valiant victors, Grant and the Viceroy of China, Li Hung Chang, meet when Grant tours the world after his second term. An immediate friendship developed between the two, both generals who had led victorious armies during civil wars. The Viceroy gave an 8-hour, 70-course dinner for his guest. Grant rated his host as "one of four great men" he met on the trip. The others: Britain's Lord Beaconsfield (Disraeli), German Chancellor Otto von Bismarck, and French statesman Léon Gambetta.

Grant received royal receptions in every port of call during the two-year global jaunt. He talked with the Emperor of Japan, climbed glaciers in Switzerland, and sailed the Nile in Egypt. But he wearied of paintings, statues, and architecture, and balked at tiger hunting in India; though hardened to war, he disliked killing animals.

Carved chest of Irish bogwood in Washington's Smithsonian Institution bears the date of Grant's visit to Dublin: January 3, 1879.

Bundled in miner's garb, Grant and his party prepare to descend into a silver mine at Virginia City, Nevada. Mrs. Grant stands between her husband and U. S. Grant, Jr. Beside the general at right: Mrs. James Graham Fair, wife of a Nevada mining banker who later became a U. S. Senator. The group includes a young Japanese lantern-bearer.

The general showed a keen interest in mines and stopped to make a personal inspection near the end of his round-the-world journey.

Before descending into the mine, Grant bet financier John W. Mackey a silver dollar that Mrs. Grant would not go down. And, indeed, at the head of the shaft, she took one look and exclaimed, "I wouldn't go down in that hole for the whole mine." But when Mrs. Grant heard that her husband had bet against her courage, she promptly entered.

Victorian elegance enriched Grant's home in Galena, Illinois, now restored. In the parlor, a horsehair sofa and chairs surround a marble-topped center table. Brussels lace curtains and rose-and-gold-brocade draperies cover the windows. In 1868 friends of Grant gathered in this parlor to congratulate the general on winning the Presidential election.

"Life at the White House," wrote Julia Dent Grant, "was like a beautiful dream...a garden spot of orchids, and I wish it might have continued forever." Her zest for living made her a good hostess and a happy First Lady.

GERALD R. BRIMACOMBE (ABOVE); CHICAGO HISTORICAL SOCIETY

administrative offices of the Government much as he had run the Army. But he displayed little of his Army shrewdness in his choice of subordinates; his Cabinet was for the most part undistinguished. An exception was Secretary of State Hamilton Fish, who succeeded in negotiating the Treaty of Washington to settle claims against Great Britain, such as those resulting from construction of the Confederate commerce raider *Alabama.* Fish also persuaded Grant to remain neutral despite provocation from Spain during a long rebellion in Cuba, but did not restrain the President in one of his major foreign policy ventures, an attempt to annex the Dominican Republic in 1869.

Personally a man of scrupulous honesty, Grant accepted handsome presents from admirers without the slightest thought that

favors might be expected in return. Worse, he allowed himself to be seen with two speculators, Jay Gould and James Fisk, who tried to corner the market in gold. When Grant awoke to their scheme, he authorized the Secretary of the Treasury to sell sufficient gold to break the corner, but the speculation had already wrought havoc with business. Other scandals tainted some of Grant's most trusted administrative officers, and even his personal secretary.

In the cause of conservation, Grant in 1872 established the Nation's first national park— Yellowstone—2,221,000 spectacular acres in northwestern Wyoming, with adjoining strips of Montana and Idaho.

During the campaign of 1872 when Grant stood for re-election, he was attacked by Liberal Republican reformers. They were, in

Mane and tail whipping like black flame, a high-stepping trotter skims over New York City's dusty Harlem Lane carrying ex-President Grant and his friend Robert Bonner. The general delighted in racing fast horses, and this road, now St. Nicholas Avenue, provided a favorite course. As President, Grant once whisked down a street some blocks from the White House and was arrested for speeding. The policeman, suddenly realizing whom he had stopped, stood flabbergasted. "Officer, do your duty," said Grant. The patrolman took the horse and rig to the station house, and the amused President walked back to the Executive Mansion. Grant's expert horsemanship had won honors for him at West Point. Riding a sorrel during graduation exercises, he set an Academy jumping record that endured for 25 years.

Grant's view, "the narrow-headed men," their eyes so close together that "they can look out of the same gimlet hole without winking." The general's friends in the Republican Party came to be known proudly as "the Old Guard."

In domestic affairs, Grant allowed Radical Reconstruction to run its course in the South, bolstering it at times with military force. Nevertheless, by the end of his second term almost all the southern states had been "redeemed" by political leaders dedicated to white supremacy.

Grant favored the conservative sound-money policies and high protective tariff advocated by eastern Republicans. In the serious depression that followed the Panic of 1873, he held firm to these policies despite increasing agitation, particularly among distressed farmers in the West. Ultimately, inflation was checked, and the national credit was restored.

Upon retiring from the Presidency in 1877, Grant went on a triumphal tour around the world; it took more than two years. After his return, his confidence again was betrayed by an unprincipled man. Grant became a silent, nonparticipating partner in an investment firm which, in 1884, went bankrupt, losing him all his own capital and all he had borrowed. At about the same time he learned that he had throat cancer.

With a will, he set about the writing of his recollections to pay off his debts and provide for his family. Racing against death, he produced a memoir of classic quality which ultimately earned his family some $450,000. Soon after completing the last page in 1885, he died. His tomb, a national memorial, stands in New York City's Riverside Park.

NINETEENTH PRESIDENT 1877-1881

RUTHERFORD B. HAYES, beneficiary of the most fiercely disputed election in American history, brought to the White House dignity, honesty, and moderate reform. His attractive wife, Lucy Webb Hayes, to the delight of the Woman's Christian Temperance Union, carried out her husband's wishes in the White House by serving no wines or liquors. As a result, she became known as "Lemonade Lucy."

Born in Delaware, Ohio, in 1822, and educated at Kenyon College and Harvard Law School, "Rud" Hayes was an earnest, diligent youth. After five years' law practice in Lower Sandusky (now Fremont), Ohio, he moved to Cincinnati, where he began to flourish as a young Whig lawyer. The Kansas-Nebraska Act, which repealed the Missouri Compromise, stirred his antislavery feelings and brought him into the Republican camp.

Hayes fought gallantly in the Civil War, was wounded in action, and rose to the rank of brigadier general. While he was still in the Army, in July, 1864, Cincinnati Republicans ran him for the House of Representatives. He accepted the nomination, but would not campaign, explaining, "An officer fit for duty who at this crisis would abandon his post to electioneer for a seat in Congress ought to be scalped. You may feel perfectly sure I shall do no such thing...."

Elected by a heavy majority, Hayes entered the House in December, 1865, disturbed by "Rebel influences... ruling the White House," but also concerned at the ultraradicalism of Pennsylvania Congressman Thaddeus Stevens. Yet, on major issues he voted as Stevens wished. In 1867 Hayes was elected Ohio Governor and intermittently served three terms.

The combination of safe liberalism, party loyalty, and a good war record made Hayes the Republican nominee in 1876, when one wing of the party clamored for reform while the other demanded a practical politician and military hero. He ran against a Democratic reformer, Governor Samuel J. Tilden of New York, who had smashed the Tweed Ring.

Although a galaxy of famous Republican speakers, and even Mark Twain, stumped for Hayes, he suspected that the Democrats had the better chance of winning. When the first returns seemed to confirm this, Hayes went to bed, believing he had lost.

The popular vote apparently was 4,300,000 for Tilden to 4,036,000 for Hayes. Whether or not Hayes was elected depended upon contested electoral votes in three southern states —Louisiana, South Carolina, and Florida—in which there had been conspicuous irregularities; there was also a dispute in Oregon. If all

Demure Lucy Hayes invited children to roll Easter eggs on the White House lawn. An advocate of abstinence, she received this portrait as a gift of appreciation from the Woman's Christian Temperance Union.

"Healer of strife," Rutherford B. Hayes drew the curtain on the Civil War by removing troops from the South. In a contested race, he won office by only one electoral vote.

Paintings by Daniel Huntington, White House Collection

122

the disputed electoral votes went to Hayes, he would win; a single one would elect Tilden.

The country was in a furor as months of uncertainty followed. Behind the scenes, hectic negotiations proceeded between southern Democrats and northern Republicans. The Republicans promised the southerners at least one Cabinet seat, Federal patronage, subsidies for internal improvements, and withdrawal of Federal troops from Louisiana and South Carolina. The southerners accepted.

At the end of January, 1877, Congress established a special Electoral Commission to rule upon the disputed votes. The commission, made up of eight Republicans and seven Democrats, decided every one of the contests in favor of Hayes by a vote of eight to seven. Only three days before the Inauguration, Congress ratified the commission's decisions.

The high-minded Hayes chose men of high caliber for his Cabinet, but outraged many Republicans, since not only was his Postmaster General an ex-Confederate (to fulfill his promise to the southerners), but one of his Cabinet officers had bolted the party as a Liberal Republican in 1872. He won a battle with Senator Roscoe Conkling, leader of a Republican faction known as the Stalwarts, over appointments to the New York Customs House, Conkling's patronage bailiwick. But Congress steadfastly ignored Hayes's pleas for overall Civil Service reform.

In his policies toward the South, Hayes pledged in his Inaugural that the rights of Negroes would be protected, but advocated the restoration of "wise, honest, and peaceful local self-government." This meant the withdrawal of troops, which Hayes hoped, together with other conciliatory policies, would lead to the building of a "new Republican party" in the South to which white business-men and conservatives would rally.

Many of the leaders of the "New South" did indeed favor Republican economic policies and approved Hayes's financial conservatism, but they faced annihilation at the polls if they joined the party of Reconstruction.

Hayes, who had announced that he would serve only one term, retired in 1881 to his 25-acre estate, Spiegel Grove, in Fremont, where he spent his last 12 years. The house is now open to the public. His papers and other historic items are preserved there in the Hayes Memorial Library and Museum.

Poised for battle, Nez Perce warriors guard the flight of their women and children during a 1,000-mile exodus from an Idaho reservation. Chief Joseph staged a bloodless raid for supplies at this Army depot on Cow Island in Montana Territory. Federal troops captured the exhausted Indians less than 50 miles from Canada and freedom.

Bewitching glow bathes the laboratory of Thomas A. Edison, as the inventor successfully tests his incandescent lamp in Menlo Park, New Jersey. The date: October 19, 1879. Edison, hand in pocket, watches as his assistant, Francis Jehl, adds mercury to a glass reservoir on the pump stand. The pear-shaped bulb burned brilliantly more than 40 hours. Electric lights were not installed in the White House until the administration of Benjamin Harrison in 1891.

First Chinese minister to the United States calls on Hayes in 1878. The President hears Chun Lan Pin express hope for East-West diplomatic relations. When Congress tried to prohibit Chinese immigration the next year, Hayes vetoed the bill, declaring that he would do nothing to wound the pride of "a polite and sensitive people."

PAINTING BY H. J. FLEMMING, COURTESY CONSOLIDATED EDISON COMPANY OF NEW YORK (ABOVE); FRANK LESLIE'S ILLUSTRATED NEWSPAPER, 1879

TWENTIETH PRESIDENT 1881

JAMES A. GARFIELD, last of the log-cabin Presidents, won back for the Presidency a measure of the prestige it had lost during Reconstruction. His attacks against political corruption, and a successful test of power against a prominent Senator, doubtless would have led to sharp contests with Congress; but before he could engage in them, he was assassinated by a disappointed office seeker.

Garfield was born in Cuyahoga County, Ohio, in 1831. Fatherless before he was two, he soon began helping his older brother Thomas work the family farm and later drove barge teams along the Ohio and Erie Canal.

Hungry for knowledge, young Garfield earned enough money to obtain a sound education in the classics. He graduated from Williams College in Massachusetts in 1856, returning to Ohio as professor of Greek and Latin at the Western Reserve Eclectic Institute (later Hiram College). Within a year he became its president.

In 1858 he married a former schoolmate, Lucretia Rudolph. Their home, Lawnfield, at Mentor, Ohio, near Cleveland, is now a state memorial. On its grounds stands a replica of the cabin in which Garfield was born.

On Sundays, as a lay preacher, Garfield delivered ornate sermons. He was young for his responsibilities, but his commanding height, broad shoulders, and heavy beard compensated for his age. The classics and poetry fascinated him; friends liked to tell how he amused them by simultaneously writing Latin with one hand and Greek with the other.

Entering Republican state politics, he was elected to the Ohio Senate in 1859, and during the secession crisis he advocated coercing the seceding states back into the Union. He learned enough law to be admitted to the bar in 1861.

An effective recruiter of soldiers, Garfield persuaded many of his students to join the 42nd Ohio Volunteer Infantry, then became their colonel. He diligently studied manuals and drilled the regiment into shape.

At the beginning of 1862, when Union military successes had been few, Garfield had command of a brigade at Middle Creek, Kentucky, against Confederate troops led by a West Pointer, and won a small victory. At age 31 he became one of the youngest brigadier generals in the Union Army.

In the next two years his skills as a staff officer brought him promotion to the rank of major general. Meanwhile, in 1862, an Ohio constituency elected him to Congress. President Lincoln persuaded the reluctant Garfield to resign his commission in the Army: It was easier to appoint major generals than

LIBRARY OF CONGRESS

From Canal Boy to President, a biography of Garfield by Horatio Alger, Jr., recounts the youthful days of the President when he drove horses along the Ohio and Erie Canal. Like all Alger heroes, Garfield epitomized the American rags-to-riches dream.

Genial scholar, James A. Garfield managed his own Presidential campaign and won by shrewdly remaining silent on key political issues. As President, he brought prestige to the office by challenging the control of state machines over Federal patronage.

Painting by Calvin Curtis, White House Collection

Breathless moment of a desperate search: As Garfield lies mortally wounded, Alexander Graham Bell listens with a telephonelike receiver for a "click" that would indicate the location of a bullet. Bell employs an electrical device he rigged for detecting metal. Steel springs in the mattress created a field of interference, rendering the examination inconclusive. Garfield died a victim of assassination after only six months in office. Below, a congressional memorial service card bears the name of William McKinley, who was elected President 16 years later and also died by an assassin's bullet.

MEMORIAL SERVICE
OF
JAMES ABRAM GARFIELD.

PRESIDENT
March 4th 1881.
Died September 19th 1881
Age 49 Years.

EULOGY BY
Hon. James G. Blaine
House of Representatives
Feb. 27th 1882.

John Sherman
Chairman Senate Committee

W.m McKinley Jr
Chairman House Committee

to obtain effective Republicans for the House of Representatives.

In the next 18 years, as Garfield was repeatedly re-elected, he became the leading Republican in the House. Although many of his Ohio constituents were opposed to the deflationary sound-money policies of the Republican Party, Garfield unflinchingly supported them; on the other hand, he was not an ardent enough advocate of the high protective tariff in his early career to suit Ohio industrialists. In addition, he was plagued with a whisper of scandal, his name having been found in a memorandum book listing men of influence, among them high officials and Congressmen, who had received stock in Crédit Mobilier, a corrupt railroad construction company.

In the 1880 Republican Convention, Garfield nominated John Sherman of Ohio for President. Sherman opposed ex-President Grant, choice of the Stalwart wing, and Maine Senator James G. Blaine, whose faction was dubbed the "Halfbreeds." When none of the candidates could win a majority, Garfield himself, on the 36th ballot, became the dark horse nominee. Chester A. Arthur, of the Stalwarts, was nominated for Vice President.

Out of the nine million votes cast, Garfield defeated the Democratic nominee, Gen. Winfield Scott Hancock, by a narrow margin. However, by carrying New York, he won a comfortable electoral majority, 214 to 155.

As President, Garfield tried to build a balanced administration, and he gave some offices to Stalwarts. But he angered the Roscoe Conkling-U. S. Grant faction by refusing to accept their choice for Secretary of the Treasury, by appointing a New York party regular to the Cabinet without prior permission from the Stalwart machine, and by making Blaine Secretary of State.

With his Cabinet settled, Garfield wrote on March 8 that he still faced the "disciplined office hunters, who draw papers on me as highwaymen draw pistols...."

Almost at once the new Postmaster General, Thomas L. James, began to expose frauds by leading Republicans who had been making money through the awarding of contracts for the delivery of rural mail. Despite protests from injured politicians, Garfield backed James in his investigation, saying, "I have sworn to execute the laws. Go ahead regardless of where or whom you hit."

Further, Garfield challenged control of patronage in the New York Customs House by Conkling, U. S. Senator from New York.

When he submitted to the Senate a list of

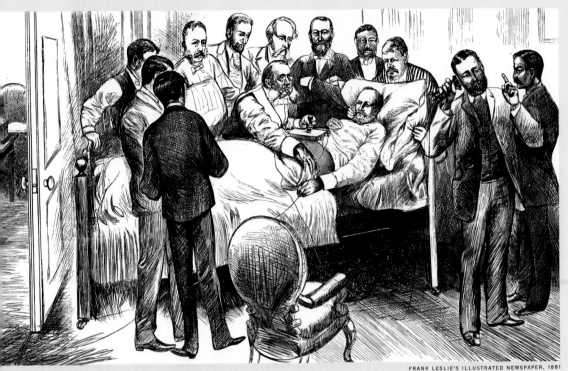

FRANK LESLIE'S ILLUSTRATED NEWSPAPER, 1881

appointments, including many of Conkling's friends, he named the Senator's arch-rival, William H. Robertson, to run the Customs House. Conkling contested the nomination, tried to persuade the Senate to block it, and appealed to the Republican caucus to compel its withdrawal.

But Garfield would not submit: "This... will settle the question whether the President is registering clerk of the Senate or the Executive of the United States.... shall the principal port of entry... be under the control of the administration or under the local control of a factional senator."

Conkling maneuvered to have the Senate confirm Garfield's uncontested nominations and adjourn without acting on Robertson. Garfield countered by withdrawing all nominations except Robertson's; the Senators would have to confirm him or sacrifice all the appointments of Conkling's friends.

In a final desperate move, Conkling and his fellow Senator from New York resigned, confident that their legislature would vindicate their stand and re-elect them. Instead, the legislature elected two other men; the Senate confirmed Robertson. Garfield's victory was complete.

Garfield, having come through this test of strength successfully, was now able to turn his attention to foreign policy. Secretary of State James G. Blaine announced the calling of a conference of the American Republics to meet in Washington in 1882.

The conference never took place. On July 2, 1881, Garfield, in a holiday mood, left the White House bound for Williams College. In Washington's Baltimore and Potomac railroad station, a lawyer from Chicago named Charles J. Guiteau, who had unsuccessfully sought a consular post, proclaimed loudly that he was a Stalwart and shot the President in the spine.

For weeks, in stifling summer heat, Garfield lay between life and death in the White House. An air-conditioning system was devised to cool his bedroom. Alexander Graham Bell, who had invented the telephone, tried to locate the bullet with an induction-balance electrical device.

The President, emaciated and helpless, was taken by special train to the New Jersey seaside, where he seemed to rally for a few days. But on September 19, 1881, he died from an infection and internal hemorrhage, wondering in his last moments about his place in history. Today's X rays, surgery, and antibiotics might have saved his life.

129

CHESTER A. ARTHUR, who had been notable only as an accomplished practitioner of the spoils system, comported himself in the White House with a dignity and competence that quite belied national forebodings. A tall, handsome man with clean-shaven chin and sidewhiskers, Arthur had always looked like a President; he proved that he could also act like one.

The son of a Baptist preacher who had emigrated from northern Ireland, Arthur was born in Fairfield, Vermont, in 1829. He graduated from Union College in the class of 1848, taught school, was admitted to the bar, and practiced law in New York City. Early in the Civil War he served as Quartermaster General of the State of New York.

For his services to the New York Republican organization, President Grant in 1871 appointed him Collector of the Port of New York. Arthur effectively marshaled the thousand Customs House employees on behalf of Senator Roscoe Conkling's Stalwart Republican machine.

Honorable in his personal life and his public career, Arthur nevertheless was a firm believer in the spoils system at the very time that it was coming under vehement attack from the reformers. President Hayes, who opposed at least the worst aspects of the spoils system, in 1878 ousted Arthur and his chief associate. Conkling and his followers tried to win redress by fighting for the renomination of Grant at the 1880 Republican Convention. Failing, they reluctantly accepted the nomination of Arthur for the Vice Presidency.

During his brief tenure as Vice President, Arthur stood firmly beside Conkling in his patronage struggle against President Garfield. But he was deeply shocked when a disgruntled job seeker shot down Garfield, crying "Arthur is President now."

When Arthur did take the Presidential oath, his outlook had changed. Undoubtedly horrified by the way he had become Chief Executive, he was anxious to prove himself above machine politics. He was to be seen most often not with his old associates, but as a man of fashion with the elite of Washington, New York, and Newport.

He had the White House redecorated in the newest style, and it became notable for elaborate Victorian hospitality. On occasion his sister, Mary Arthur McElroy, acted as hostess—his wife, Ellen Herndon Arthur, had died the previous year.

To the indignation of the Stalwart Republicans, the Presidency transformed the former Collector of the Port of New York into an insistent champion of Civil Service reform. Public pressure, heightened by Garfield's death, forced Congress to heed the President.

In 1883 Congress passed the Pendleton Act, which established a bipartisan Civil Service Commission, forbade levying political assess-

Tall and stylishly groomed, Chester A. Arthur won a reputation for elegance and pleasant, easy manners. He pushed a fearless reform policy that led to the first national Civil Service law.

To relieve his solitude in the White House, Arthur reads to Nell, his 13-year-old daughter. The President's wife died a year before he took office. Nell occasionally attended official ceremonies with him; his son Chester Alan was away at college.

Painting by Daniel Huntington, White House Collection

FRANK LESLIE'S ILLUSTRATED NEWSPAPER, 1885

ments against officeholders, and provided for a "classified system" that made certain Government jobs obtainable only through the taking of competitive written examinations. The act also protected employees against dismissal for political reasons.

Out of a total of 133,000 Federal positions, only 14,000 were classified at first, but the act provided that subsequent Presidents could increase the number by executive order. Over the next six decades, as Presidents leaving office extended the list to protect their appointees, a majority of Federal employees came under Civil Service.

Acting independently of party dogma, Arthur also tried to revise existing tariff rates downward. He wished them to be high enough to protect American industries but low enough so that the Government would not be embarrassed by annual surpluses of revenue.

The surpluses had encouraged reckless appropriations. Congressmen habitually expended the extra tax money on river and harbor improvements in their districts. These bills, though sometimes meritorious, were generally believed to be so worthless that the term "pork barrel" came to be applied to them. When President Arthur vetoed a large pork barrel bill, an incredulous Congress overrode his veto.

In 1882 Arthur appointed a commission to study tariff revision. The commission, made up of protectionists, recommended a 20 to 25 percent cut, but during the process of revision, lobbyists persuaded Congressmen to raise about as many rates as they lowered. When Arthur signed the resulting Tariff Act of 1883, aggrieved westerners and southerners, who blamed the tariff for their having to buy manufactured goods dearly and sell farm products cheaply, looked to the Democratic Party for redress. Thus the tariff began to emerge as a major issue between the parties.

The Arthur Administration enacted the first general Federal immigration law. Arthur approved a measure in 1882 excluding immigrants who were paupers, criminals, idiots, or insane. Congress suspended Chinese immigration for a ten-year period; later it extended and strengthened the restriction.

The conduct of foreign affairs continued to be dull and quiet, but a portent of the future was Arthur's approval of legislation in 1883 to construct four steel warships—the first vessels of a modern American Navy.

Arthur demonstrated as President that he was above factions within the Republican Party, if indeed not above the party itself. Perhaps in part his reason was the well-kept secret he had known since a year after he succeeded to the Presidency, that he was suffering from a fatal kidney disease. He kept himself in the running for the Presidential nomination in 1884 in order not to appear that he feared defeat, but was not renominated, and died in 1886. Publisher Alexander K. McClure recalled, "No man ever entered the Presidency so profoundly and widely distrusted, and no one ever retired ... more generally respected."

Sidewhiskers grayed by the cares of his office, Arthur vacations in 1883 at Upper Geyser Basin in Yellowstone National Park. Lt. Gen. Philip H. Sheridan (seated at left) arranged the Presidential visit. Arthur's Secretary of War, Robert T. Lincoln, son of Abraham Lincoln, sits at right.

Spray and splinters fly as an explosion shatters the hulk of the *Joseph Henry* in the harbor of Newport, Rhode Island. Aboard the *Triana,* Arthur and his daughter Nell review the Navy's 1884 demonstration of a newly developed torpedo. His endeavors to update the fleet laid the beginnings of the modern United States Navy.

F. JAY HAYNES, PIONEER PHOTOGRAPHER OF THE OLD WEST, FROM "FOLLOWING THE FRONTIER," BY FREEMAN TILDEN (ALFRED A. KNOPF, 1964); HARPERS WEEKLY, 1884

TWENTY-SECOND 1885-1889 and TWENTY-FOURTH PRESIDENT 1893-1897

GROVER CLEVELAND, the first Democrat to be elected President after the Civil War, believed that the Government could best contribute to prosperity by not interfering with the free functioning of economic forces.

He ceaselessly fought what he regarded as the evils of governmental "paternalism," whether tariff protection to large corporations or relief to drought-stricken farmers. His were the most widely accepted economic views of the time.

Courageous, resolutely independent, Cleveland was the only President to leave the White House and return four years later, elected for a second term.

One of nine children of a Presbyterian minister, Cleveland was born in Caldwell, New Jersey, in 1837, and was raised in upstate New York. As a lawyer in Buffalo, he became notable for his single-minded concentration upon whatever task faced him.

At age 44 he suddenly emerged into a political prominence that carried him to the White House in less than four years. In 1881 he was elected as a reform Mayor of Buffalo, and a year later, reform Governor of New York, in both positions distinguishing himself by his frequent use of the veto to curb political favoritism and corruption.

As candidate for President, Cleveland enjoyed not only Democratic support but also aid from a number of reform Republicans, the "Mugwumps," who disliked the record of the Republican nominee, James G. Blaine, "the plumed knight from Maine." In spite of this, Cleveland received a plurality of only 29,000 popular votes; he had 219 electoral votes to Blaine's 182.

While living in Buffalo, Cleveland had been content to lead a bachelor's existence, but in the White House, where he had inherited President Arthur's French chef, he was not entirely at ease at first.

"I must go to dinner," he wrote a friend, "but I wish it was to eat a pickled herring Swiss cheese and a chop at Louis' instead of the French stuff I shall find."

In June, 1886, he married 21-year-old Frances Folsom, becoming the only Chief Executive whose wedding was held in the White House. They had five children.

THOMAS NAST, HARPER'S WEEKLY, 1886

Resolute reformer, Grover Cleveland despised political corruption and attacked it at every opportunity. "He sailed through American history like a steel ship loaded with monoliths of granite," wrote H. L. Mencken. One of the hardest working Presidents, he often labored at his desk until 2 a.m. Though his brusque use of veto powers angered many factions, Cleveland proved a masterful public servant.

Tower of integrity, Cleveland in caricature guards the U. S. Treasury. For years veterans of the Civil War had been raiding the Federal vaults with fraudulent pension claims. Cleveland took the trouble to read the pension bills and, outraged by the deceit, vetoed hundreds of them.

Painting by Eastman Johnson, White House Collection

135

Vigorously Cleveland pursued his credo that the Government must not give special favors to any economic group, whether powerful or weak. He even vetoed a bill to appropriate $10,000 to distribute seed grain among drought-stricken farmers in Texas.

Demonstrating phenomenal industry, he tried to end waste and corruption in the granting of pensions through private bills to Civil War veterans who failed to meet lenient Government requirements. On one busy day, the Senate voted 400 of these bills, some of them having a basis, but many of dubious or spurious merit.

Cleveland, working late into the night, read through hundreds of documents supporting such bills, and while he signed 1,453, he returned hundreds with tart veto messages. The pension list, he wrote, ought to remain "a roll of honor."

When Congress, pressured by the Grand Army of the Republic, passed a bill granting pensions for disabilities not caused by military service, Cleveland vetoed it, too, risking strong opposition in the next Presidential campaign from the old soldiers.

He also incurred the wrath of the railroads by ordering an investigation of their Federal land grants, forcing the return of 81,000,000 acres. In 1887 he signed the Interstate Commerce Act, which provided for the first Federal regulation of the railroads.

Cleveland angered business when, in his Annual Message to Congress in December, 1887, he called for a reduction of high protective tariffs. It was pointed out to him that he had given the Republicans an effective issue for the 1888 campaign, but he retorted, "What is the use of being elected or re-elected unless you stand for something?"

And Democratic politicians often found him painfully blunt. Just before the campaign, he wrote to tell one of them, "I am satisfied that I can improve my time much more profitably at this extremely busy period than by talking politics with you."

Cleveland lost in 1888, though he received a larger popular vote than his opponent, Benjamin Harrison; electoral votes in New York and Indiana swung the election to the Republican candidate.

As a "lame-duck" President, Cleveland spoke before Congress in December of 1888 and again poured his wrath upon the corporate beneficiaries of tariff protection:

"He mocks the people who proposes that the Government shall protect the rich and that they in turn will care for the laboring

Youngest First Lady, Frances Folsom Cleveland, 21, wears a satin wedding gown with a 12-foot train and a border of orange blossoms. Her marriage to the 49-year-old bachelor in 1886 marked the only wedding ceremony of a Chief Executive in the White House. Cleveland finished a day's work before the 7 p.m. wedding. Fewer than 40 persons attended the rites, which the President altered by deleting the word "obey" from the bride's vows. During his second administration, Mrs. Cleveland became the first wife of a President to give birth to a child in the White House.

Shower of shoes and rice rains down on Cleveland and his wife as they leave the White House (lower right). Following a dinner reception, the bride changed into a gray silk traveling dress for a honeymoon trip to Deer Park in the mountains of Maryland. The bridal couple left from a private exit in the Red Room at the top of the steps. Wedding guests shout blessings as the President and First Lady board their closed carriage.

Hopeful, huddled masses of immigrants gaze at the Statue of Liberty as they enter the harbor of New York City aboard the liner *Germanic*. A year earlier, in 1886, President Cleveland had dedicated the impressive structure on Bedloe's Island (now Liberty Island). A gift from France, the Lady of Liberty stretches skyward 152 feet above her 150-foot-high pedestal. In the late years of the 19th century, she welcomed more than a million immigrants from Germany—more than any other nationality.

137

First Democratic Presidential victor in 28 years, Cleveland watches his Inaugural parade from a stand in front of the White House. Only the grand review of General Grant's troops at the end of the Civil War surpassed the Cleveland procession that pounded down Pennsylvania Avenue in 1885. A few hours earlier, a crowd of some 30,000 at the Capitol heard Cleveland sworn in as President for the first time. Four years later he lost the election, but won in 1892, thus becoming the only President to serve nonconsecutive terms.

Cleveland scowls at a representative of Tammany Hall who has posted a petition for political appointments at the White House gate: a magazine cartoon depicting his ceaseless vigilance against corruption. As Governor of New York, Cleveland had blasted New York City's political machine, with its Tammany tiger symbol. As President, he continued to fight pressure groups, and the penchant for honesty made his first Presidential term the embodiment of reform. His forthright stands proved him the strongest President between Abraham Lincoln and Theodore Roosevelt.

PUCK, 1885, FROM THE COLLECTION OF ASSOCIATE JUSTICE POTTER STEWART

138

poor.... A just and sensible revision of our tariff laws should be made for the relief of those of our countrymen who suffer under present conditions."

In 1892, Cleveland and Harrison faced each other again, this time with Cleveland winning. Soon after his return to the White House, he had to cope with an acute economic depression, and a crisis in his health. Secretly hospitalized aboard a yacht cruising the East River, he had a malignant growth removed from the roof of his mouth.

As he made a rapid and full recovery— though it was 25 years before the whole story was made public—he focused his attention not upon business failures, farm foreclosures, and unemployment, but upon the Treasury crisis. Exerting his Presidential authority, he obtained repeal of the mildly inflationary Sherman Silver Purchase Act, and, with the aid of Wall Street loans, maintained the Nation's gold reserve.

When Coxey's Army, seeking unemployment relief, marched on Washington, Cleveland had the leader, Jacob S. Coxey, arrested for walking on the grass. And when the Pullman strike against wage cuts in Chicago tied up railroads, Cleveland authorized his Attorney General to obtain an injunction against the strike. The injunction was violated, and he sent Federal troops. "If it takes the entire Army and Navy of the United States to deliver a postal card in Chicago," he declared, "that card will be delivered."

In 1895 Cleveland invoked the Monroe Doctrine, requiring Great Britain to accept arbitration of a disputed boundary in Venezuela. This action won him public acclaim, but, overall, his policies during the depression of the 1890's were unpopular. His party deserted him in 1896, nominating William Jennings Bryan of Nebraska.

At the end of his first term Cleveland had told Washington newspaper correspondents, "The animating spirit of the Administration was administrative reform."

He did succeed in bringing new high standards of service to the executive branch, but the conservative economic policies which he pursued with such incorruptible courage failed to bring the Nation the widespread prosperity he sought for it.

After leaving the White House, Cleveland lived in retirement in Princeton, New Jersey, and died in 1908. His last words were:

"I have tried so hard to do right."

139

BENJAMIN HARRISON, nominated for President on the eighth ballot at the 1888 Republican Convention, conducted what became known as a "front-porch" campaign, delivering short speeches to delegations that came to visit him in Indianapolis.

Since he was only 5 feet, 6 inches tall, Democrats called him "Little Ben"; Republicans replied that he was big enough to wear the hat of his grandfather, "Old Tippecanoe." Cartoonists drew him as a diminutive figure almost hidden under a huge beaver hat.

In the election, although he received 90,000 fewer popular votes than Cleveland, he carried the electoral college, 233 to 168.

Benjamin Harrison was born in 1833 on William Henry Harrison's farm near North Bend, Ohio. He was seven when his grandfather was elected President. He attended school in Cincinnati and graduated from Miami University at Oxford, Ohio. In 1853, the year he was admitted to the bar, he married Caroline Lavinia Scott, who later became the first President General of the Daughters of the American Revolution.

The newlyweds moved west to Indianapolis, where Harrison became an industrious lawyer, beginning his *Indiana Reports,* records of state court proceedings, and ultimately completing ten volumes. He campaigned for the new Republican Party.

During the Civil War the Governor of Indiana appointed him colonel of the 70th Regiment, Indiana Volunteer Infantry, which engaged in severe combat as part of Gen. William Tecumseh Sherman's army. Within a month he fought more battles than his grandfather saw in a lifetime. When Atlanta fell, he hurried back to Indiana, at the governor's request, to enlist recruits and engage in political combat against the Copperheads—northerners who sympathized with the South—in the campaign of 1864.

After the war, he became a moral pillar of Indianapolis. He built a fine home—although the front porch wasn't added until after he became President.

Concentrating intently upon legal cases, Harrison sometimes passed friends in the street without noticing them. Democrats turned this characteristic against him, defeating him for governor in 1876 by unfairly stigmatizing him as "Kid Gloves" Harrison.

Nevertheless, his political stature grew. President Garfield considered him for a Cabinet post, but Harrison preferred to serve the Senate term he had won in 1880. As Senator he championed the causes of Indians, homesteaders, and Civil War veterans.

First President General of the Daughters of the American Revolution, Caroline Scott Harrison enjoyed painting watercolors and started the White House china collection.

Heritage of public service distinguished Benjamin Harrison. He filled the shoes of his grandfather, William Henry Harrison, who 48 years earlier had served as the Nation's ninth President. His great-grandfather had signed the Declaration of Independence. Benjamin Harrison favored a vigorous foreign policy and extended the National Park System in the American West.

Paintings by Eastman Johnson (opposite) and Daniel Huntington, White House Collection

In a frenetic dash for free land, 50,000 pioneers race to claim home sites in Oklahoma Territory,

As President, Harrison resisted strong pressure for patronage by Republican leaders, who were hungry for spoils after four years of Democratic rule. Although he had made no political bargains, his supporters had given innumerable pledges in his behalf. When Boss Matt Quay of Pennsylvania heard that Harrison ascribed his victory to Providence, he exclaimed that Harrison would never know "how close a number of men were compelled to approach the gates of the penitentiary to make him President."

Harrison favored extension of Civil Service, but the pressure against it was too great. Within a year, his own Postmaster General, John Wanamaker, had dispensed postmasterships to 30,000 deserving Republicans.

Harrison signed the Sherman Antitrust Act, which would later figure dramatically in domestic affairs, but his own times were not ripe for its enforcement. He also initiated rural free delivery of mail.

A vigorous foreign policy marked Harrison's administration, and he personally helped shape it, since Secretary of State James G. Blaine was frequently ill. The first Pan-American Congress, meeting in Washington in 1889, established an information center, which later became the Pan-American Union.

Harrison guided Blaine in asserting American claims in Samoa and in seeking, unsuccessfully, to obtain a harbor in Haiti. At the end of his administration he sent the Senate a treaty annexing Hawaii, but President Cleveland withdrew it.

The perplexing domestic problem President Harrison faced was that of trying to maintain a protective tariff and at the same time to reduce the Treasury surplus being built by the high rates.

Republican leaders in Congress successfully met the challenge. Representative William McKinley of Ohio and Senator Nelson W. Aldrich of Rhode Island framed a still higher tariff bill, containing some rates that were intentionally prohibitive. Harrison, who believed in protection, nevertheless tried to make the tariff more acceptable to other nations by writing in reciprocity provisions.

To help spend the surplus, Harrison signed substantial appropriation bills for the improvement of rivers and harbors, building a two-ocean Navy, and subsidizing steamship lines; and for the first time except in war,

142

opened by Harrison for settlement in 1889.

Congress appropriated a billion dollars. When critics attacked it as the "billion-dollar Congress," Speaker Thomas B. Reed replied, "This is a billion-dollar country."

By the end of the Harrison Administration, the surplus had evaporated, and prosperity seemed about to disappear as well.

The year 1892 was a bleak one for Harrison. His wife died in October. In November, abandoned by his party leaders, he was defeated by Grover Cleveland.

Back home in Indianapolis, Harrison became a notable speaker and writer, and he brilliantly upheld Venezuela's claims against Great Britain in a boundary dispute with British Guiana. In 1896 he married a widow, Mary Lord Dimmick, niece of his first wife. Five years later he died.

Centennial President, Harrison in 1889 stands on the site of old Federal Hall in New York City to re-enact the Inauguration of George Washington. Show of flags dressing Wall Street so impressed Harrison that he started the custom of flying the national colors from all public buildings.

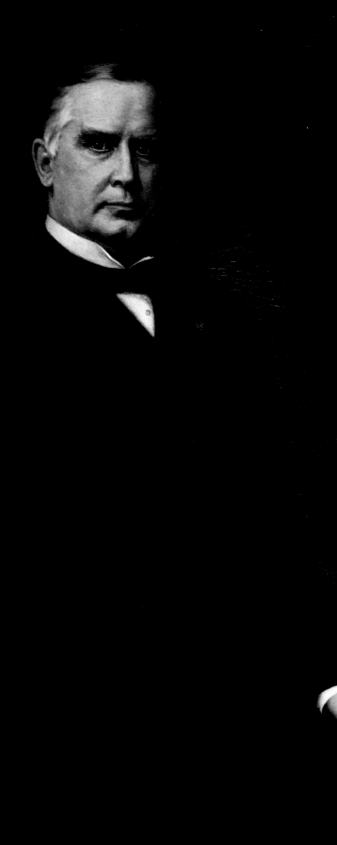

William McKinley

TWENTY-FIFTH PRESIDENT 1897-1901

WILLIAM McKINLEY was a transitional figure as Chief Executive. Last in a long succession of Civil War veterans to hold office, first of the 20th-century Presidents, he witnessed a new order, born of the vast economic changes and developments of the 19th century. He launched the Nation, now a power, into world affairs, saying: "Isolation is no longer possible or desirable. . . . The period of exclusiveness is past."

At home, trusts proliferated and prosperity returned. Overseas, the United States defeated Spain and acquired a tropical empire, which it retained for a few decades.

McKinley rode the crest of the Republican "full dinner pail" popularity and easily won a second term. But before a year had passed, he was dead from an assassin's bullet.

McKinley was born in 1843 in Niles, Ohio, where now stands a memorial library and museum. The son of an iron founder, he briefly attended Allegheny College, and was teaching in a country school when the Civil War broke out. He enlisted as a private in the Union Army at the age of 18, and was mustered out as a major.

He studied law, opened an office in Canton, Ohio, and married Ida Saxton, daughter of a local banker. His attractive personality, exemplary character, and marked intelligence enabled him to rise rapidly in the U. S. House of Representatives, where he took his seat at 34. Within three years he was appointed to the powerful Ways and Means Committee, of which he was later chairman.

Robert M. La Follette, Sr., of Wisconsin, who served on the committee with him, recalled that he "represented the newer view," and "on the great new questions . . . was generally on the side of the public and against private interests."

During his 14 years in the House, McKinley became the leading Republican tariff expert, giving his name to the measure enacted in 1890. In the election a few weeks later, the Republicans were voted out of control of the House; the public feared the bill would increase retail prices. McKinley, also a victim of a Democratic gerrymander in his district, lost his seat along with the other Republicans. But he was promptly elected Governor of Ohio and served two terms, gaining national prominence as an administrator.

For several years wealthy Marcus Alonzo Hanna of Cleveland promoted his friend McKinley for the Presidency. At the 1896 Republican Convention, in time of depression, Hanna ensured the nomination of McKinley as "the advance agent of prosperity." The Democrats, advocating the "free and

He resembles a young Napoleon," said journalists of the pale, short, and purposeful William McKinley. To enhance his dignified deportment, the President wore a boutonniere and glasses suspended on a neat black cord.

Horrendous blast hurls bodies and debris skyward as the U. S. battleship *Maine* explodes in Havana, Cuba; a contemporary print portrays the fiery scene.

Aroused Americans cried, "Remember the *Maine*," and pressured McKinley to punish Spain for the disaster. Congress declared war April 25, 1898. At the end of the hundred-day hostilities, the United States acquired its first overseas possessions: the Philippines, Puerto Rico, and Guam.

Painting by William D. Murphy, White House Collection

unlimited coinage of both silver and gold" at a ratio of 16 to 1, nominated 36-year-old William Jennings Bryan, the silver-tongued orator from Nebraska, who created feverish excitement wherever he spoke. Hanna used large contributions from eastern Republicans frightened by Bryan's views on silver. McKinley—meeting delegations on his front porch in Canton, Ohio—defended the gold standard of the Republican platform. On election day, McKinley defeated Bryan and both Houses of Congress were Republican.

When President McKinley took office, the depression had almost run its course and with it the extreme agitation over silver. Deferring any action on the money question, McKinley instead called Congress into special session to enact the Dingley Tariff, at that time the highest in history. It remained in force during 12 ensuing years of business expansion.

In the friendly atmosphere of the McKinley Administration toward industrial combina-

tions, "trusts"—as they were popularly called —came into existence at an unprecedented pace. In the six years beginning with 1898, no fewer than 236 "important and active Industrial Trusts" were incorporated, so that by 1904 there were listed 318 trusts with capitalization exceeding seven billion dollars.

Newspapers caricatured McKinley as a little boy led around by "Nursie" Hanna, representative of the trusts. Actually, McKinley was not that greatly dominated by Hanna; he firmly condemned the trusts as "dangerous conspiracies against the public good."

Not prosperity, as anticipated, but foreign policy became the dominant concern of the McKinley Administration. Americans became increasingly indignant as the protracted, stalemated struggle between Spanish forces and the revolutionaries in Cuba brought disease and starvation to the Cuban people.

With the sinking of the battleship *Maine* in Havana harbor, public excitement and

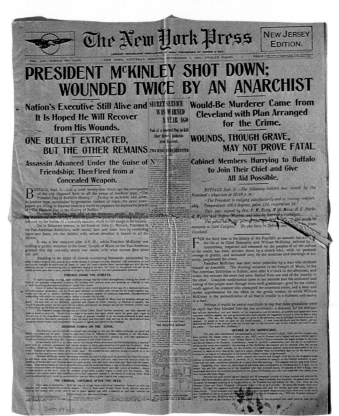

Assassin fells the President, scream headlines in 1901. McKinley was shot September 6 at the Pan-American Exposition in Buffalo, New York. He died eight days later.

Bustling young giant: A cartoon captures the brisk pace at the turn of the century as the Nation becomes a world power. McKinley prepares to dig a canal across Nicaragua, but pauses to consider a shorter route through Panama.

anger brought upon the President a pressure for war. Unable to restrain Congress, McKinley delivered a message of "neutral intervention" in April, 1898. Congress thereupon voted three resolutions tantamount to a declaration of war for the liberation and independence of Cuba.

In the hundred-day war that followed, the United States Navy intercepted the Spanish warships fleeing out of Santiago Harbor, Cuba, and completely destroyed them. Ashore, "Rough Rider" Theodore Roosevelt became a hero at the battle of San Juan Hill. Puerto Rico was also occupied, and strategic Hawaii annexed. In the Philippine Islands, Commodore George Dewey had defeated the Spanish in Manila Bay. The United States, as decided by the Treaty of Paris of 1898, annexed the Philippines as well as the islands of Guam and Puerto Rico.

Rebelling Filipinos, who had fought with the U. S. forces against the Spanish, in 1899 precipitated the United States into a conflict longer and bloodier than the Spanish-American War. Decades later, in 1946, the Philippines gained independence, and in 1952 Puerto Rico achieved commonwealth status.

In 1900 McKinley again campaigned against Bryan, who inveighed against imperialism and the Republican candidate for Vice President, Theodore Roosevelt. McKinley quietly stood for the "full dinner pail."

Victory in the election left him thinking soberly of the problems that followed victory in war, and warning that they would be a task for "the whole American people."

His second term came to a tragic end in September, 1901. Standing in a receiving line at the Buffalo Pan-American Exposition, he had just given a little girl the red carnation from his buttonhole when an anarchist named Leon Czolgosz, his gun concealed in a handkerchief, shot him twice. McKinley died eight days later.

4

AMERICA ENTERS THE MODERN ERA

Theodore Roosevelt through Herbert Hoover

IN THE FIRST TWO DECADES of the 20th century, Theodore Roosevelt and Woodrow Wilson endowed the American Presidency with a powerful leadership the Nation had not known since Lincoln. Several of their successors gave nostalgic tugs backward, but these two—one a Republican, the other a Democrat—established a pattern for succeeding strong Presidents.

At home both sought a larger measure of political democracy and economic justice, and abroad a share in responsibility for world order. They moved to assume the sober duties of the United States in its new status as an industrial giant and major world power.

Roosevelt expressed the President's new progressive role: "In a century and a quarter as a nation, the American people have subdued and settled the vast reaches of a continent; ahead lies the greater task of building up on this foundation, by themselves, for themselves, and with themselves, an American commonwealth which in its social and economic structure shall be four square with democracy."

Wilson developed the progressive theme in his Inaugural Address of March, 1913. He noted that while "Our life contains every great thing, and contains it in rich abundance," unnecessary evil had come with the blessings.

"With riches has come inexcusable waste. We ... have not stopped to conserve the exceeding bounty of nature. ... We have been proud of our industrial achievements, but we have not hitherto stopped thoughtfully enough to count the human cost. ... The great Government we loved has too often been made use of for ... selfish purposes, and those who used it had forgotten the people."

Both these Presidents and their supporters, the progressive generation, believed that, without abandoning the free-enterprise system, they could perfect the dream of the Founding Fathers by combining a scientific approach to the problems of the age with positive Government action. They wished to reform, not destroy, the American way of life.

In 1906 Finley Peter Dunne quoted his fictitious Mr. Dooley, Irish sage and bartender, as saying, "Th' noise ye hear is not th' first gun iv a rivolution. It's on'y th' people iv th' United States batin' a carpet."

For the most part, the leaders of this generation were successful young men and women

---

"You may fire when you are ready, Gridley." Gripping a railing of the flagship *Olympia,* Commodore George Dewey, under orders from Assistant Secretary of the Navy Theodore Roosevelt, closes for action at Manila Bay in 1898. When *Olympia*'s captain, Charles V. Gridley, gave the command to fire, Dewey's U. S. Asiatic Squadron blew the antiquated Spanish fleet out of Philippine waters. Thus the United States ended Spain's colonial era in a 100-day war and entered the 20th century destined to be a world power.

PAINTING BY RUFUS ZOGBAUM, COURTESY STATE OF VERMONT

Child at work changes cotton bobbins. In southern textile mills one-third of the workers were under 16. Children sometimes labored 12 hours a day for only a few cents. Photographer Lewis Hine's portrayal led to laws regulating such conditions. The first Federal child labor law was passed during Wilson's Presidency.

The man and the car: Henry Ford, apostle of mass production, sits in his first model of 1896. Ford's low-cost Model T put America on wheels.

LEWIS W. HINE COLLECTION, LIBRARY OF CONGRESS

Frail flying machine lifts off for a momentous 12-second trip above the dunes at Kill Devil Hill on North Carolina's Outer Banks. During Theodore Roosevelt's administration, Orville Wright —prone at the controls—made man's first powered flight in a heavier-than-air craft. His brother Wilbur runs alongside to steady the wing. The historic date: December 17, 1903.

UNDERWOOD AND UNDERWOOD (ABOVE); LIBRARY OF CONGRESS

of good education and family background who wished to extend the abundance of the Nation more widely to the poor. Their ideals were clean government and social justice.

They achieved reform legislation in city, state, and Federal Government—to guarantee citizens greater political participation, to protect their health and morals, to restrict corporate encroachments on their rights, and to conserve the national heritage of natural resources. These reformers sought also to propagate democracy and prosperity in other nations, and ultimately enlisted in a great crusade to make the world, in Wilson's words, "safe for democracy."

Inevitably reaction followed, and voters seemed to tire of Presidents like Roosevelt and Wilson. They turned to Warren G. Harding, who tried to lead them back toward a "normalcy" no longer to be found, and then they voted to "Keep Cool With Coolidge."

By 1928 their mood had changed again,

"We want the vote!" Suffragettes parade through Washington, D. C. The Nineteenth Amendment to the Constitution gave women the franchise in 1920.

"The Pole at last!" Robert E. Peary, with a "Godspeed" from Theodore Roosevelt, became the first to reach the North Pole, on April 6, 1909. The explorer planted the Stars and Stripes, then photographed Matthew A. Henson (center), his Negro assistant, and the four Eskimos who shared in the achievement.

WIDE WORLD

ADMIRAL ROBERT E. PEARY

and they elected Herbert Hoover, who admired both Theodore Roosevelt and Wilson. Hoover's campaign nickname, the "Great Engineer," signified his intent to bring a technical solution to the Nation's difficulties.

Like his progressive predecessors in the White House, Hoover believed the Government should guarantee a free working of the economy; he hoped for a voluntary rather than compulsory way to efficiency. It was his misfortune to be President when the Great Depression struck. Although in time he proposed remedial legislation in the progressive tradition, his defeat in 1932 showed the people's desire for more drastic measures.

Facing deep troubles at home and abroad, where the depression was bringing Adolf Hitler and other aggressors to power, the American people were again ready for leadership reminiscent of the Wilson and Theodore Roosevelt Administrations. Once more they were determined to beat the national carpet.

TWENTY-SIXTH PRESIDENT 1901-1909

THEODORE ROOSEVELT brought new excitement and strength to the Presidency. Vigorously he led Congress and the public toward progressive reforms and a strong foreign policy, taking the view that he was a steward of the people, limited only by specific constitutional restrictions. In the popular eye he was the "buster of trusts" and wielder of a "big stick."

"I did not usurp power," he later wrote, "but I did greatly broaden the use of executive power."

Roosevelt's youth differed sharply from that of the log-cabin Presidents. He was born to a well-to-do family in New York City in 1858; his brownstone home on East 20th Street is a national historic shrine. But Roosevelt, too, had to struggle—against ill health. When his father told him he had the mind but not the body to sustain a worth-while career, he replied, "I'll make my body."

From early childhood Roosevelt was a naturalist, and he learned to ride, hunt, and thrive in the wilderness. He eventually did build a strong body and became a lifelong advocate of physical and moral excellence.

While a senior at Harvard University he began work on *The Naval War of 1812,* published two years later in 1882—the first of some 40 books. Using his earnings from writing to supplement his income, he decided to devote himself to public service.

Backed by a Republican club in New York City, Theodore Roosevelt, at 23, won election to the New York State Assembly. The colorful, energetic way he fought for clean government projected him into the headlines. Nearly all the rest of his life he was in them, except for one tragic interlude.

In 1884 his first wife, Alice Lee Roosevelt, and his mother died within a few hours of each other. Roosevelt left New York for the Badlands of Dakota Territory, and there in the next two years he mastered his sorrow as he lived in the saddle, driving cattle, hunting, and capturing three thieves. The Theodore Roosevelt National Memorial Park in North Dakota, which includes T. R.'s ranch, was created in his memory.

In all his adventures, both in his youth and as a man, he showed utter fearlessness.

"There were all kinds of things of which

Many-sided man—war hero, writer, reform politician—Theodore Roosevelt at 42 became the Nation's youngest Chief Executive, succeeding the assassinated President McKinley on September 14, 1901. He had served as McKinley's Assistant Secretary of the Navy, won the governorship of New York in 1898, and two years later was elected Vice President. Entering the White House, he labored to earn election there "in my own right."

"Trust-busting Teddy" smashes burgeoning monopolies in American business. A New York *Globe* cartoonist captures T. R.'s energetic onslaught on "malefactors of great wealth." He worried Wall Street but won support on Main Street, U.S.A. Roosevelt had a flair for awakening public interest in the problems of the day.

LIBRARY OF CONGRESS

Fearless under fire, Col. Theodore Roosevelt on horseback leads the Rough Riders against a Spanish force in Cuba on July 1, 1898. Artist Frederic Remington captured the Roosevelt gallantry in the San Juan charge that endeared him to fellow Americans and

I was afraid at first," he said, "ranging from grizzly bears to 'mean' horses and gunfighters; but by acting as if I was not afraid I gradually ceased to be afraid. Most men can have the same experience if they choose."

In December, 1886, Roosevelt married Edith Kermit Carow, a childhood friend. Returning to politics, he served a lengthy apprenticeship as United States Civil Service Commissioner, President of the New York City Board of Police Commissioners, Assistant Secretary of the Navy, and Governor of New York. To each position he brought glamour and publicity.

At the Navy Department, he moved even faster than John D. Long, the competent Secretary, to get ready for possible war with Spain, sending orders to Commodore George Dewey that, if hostilities began, he was to attack the Spanish fleet in the Philippines.

When war came, Roosevelt became lieutenant colonel of the Rough Rider Regiment. Advanced to colonel, he got the Rough Riders into the thick of the fight in Cuba. Flam-

boyantly brave and devoted to his men, he was the favorite of the war correspondents.

In the path of heavy fire from the Spanish on the San Juan ridge, Roosevelt, on horseback, paraded conspicuously before his troops as he marshaled them and gave the order to charge. Up Kettle Hill they went, "cheering and running forward between shots."

In a few minutes the Rough Riders were at the top, and Roosevelt became one of the most popular heroes of the war. A monument on San Juan Hill near Santiago was erected in memory of the valiant charge.

Boss Tom Platt, needing a hero to draw attention away from scandals in New York State, accepted Roosevelt as the Republican candidate for governor in the fall of 1898. Roosevelt won, "played fair" with Platt, as he had promised, yet brought distinction to his administration. In 1900, Platt, with the aid of other bosses, managed to push Roosevelt out of New York and into the Vice Presidency, despite the protests of President McKinley's manager, Mark Hanna.

earned him world-wide fame. For the strenuous T. R., every challenge evoked a similarly vigorous response. He wrote to his son Kermit: "I always believe in going hard at everything"—this despite ill health and poor eyes that required him to wear glasses.

With the assassination of McKinley, Roosevelt, at 42, became the youngest President in the Nation's history.

"Now look," moaned Hanna, "that damned cowboy is President of the United States."

Nevertheless, Roosevelt heeded Hanna's advice to go slowly. He also enlisted in Government service capable men like Henry L. Stimson, men of a sort too seldom recruited earlier. At the same time he built a national organization loyal to himself rather than to Hanna. This served him well in the election of 1904, when he won the Presidency in his own right, against Alton B. Parker, polling more than 56 percent of the popular vote.

Roosevelt showed the proper respect for the powerful conservative leaders of Congress —Speaker "Uncle Joe" Cannon and Senator Nelson Aldrich—but tried to edge them toward his own policies.

"These men," Roosevelt explained years later, "still from force of habit applauded what Lincoln had done in the way of radical dealing with the abuses of his day; but they

THEOBALD CHARTRAN,
WHITE HOUSE COLLECTION

Poised, self-assured Edith Kermit Carow Roosevelt joined in the vigorous fun of husband and six children, yet firmly asserted herself when things got out of hand.

Roosevelt exuberance echoed in the 22 rooms of Sagamore Hill on Long Island, T. R.'s summer White House. His daughter-in-law Eleanor Alexander recalled the Sagamore scene: "The Roosevelt family enjoyed life far too much to . . . waste time sleeping. Every night they stayed downstairs until midnight; then, talking at the tops of their voices, they trooped up the wide, uncarpeted staircase and went to their rooms. For a brief ten minutes all was still; and, just as I was dropping off to sleep for the second time, they remembered things they had forgotten to tell each other and rushed shouting through the halls."

Tusks and game heads, esteemed by Roosevelt as "proof of the hunter's prowess," fill Sagamore Hill, now a national shrine.

did not apply the spirit in which Lincoln worked to the abuses of their own day."

Roosevelt's ideal was to use the Government as the arbiter among conflicting economic forces in the Nation, especially between capital and labor, guaranteeing justice to each and dispensing favors to none. Thus he emerged as a "trust buster." He shared American pride in the enormous productivity of factories, with consequent high living standards, but he realized that the abuses growing out of the new industrial combinations— the trusts—must be curbed. He insisted that moderate reform was the only conservative way to prevent drastic upheaval.

Roosevelt fought for legislation to investigate large interstate corporations and to impose supervision on them; in 1903 Congress established a Department of Commerce and Labor which contained a Bureau of Corporations to investigate trusts. Roosevelt also initiated numerous antitrust suits.

The first and most spectacular of these was the Government case against the Northern Securities Company, a great railroad combination in the Northwest. To the distress of J. P. Morgan of Wall Street, the Government won. The Supreme Court later upheld the decision to break up the combine.

In 1906, Roosevelt proposed stronger Government regulation of the railroads. Through adroit maneuvering, he obtained the Hepburn Act, giving firmer regulatory power to the Interstate Commerce Commission, established in 1887 under Grover Cleveland.

In dealing with labor problems, Roosevelt pursued a similar course. In May, 1902, the miners in the anthracite coal fields struck for an eight-hour day, a wage increase, and union recognition. By October the coal shortage threatened the country. Roosevelt forced the mine operators to confer with labor leaders, and used Government influence for the first time to gain impartial arbitration.

Some of Roosevelt's highest achievements were in conservation. He believed in both the scientific development of national resources and the preservation of wilderness areas.

In the spring of 1903, Roosevelt toured the West, noting in many places how the uncontrolled exploitation of lands, forests, minerals, and water was threatening our natural resources. He camped in Yosemite Park with naturalist John Muir and became converted to Muir's view that it could best be preserved under Federal control. With the approval of most Californians, Roosevelt brought Yosemite under national administration in 1906. He also added enormously to the national forests in the West, reserved coal deposits and future sites for power dams for public use, and fostered great irrigation projects.

In foreign policy, Roosevelt steered the United States toward more active participation in world politics. He liked to quote what he called a West African proverb, "Speak softly and carry a big stick, you will go far." The "big stick" was the new American Navy, which he prodded Congress to build up to a strength equaling that of other world powers.

NATIONAL GEOGRAPHIC PHOTOGRAPHER WILLIAM ALBERT ALLARD (ABOVE AND BELOW)

Riding a steam shovel, the President in 1906 inspects a pet project, the Panama Canal. Crews worked on the strategic short cut between the Atlantic and Pacific for 16 years despite tropical heat, yellow fever, and opposition from Colombia, former owner of the Isthmus.

To enable the fleet to move readily between the Atlantic and Pacific Oceans, Roosevelt took drastic measures (keenly resented in Latin America) to begin construction of a canal across the Isthmus of Panama. And to forestall the intervention of European creditors and the establishment of unfriendly foreign bases in the Caribbean, he sent an American official to police the finances of the Dominican Republic.

At the request of Japan, in 1905 he mediated the Russo-Japanese War, winning the Nobel Peace Prize—and the ill will of the Japanese, who did not gain as much as they had hoped. When, later, war with Japan threatened over the separation of Japanese from Americans in San Francisco schools, Roosevelt persuaded the school board to back down and negotiated immigration restrictions with Japan. He then sent the Great White Fleet on a goodwill tour of the world. At Yokohama it was received with acclaim.

"Teddy" brought a new vibrancy to the Presidency. His high-pitched, earnest voice, jutting jaw, and pounding fist captivated audiences. And he was a brilliant conversationalist of almost limitless range.

Rudyard Kipling recalled listening to Roosevelt in the early 1890's at Washington's Cosmos Club: "I curled up on the seat opposite," Kipling said, "and listened and wondered, until the universe seemed to be spinning round and Theodore was the spinner."

The strenuous life was a necessity for Roosevelt and those associated with him. In February, 1908, he described a visit to Rock Creek Park, where the ice had "just broken .... We did the usual climbing stunts at the various rocks, and then swam the creek; and it was a good swim, in our winter clothes and with hobnail boots and the icy current running really fast."

Leaving the Presidency in 1909, he was not content to settle down at Sagamore Hill, his home at Oyster Bay, Long Island, today a national historic site. Instead, he departed

Staunch advocate of a strong Navy, Roosevelt dispatched 16 American battleships on a 14-month world cruise in 1907. The President used the spectacular voyage of the Great White Fleet to impress potential enemies with United States naval might —and to persuade Congress to authorize two dreadnoughts. Here, aboard the Presidential yacht *Mayflower,* Roosevelt reviews the fleet at Hampton Roads, Virginia.

UNDERWOOD AND UNDERWOOD (ABOVE); KERMIT ROOSEVELT

"Last chance to be a boy." The Huck Finn in T. R. took him down rapids on Brazil's River of Doubt in 1914. Three men died; Brazilian Colonel Candido Rondon (center), co-leader with Roosevelt, lost a toe; and T. R. shortened his life with an abscess and jungle fever.

Camping conservationist, the President visits Yosemite National Park in 1903 (left). Although he was attacked by the press for his interest in hunting, it was Roosevelt who set aside the first 51 wildlife refuges in the United States.

for Africa at the head of an expedition to hunt big game. He bagged probably the world's most comprehensive collection of East African animals, now housed in the Smithsonian Institution.

In 1914 Roosevelt explored the unknown River of Doubt in the Amazon wilds. Of the trip he wrote: "No less than six weeks were spent in slowly and with peril and exhausting labor forcing our way down through what seemed a literally endless succession of rapids and cataracts."

He did not relate that he himself had been injured and ill; at one perilous point he even suggested that the others leave him behind to die. In a voice still weak with fatigue, Roosevelt gave his first public account of his Amazon trip in a lecture to the National Geographic Society.

T. R. was proud of having put the River of Doubt (later named the Theodore Roosevelt) "on the map," as he phrased it. "I had to go. It was my last chance to be a boy."

But he had not ignored politics. By 1910, he was advocating a "New Nationalism," which led to the Progressive program. "I stand for the square deal," he asserted. In 1912 he ran for President on a Progressive ticket, splitting off from the Republican Party, which nominated Taft. To reporters he remarked that he felt as fit as a bull moose, and the new party became known as the Bull Moose Party.

While campaigning in Milwaukee, T. R. was shot in the chest by a fanatic, but insisted on speaking before being taken to the hospital.

"The bullet is in me now," he told his audience, "so that I cannot make a very long speech...I am ahead of the game, anyway. No man has had a happier life than I have led; a happier life in every way."

Roosevelt recovered, but lost to Wilson in the election, and was never able to resume fully the strenuous life he loved. He died in 1919 and was buried at Youngs' Memorial Cemetery, Oyster Bay, Long Island.

TWENTY-SEVENTH PRESIDENT 1909-1913

WILLIAM HOWARD TAFT, a large, jovial, conscientious man, was a distinguished jurist and accomplished administrator whose real aspirations were in the direction of the Supreme Court rather than the Presidency. He achieved his fondest dream eight years after he left the White House, becoming Chief Justice of the United States in 1921.

His four years in the White House were extremely uncomfortable—primarily because he was caught in the middle of an intense battle between progressives and conservatives. Taft disliked resorting to political means to gain his worthy ends. He once explained: "Political considerations have never weighed heavily with me. I have tried to do in each case what seemed to me the wisest thing, regardless of its effect upon my own future."

As a result, Taft received scant credit for the considerable achievements of his administration. In four years he initiated double the number of antitrust suits that had marked Theodore Roosevelt's seven years in office, and dissolved the giant oil and tobacco trusts. As a conservationist, he reserved oil and coal deposits on Federal lands, established a Bureau of Mines to guard mineral resources, and encouraged irrigation projects. To aid the "common man," he obtained parcel post and a postal savings system, and established the Children's Bureau and a Commerce Court.

And he chose a woman, Julia Lathrop, to direct the Children's Bureau, after consulting his Attorney General to be certain that such an appointment would be legally valid.

Genial, gregarious William Howard Taft, a veteran public servant before he reached the White House, believed that the only lasting reward of the Presidency lay in "the thought that one has done something permanently useful to his fellow countrymen."

Cultured Helen Herron Taft enjoyed traveling with her diplomat husband in the Far East. As First Lady, she received from the Mayor of Tokyo 3,000 Japanese cherry trees, an enduring gift to the Nation's Capital.

Taft created a commission to promote efficiency and economy in Government, and fostered successfully two constitutional amendments, providing for a Federal income tax and for popular election of Senators. It was a substantial record, but progressives, demanding far more, assailed it as deficient.

In Taft, the National Geographic Society found a friend and champion in its early days. He lectured before the Society ten times and contributed 13 articles to its magazine, on subjects ranging from the League of Nations to the Lincoln Memorial. He was also the first ex-President to become a Trustee of the Society, serving on the Board from 1917 until his death in 1930.

Taft was born in 1857 in Cincinnati, the

Paintings by Anders L. Zorn (left) and Bror Kronstrand, White House Collection   161

Respect and affection bound Filipinos to Taft during his four-year tour of duty. Appointed first Civil Governor of the Philippines in 1901, Taft vastly improved the islands' roads, schools, and standard of living.

Top-hatted delegates, headed by Secretary of War Taft, take a flat-car tour of the Panama Canal. During his four years as Secretary, Taft championed the project. The "big ditch" opened for business in 1914 on the eve of World War I.

Sheet music for Taft's 1908 campaign features a portrait of the personable, portly Republican—at some 300 pounds the largest of all Presidents.

son of a prominent, well-to-do Ohio judge who had served in Grant's Cabinet. He was graduated second in his class at Yale and returned home to study and later to practice law. He rose in politics through Republican judiciary appointments, through competence and availability, and because, as he once wrote facetiously, he always had his "plate the right side up when offices were falling."

He was appointed, before he was 35, to be a Federal circuit court judge. His decisions, though tending to be verbose, were notable for their conservative legal scholarship. Taft aspired only to be a member of the Supreme Court, but his wife, Helen Herron Taft, held other ambitions for him.

His route to the White House was via administrative posts. President McKinley sent him to the Philippines, and in 1901 he became Civil Governor. Sympathetic toward the Filipinos, he made a splendid reputation by improving the economy, building roads and schools, and giving the people at least limited participation in their government.

Taft loved the Filipinos and they loved him.

With bands and flags, 6,000 islanders marched to the governor's palace on January 10, 1903, to demonstrate their affection. Florid speeches in Spanish praised the beloved Taft. One declared that Governor Taft was a "saint with the power to perform the great miracle" of uniting all of the factions in the islands. Pedro A. Paterno, whom Taft had been forced to chastise for his revolutionary activities, declared that "as Christ had converted the cross into a symbol of glory and triumph, so had Governor Taft turned a dying people to the light and life of modern liberties."

President Roosevelt brought Taft to Washington in 1904 to be Secretary of War, in charge of work on the Panama Canal. One magazine called Taft an "ambassador to stubborn tasks at far corners of the earth."

By 1907, Roosevelt had decided that Taft should be his successor and easily obtained his nomination at the 1908 Republican Convention. Taft disliked the campaign, "one of the most uncomfortable four months of my life." He pledged his fealty to the Roosevelt program, especially popular in the West,

TAFT PRESIDENTIAL PAPERS, LIBRARY OF CONGRESS

while his brother Charles Taft assured eastern Republicans they had nothing to fear. William Jennings Bryan, who was running on the Democratic ticket for a third time, complained that he had to oppose two candidates, a western progressive Taft and an eastern conservative Taft.

Progressives at first were well pleased with the election of Taft. "Roosevelt has cut enough hay," they said. "Taft is the man to put it into the barn." Conservatives were delighted to be rid of Roosevelt.

From the outset, Taft recognized that his techniques as President would differ from those of his predecessor. To Roosevelt, departing for Africa, he sent a revealing farewell letter: "I have not the facility for educating the public as you had through talks with correspondents, and so I fear that a large part of the public will feel as if I had fallen away from your ideals; but you know me better and will understand that I am still working away on the same old plan. . . ."

But Taft did not approve of Roosevelt's stretching of Presidential powers, and when confronted with Congressional opposition inherited from Roosevelt, he moved cautiously.

Taft became President shortly after a variety of Roosevelt proposals dealing with such matters as labor reforms and conservation had been killed in the House Rules Committee by Speaker "Uncle Joe" Cannon. Taft alienated the progressives when he refused to help them curb the Speaker's power.

Keeping his campaign promise to lower tariffs, Taft called Congress into special session to enact the legislation. But then, with his view of a limited Presidential role, he would not marshal his powers behind the progressives as they battled for lower rates. Taft worked privately to improve the bill, but refused to publicize his achievements. The resulting Payne-Aldrich tariff seemed another triumph for eastern industrialists, yet in Winona, Minnesota, he opened himself to criticism by defending it as "on the whole . . . the best bill that the Republican Party ever passed."

Taft added to his political miseries by replacing Roosevelt's conservationist Secretary

163

First former President to be named a Trustee of the National Geographic Society, Taft (seated fourth from left) meets with fellow board members in 1921. Six months earlier he had been appointed Chief Justice—the only man to head both the executive and judicial branches of the Government. To Taft's right sits inventor Alexander Graham Bell, to his left Society President Gilbert H. Grosvenor.

After his White House term, Taft had happily departed politics to become a professor of constitutional law at Yale. Appointment to the Supreme Court fulfilled a lifelong dream. As Taft the Chief Justice wrote decisions, Taft the administrator zestfully set about reorganizing a court system clogged with litigation. Before he died in 1930, he secured Congressional approval for today's Supreme Court Building.

"A shrine at which all can worship," proclaimed ex-President Taft (left), Chairman of the Lincoln Memorial Commission. To President Warren Harding (center), Taft said, "I have the honor to deliver this Lincoln Memorial into your keeping." A distinguished guest was Robert Todd Lincoln (right), son of the Great Emancipator. Thousands witnessed the ceremony on May 30, 1922 (below).

of the Interior with a Seattle lawyer, Richard A. Ballinger. Soon the progressives were charging Ballinger with failure to carry out Roosevelt's policies on conservation. When Taft defended him, he became an anticonservationist himself to the progressives, despite his solid conservation achievements.

In his foreign policy, Taft was a strong advocate of arbitration as a means of settling international disputes. In 1910 he made a notable speech calling for treaties to set up arbitral courts. At its close, French Ambassador Jules Jusserand declared, "We will make such a treaty with you." Taft replied, "I'm your man." He negotiated treaties with both France and England, but the Senate amended them to death.

Later Taft declared, "It was not that those treaties would have abolished war; nobody said they would; but it was that they were a step in the right direction toward the practical ideal under which war might have been impossible."

In reply to the critics who complained that Taft was dedicating his foreign policy to American exporters and investors overseas, he asserted, "To call such diplomacy 'dollar diplomacy'... is to ignore entirely a most useful office to be performed by a government in its dealings with foreign governments."

In 1912, when the Republican Convention renominated Taft, many progressives left the party to support the Bull Moose candidacy of Roosevelt, thus guaranteeing the election of Woodrow Wilson. While under attack from his old friend Roosevelt, Taft took solace from a remark of Abraham Lincoln's that he kept framed on his desk: "I do the very best I know how—the very best I can; and I mean to keep on doing so until the end."

In 1918, when he discovered T. R. in the same Chicago hotel, he threaded his way through the dining room, amid applause, to grasp his hand. Later Roosevelt exclaimed, "Wasn't it a gracious thing for him to do?"

To Taft's delight, President Harding in 1921 appointed him Chief Justice of the United States, making him the only man to serve both as President and as head of the Supreme Court. Taft planned reforms to make the Federal judiciary more efficient, and Congress enacted them. He was so happy at the Court, where he served until just before his death in 1930, that he once wrote, "I don't remember that I ever was President."

Taft lies in Arlington National Cemetery, across the Potomac from Washington. His birthplace is now a national historic site.

165

TWENTY-EIGHTH PRESIDENT 1913-1921

WOODROW WILSON was a great war leader and crusader for world peace who insisted that the United States must share responsibility for maintaining international stability. In his first term he brought to fruition a basic program of progressive reform, the New Freedom. In his second term, he mobilized the manpower and industrial might of the United States, which helped bring an Allied victory in the war to make the world "safe for democracy."

Wilson sought to implement that ideal through the League of Nations, but the Senate blocked the entrance of the United States into the League and frustrated his dream.

Perhaps because his earliest memories were of the Civil War and its tragic consequences, Wilson's most earnest hope was for permanent peace. He was born in Staunton, Virginia, in 1856, the son of a Presbyterian minister who during the Civil War had a church in Augusta, Georgia, and during Reconstruction taught theology in the charred city of Columbia, South Carolina. The boyhood home of Wilson can still be seen in Augusta, and the Staunton birthplace and Columbia home have become Woodrow Wilson memorial museums.

Wilson was raised in the traditions of the South; he was proud the Confederates had fought, but glad the Union had survived.

After being graduated from Princeton—known then as the College of New Jersey—and attending the University of Virginia Law School, Wilson practiced law in Atlanta. But finding the law an uncongenial profession, he earned a Ph.D. at the Johns Hopkins University and began an academic career. His hope, as he told his future wife, Ellen Louise Axson, was to move on to statesmanship. As a law student he had expressed his daydreams by inscribing calling cards, "Thomas Woodrow Wilson, Senator from Virginia."

Wilson rose rapidly as a conservative professor of political economy, popular both in the classroom and as a writer. Although Wilson disparaged his own appearance, he was a striking figure. His wife described him

Quest for peace guided Woodrow Wilson; he had seen the frightfulness of conflict as a child during the Civil War. But destiny cast him as a wartime President. He came to the White House on the eve of battle in Europe. By April, 1917, only five months after re-election, he found himself asking Congress to declare war on Germany.

Childhood friend of the President, Ellen Louise Axson gave up a career in art to marry the young professor. Their three daughters, seen here at their Princeton, New Jersey, home, were in their twenties when the family moved to the White House. As First Lady, Ellen Wilson saw two of the girls married before her death at 54.

Painting by Sir William Orpen, White House Collection

with a line from Wordsworth, "a noticeable man, with large gray eyes."

A contemporary, W. S. Couch, saw his face as "curiously geometrical. . . . The mouth is small, sensitive, with full lips, a mouth almost too well shaped for a man, and a woman might envy the arched eyebrows. But the almost brutal strength of the general bony structure of the face, and that aggressive jaw promise an active, iron willed, fighting man. . . ."

Elected President of Princeton in 1902, Wilson threw his energies into remodeling the university into an eminent intellectual institution. Faculty and alumni received many of his reforms warmly, but opposed others. The resulting unrest perhaps influenced his decision to accept a call from conservative Democrats to run for Governor of New Jersey in 1910.

Even during the campaign, he asserted his independence of the conservatives and of the machine that had nominated him. "I should deem myself forever disgraced," he announced, by cooperating "in even the slightest degree" with the "boss system" of his own party. He

endorsed an extensive progressive platform. As governor he made good his pledges, speedily moving New Jersey into the vanguard of the progressive states.

After a stiff fight at the 1912 Democratic Convention, he was nominated for President and campaigned on a program called the New Freedom. Wilson claimed this placed greater stress on individualism and states' rights than did Theodore Roosevelt's competing New Nationalism. It was a New Freedom, asserted Wilson, for "the man who is knocking and fighting at the closed doors of opportunity." In the three-way election, against Roosevelt and Taft, he received only 42 percent of the popular votes, but an overwhelming proportion of electoral votes.

In his first Inaugural Address, President Wilson criticized the "inexcusable waste" that accompanied American prosperity and the use of the Government "for private and selfish purposes." He called for a reform program that would be a return to early ideals, declaring, "Our work is a work of restoration."

He followed with a bill of particulars that he translated into legislation a year later. President Wilson, like Roosevelt before him, regarded himself as the personal representative of the American public. "No one but the President," he wrote in the summer of 1913, "seems to be expected . . . to look out for the general interests of the country."

Wilson skillfully maneuvered through Congress three major pieces of legislation. The first was a lower tariff, the Underwood Act, which he obtained despite lobbies and logrolling. In support of the bill, he appeared in person to deliver a message to Congress, the first President to do so since John Adams. Attached to the measure was the first graduated income tax as we know it today, beginning with a one percent tax and ranging to a six percent maximum.

Next Wilson obtained legislation of great lasting importance, the Federal Reserve Act. This provided the Nation with the more elastic money supply it badly needed by creating 12 regional "bankers' banks," supervised by a board in Washington. In 1914 he won stronger antitrust legislation, including establishment of a Federal Trade Commission to guard against unfair business practices.

Courage and stubbornness, traits that marked his years as Chief Executive, seem to show in Wilson's walk. In cap and gown, he strides across the campus at Princeton, where he was a bold, innovating president.

Birthplace of the 28th President, the manse of the First Presbyterian Church in Staunton, Virginia, wears the look of Dixie with its balconies and stately Greek Revival columns. From the house, maintained as a public shrine, the gardens descend in three terraces. Son of a minister, Wilson spent his formative years in the South and as a young lawyer practiced in Georgia.

169

Versatile helpmate, dark-eyed Edith Bolling Galt married Wilson, a widower, in 1915. His confidante during the 18-hour workdays of the war, she became both nurse and executive secretary after a stroke crippled the President in the fall of 1919.

In gratitude for U. S. food, Belgian children embroidered this flour sack from a Waitsburg, Washington, mill and sent it to Wilson.

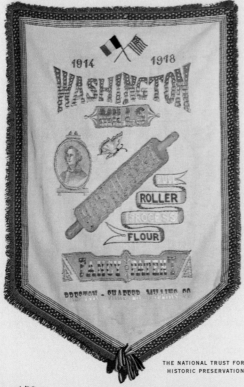

In 1916, an election year, Wilson loosed another burst of legislation; out of conviction as well as political shrewdness, he took up the views of the 1912 Bull Moosers on the strong exercise of Federal power. Among the new acts was one to end child labor throughout the Nation—a law the Supreme Court invalidated by a 1918 decision it subsequently overruled. Another law limited interstate railroad workers to a maximum eight-hour day. By virtue of such domestic legislation and the Democratic campaign slogan, "He kept us out of war," Wilson narrowly won re-election over Charles Evans Hughes.

Wilson knew both great happiness and acute sorrow in the White House. During the early months, surrounded by the wife he adored, his three grown daughters, and often by numerous Southern relatives, he would frolic within the circle, singing at the piano, laughing and reciting limericks, and doing imitations, including one of fist-shaking Theodore Roosevelt. But in August, 1914, Mrs. Wilson died, and Wilson was brokenhearted.

Without his wife he seemed lost until he met a charming widow, Edith Bolling Galt. They were married in December, 1915.

"He believed that God had given her to him for companionship, strength, and joy," Wilson's biographer, Arthur S. Link, has written. "Her love made him whole again."

Throughout his years in the White House, Wilson worked long hours, often until late at night. He drafted his own speeches, press statements, and important correspondence, first setting them down in Graham shorthand, then transcribing them on his typewriter.

As the war in Europe impinged increasingly upon the United States, Wilson's burden became heavier and heavier. "All the rest of the world is on fire," he said, "and our own house is not fireproof." He had urged the American people to be neutral in thought as well as in deed, but became involved in a struggle to maintain the Nation's neutral rights on the high seas. In 1916, against Congressional opposition, he launched a preparedness program, enlarging the Army and greatly increasing the size of the Navy.

From the war's beginning, Wilson hoped for a just peace, and as late as January, 1917, called for "peace without victory." But Germany made a bold gamble, and on January 31 announced that in certain waters its submarines would sink any ship, Allied or neutral, without warning—knowing this would bring American intervention. Wilson reluctantly concluded that Germany was flouting

U. S. SIGNAL CORPS, NATIONAL ARCHIVES (ABOVE); THE BETTMANN ARCHIVE

Jubilant doughboys on the front line cheer news of the Armistice in November, 1918. Had this truly been the war to end wars? Wilson fervently hoped so and sought to build an enduring peace safeguarded by a League of Nations.

First President to visit Europe while in office, Wilson arrived in Paris for the Peace Conference in December, 1918. French Premier Georges Clemenceau points out landmarks to the American leader (right) and to David Lloyd George, Prime Minister of Great Britain.

Throngs cheered Wilson in the Paris streets, but at the conference table the victors bickered over borders and reparations, and his hopes for a "just and stable peace" dimmed. Though the Allies acclaimed his proposed covenant creating the League of Nations, he saw other peace aims ignored or compromised. Returning home a weary man, he faced the task of winning Senate ratification of the peace pact—the Treaty of Versailles.

America's neutral rights and that peace and the preservation of democracy could come only through the destruction of German autocracy. On April 2, 1917, he asked Congress for a declaration of war.

As the massive American effort brought nearly five million men under arms and produced vast quantities of war materiel, the balance slowly tipped in favor of the Allies. Wilson went before Congress in January, 1918, to enunciate American war aims, the Fourteen Points. The most important was the fourteenth, the establishment of "a general association of nations...affording mutual guarantees of political independence and territorial integrity to great and small states alike."

After the Armistice in November, 1918, Wilson went to Paris to try to fabricate in person an enduring peace. On his return he presented to the Senate the Versailles Treaty, containing the Covenant of the League of Nations. He asked, "Dare we reject it and break the heart of the world?" But the election of 1918 had shifted the balance in Congress to the Republicans—partly because of farmers' discontent with grain prices, not opposition to Wilson's peace aims. A militant minority in the Senate believed the United States should stay out of the League. By seven votes the treaty failed to obtain the requisite two-thirds Senate majority.

The President, against his doctor's warnings, had made a national tour to mobilize public sentiment, but became exhausted and collapsed at Pueblo, Colorado, September 25, 1919. Shortly after, he suffered a stroke and nearly died. For two months Wilson's wife and physician tried to shield him from matters

Always a crusader, Wilson was the first President since John Adams to address Joint Sessions of Congress. Here in the House Chamber he appeals for legislation soon after taking office. From this same dais on January 8, 1918, he presented his famous Fourteen Points, outlining American peace hopes. Congressional controversy engulfed the fourteenth point, which called for establishment of an international "association"—the League of Nations.

Exhausted but still a fighter, Wilson ignores his doctor's advice and makes a whistle-stop tour of the United States. His aim: to mobilize public opinion and force the Senate to act favorably on the League of Nations. He would be glad to give his life for the cause, he said. After stumping the Midwest and Far West, he collapsed and was whisked back to Washington, where he was invalided by a stroke four days later. He gradually regained strength, but suffered another blow when, on March 19, 1920, the Senate voted down the Versailles Treaty with its League Covenant.

that would upset or tire him. Once Mrs. Wilson turned away officials, saying, "I am not interested in the President of the United States. I am interested in my husband and his health." Wilson's illness has since been cited by those seeking to provide constitutional safeguards against the incapacity of a President.

Nursed by his wife, the ex-President lived on until 1924 at 2340 S Street in Washington, now a national historic landmark. He is buried at the Washington Cathedral, where his tomb and memorial bay may be seen.

On Armistice Day, 1923, he spoke briefly to the crowd that gathered outside his home. "I am not one of those who have the least anxiety about the triumph of the principles I have stood for," he said. "That we shall prevail is as sure as that God reigns."

Warren G Harding

TWENTY-NINTH PRESIDENT 1921-1923

WARREN GAMALIEL HARDING, a well-meaning man, promised a Nation troubled by the inflation and dislocations following World War I that he would take it back to "normalcy." But there was to be no turning back from the profound economic and social changes that the war had wrought. Harding, unwise in some of his appointments, was betrayed by corrupt friends and died heartsick and disillusioned before the end of his term.

He was born in the Ohio village of Blooming Grove in 1865, the son of a farmer who turned homeopathic doctor. After graduation from Ohio Central College, Harding became, at 19, the publisher and co-owner of the Marion, Ohio, *Star*. As the little town of 4,000 steadily grew and prospered, so did the *Star* and Warren Harding. In 1891 he married Florence Kling De Wolfe, daughter of the town's richest banker. He became a director of almost every important business in town, a leader in fraternal organizations and charitable enterprises.

Tall, handsome, and likable, Harding was ideally suited to be the most prominent citizen of Marion. His undeviating Republicanism and vibrant speaking voice, together with more political skill than has been generally recognized, carried him far. He served in the state Senate and in 1902 became Lieutenant Governor of Ohio. He delivered the nominating address for President Taft at the 1912 Republican Convention, and the keynote speech four years later. In 1914 he was elected to the United States Senate, which he found to be "a very pleasant place."

An Ohio admirer, Harry Daugherty, began to promote Harding for the 1920 Republican nomination because, as he later explained, "He looked like a President."

When the principal candidates of the 1920 Republican Convention deadlocked, Harding obtained the nomination. The call for "normalcy" became the theme of his campaign. He declared, "America's present need is not heroics, but healing; not nostrums, but normalcy; not revolution, but restoration; not agitation, but adjustment; not surgery, but serenity; not the dramatic, but the dispassionate; not experiment, but equipoise; not submergence in internationality, but sustainment in triumphant nationality. . . ."

Actually, the very murkiness of such statements was effective. While the Democratic candidates, Governor James M. Cox of Ohio and Franklin D. Roosevelt, conducted crusades for the League of Nations, both opponents and proponents of American entrance into the League could find in Harding's speeches reasons to vote for him. Most voters, however, were chiefly interested in protesting uncomfortable living conditions. Harding

"He looked like a President," political friends said of Warren Harding, and the polls bore them out in 1920, when the Ohioan won by a landslide. Plagued by scandals involving high Government officials, he died disillusioned after 2½ years in office.

"I have only one real hobby — my husband," said Florence Kling De Wolfe Harding. Ambitious, enthusiastic, she helped him to the top. Her frequent garden parties gave the White House a country-club air.

Painting by F. Luis Mora, White House Collection

175

won by the greatest landslide in a century, more than 60 percent of the popular vote.

He promised to enlist the best brains in the country in his administration; he did, in choosing such distinguished men as Charles Evans Hughes to be Secretary of State and Herbert Hoover to be Secretary of Commerce. Unfortunately he also appointed some officials who turned out to be false to their trusts.

Despite the pleas of Hughes, President Harding interpreted his election as a mandate to stay out of the League of Nations. Hughes, loyal to the President, was cold to European proposals for cooperation in collective security. As a substitute, he proposed at the Washington Conference on the Limitation of Armaments a drastic reduction of the fleets of the United States, Great Britain, and Japan.

A British observer declared that Secretary Hughes sank more British battleships than "all the admirals of the world had destroyed in a cycle of centuries."

The United States thus eased tensions in the Pacific, and in so doing postponed for 15 years a serious naval race with Japan.

With similar skill, Secretary Hoover ran Harding's Department of Commerce in the interests of small business. Further, he persuaded the President to pressure steel companies into eliminating the 12-hour day and 7-day week, then still in effect at some mills.

Republicans in Congress easily obtained the President's signature on their bills. They eliminated wartime controls and slashed taxes, established a Federal budget system, restored the high protective tariff, and imposed tight limitations on immigration. By 1923 the postwar depression seemed to be giving way to new prosperity, and newspapers hailed Harding as a wise statesman, effectively carrying out his campaign promise, "Less government in business and more business in government."

But behind the façade, some of Harding's friends brought to their offices and even to the White House something of the less savory atmosphere of a rural county seat. Word began to reach him that some of his cronies were using their offices for their own enrichment. Alarmed, he complained to editor William Allen White, "My . . . friends . . . they're the ones that keep me walking the floors nights!"

Fortunately for himself, Harding did not live to face the public reaction to the Teapot Dome affair, concerning the leasing of Government oil reserves, and other scandals of his administration. On August 2, 1923, he died in San Francisco following a heart attack. By the time the scandals were exposed, the damage to the Republican Party was offset by the obvious moral rectitude of his successor, Calvin Coolidge.

Harding was buried at Marion amid national mourning, and the Harding Memorial there marks his burial site. His Marion home is a national historic landmark.

Bareheaded in soft spring rain, President Harding (center) attends the unveiling on April 6, 1922, of a National Geographic Society memorial honoring explorer Robert E. Peary in Arlington National Cemetery. Mrs. Harding watches at his right; on the President's left stand Society President Gilbert H. Grosvenor; the French Ambassador and Mme Jusserand; Chief Justice Taft; and Secretary of State and Mrs. Charles Evans Hughes.

Unknown soldier lies in state in the Capitol Rotunda on the same catafalque that had borne three assassinated Presidents—Lincoln, Garfield, and McKinley. Here on November 11, 1921, President Harding pays his respects to an American soldier, "known but to God," who fell in France in World War I. Shortly after, the casket rode a caisson across the Potomac River to Arlington.

Wan and depressed on a speaking tour, the President cruises Alaskan waters with Mrs. Harding and Territorial Governor Scott C. Bone (in Eskimo parka). A few weeks later, in San Francisco, the Nation's 29th President died of a heart attack.

CALVIN COOLIDGE as President was the embodiment, in an urban age, of the frugality, industry, and morality of an earlier, rural America. In keeping with his credo, Coolidge took an essentially hands-off view of the role of Government, asserting, "The business of America is business."

Born in Plymouth, Vermont, on July 4, 1872, Coolidge was the son of a hard-working village storekeeper. Parts of the house in which he was born, and his father's adjoining store, are maintained as a museum. "My boy was always shy and quietlike and never put himself forward," his father later reminisced. "He was a trusty kind of a boy.... all he wanted was a good education.... Calvin could get more sap out of a maple tree than any of the other boys around here."

Coolidge was graduated from Amherst College with honors, and entered law and politics in Northampton, Massachusetts. It was there that he met Grace Goodhue, who became his wife in 1905. "She has kept me running for public office ever since I married her," Coolidge jested in later years. In truth, as Mrs. Coolidge wrote, she had at times "protested against further advancement up the political ladder." Over the years he won election to a score of offices, ranging from councilman in Northampton to Governor of Massachusetts. En route he became thoroughly conservative.

Boston merchant Frank W. Stearns explained privately in 1916: "He told me once that when he first went into the Legislature he supposes he was considered a radical, especially along the lines of legislation in favor of social betterment. There came a time about the middle of his legislative experience when he came to the conviction *not* that his previous ideas were wrong but that Massachusetts, at any rate, was going too fast. As he put it, legislation was outstripping the ability to administer. He felt that unless we were willing to get into serious trouble that would take years to rectify, a halt must be called.... He said he supposed at the time that his career in public life was ended...."

As President, Coolidge took this same view of the Federal Government—that enough reform legislation had been enacted and that it was up to him to call a halt.

Coolidge first became a national figure during the Boston police strike of 1919. When Samuel Gompers, president of the American Federation of Labor, urged that the strikers be re-employed, Coolidge wired, "There is no right to strike against the public safety by anybody, anywhere, any time." After the nomination of Harding for President at the 1920 Republican Convention, delegates ignored the leaders and nominated Governor Coolidge for Vice President.

In the early morning hours of August 3, 1923, while visiting his father in Plymouth, Coolidge received word that

Frugal New Englander, Calvin Coolidge occupied the White House in an era of extravagance and waste but offered the Nation an example of near-Spartan rectitude in public and private life. Delighting in his Yankee twang, the Nation affectionately called him "Cal."

Lighted by this lamp, the family Bible by his hand, Vice President Coolidge was sworn in as 30th President at 2:47 a.m., August 3, 1923, in his native Plymouth, Vermont. His father, a notary, administered the oath when President Harding died.

COURTESY CALVIN COOLIDGE
MEMORIAL FOUNDATION

Coolidge revisits Vermont: "I found that the love I had for the hills where I was born touched a responsive chord in the heart of the whole nation."

Window sticker struck a popular note. Coolidge polled 54 percent of the vote in 1924.

Indian headdress replaces straw hat as Coolidge powwows with the Sioux at Deadwood, South Dakota, in 1927.

While vacationing in the Black Hills that year he announced that he would not seek re-election. The death in 1924 of 16-year-old Calvin, Jr.—a blister on his toe from playing tennis led to blood poisoning—had left enduring sorrow. "When he went," lamented Coolidge, "the power and the glory of the Presidency went with him."

Harding was dead, and that he was President. By the light of a kerosene lamp, his father, a notary public, administered the oath of office.

The Coolidge Homestead, across the street from the birthplace, appears today much as it did then. In the "oath" room visitors see original furnishings—a day bed, a brown rug, a wood-burning stove. In these simple surroundings, Coolidge began his administration.

Of Coolidge as President, a Democratic admirer, Alfred E. Smith, wrote: "His great task was to restore the dignity and prestige of the Presidency when it had reached the lowest ebb in our history, and to afford, in a time of extravagance and waste, a shining public example of the simple and homely virtues which came down to him from his New England ancestors."

President Coolidge was determined to preserve the old moral and economic precepts amid the Nation's material prosperity. He refused to use the economic power of the Federal Government to check the growing boom and did not believe that Government action was the solution to the depression in agriculture and certain industries. His first message to Congress, in December, 1923, called for a foreign policy of attending "to our own affairs," and for tax cuts, economy, and only limited aid to farmers; it was hailed by Chief Justice Taft as "great in the soundness of its economic statesmanship."

Coolidge rapidly became so popular that the Harding scandals, as they were gradually exposed, seemed to damage the Democratic investigators more than they discredited the Republican Party. In 1924, benefiting from "Coolidge prosperity," he defeated John W. Davis, winning 54 percent of the popular vote.

In his Inaugural Address Coolidge asserted that the Nation had achieved "a state of contentment seldom before seen," and pledged himself to maintain the status quo. He vetoed two farm-relief bills and Senator George Norris's scheme to produce cheap Federal electric power on the Tennessee River. During his years as Chief Executive, the Federal budget hardly varied, while the national debt dropped by almost one-fourth.

In a speech to the Daughters of the American Revolution, Coolidge formulated the deeply conservative political philosophy behind such vetoes:

"Whenever some people find that abuse needs correction in their neighborhood, instead of applying a remedy themselves, they seek to have a tribunal sent on from Washington to discharge their duties for them, regard-

PAINTING BY HOWARD CHANDLER CHRISTY, WHITE HOUSE COLLECTION

Grace Goodhue Coolidge, charming and radiant, was among the most popular of First Ladies. She taught at the Clarke School for the Deaf in Northampton, Massachusetts, before marrying the future President.

less of the fact that in accepting such supervision they are bartering away their freedom."

Walter Lippmann, in 1926, sought to explain the success of the Coolidge credo: "It suits all the business interests which want to be let alone.... And it suits all those who have become convinced that government in this country has become dangerously complicated and top-heavy."

President Coolidge himself put it with characteristic succinctness: "When things are going along all right, it is a good plan to let them alone."

Coolidge was both the most remote of

181

Lines of curious Americans crowd the White House sidewalk to attend a New Year's Day reception during the Coolidge Administration. The President met the public almost daily. "On one occasion I shook hands with nineteen hundred in thirty-four minutes," the Vermonter recalled in his *Autobiography,* "which is probably my record. Instead of a burden, it was a pleasure . . . to meet people in that way and listen to their greeting. . . ."

Presidents and one of the most accessible. He once told Bernard Baruch why he often sat silently through interviews in his office: "Well, Baruch, many times I say only 'yes' or 'no' to people. Even that is too much. It winds them up for twenty minutes more."

On the other hand, no President was kinder in permitting himself to be photographed in Indian war bonnets or cowboy dress, and in greeting innumerable delegations. And he was the last President whom every visitor to Washington could meet. At about 12:30 most afternoons a line-up of several hundred persons filed through the President's office to shake his hand.

Coolidge's dry Yankee wit and his frugality with words became legendary. The story of the young woman who sat next to Coolidge at a dinner party is typical. She told him she had bet she could get at least three words of conversation out of him. Without looking at her, he quietly retorted, "You lose." And in 1927,

while vacationing in the Black Hills of South Dakota, he called a special press conference to issue the most famous of his statements, "I do not choose to run for President in nineteen twenty eight."

He retired from the Presidency in 1929, and that year became a member of the National Geographic Society's Board of Trustees.

His biographer, Claude M. Fuess, who calls him "a great and good man," sums up the Coolidge Presidency: "He was a safe pilot, not a brilliant one. Under him the nation was not adventurous, but it was happy. He won no battles, challenged no traditions, instituted few reforms. What he would have done with a war or a depression on his hands is a fascinating subject for speculation."

But when the Great Depression hit, Coolidge was in retirement; shortly before his death in January, 1933, he confided to an old friend, "I feel I no longer fit in with these times." He is buried in Plymouth, Vermont.

FROM RICHARD E. BYRD (ABOVE); INTERNATIONAL NEWSREEL

Off for the top of the world. Ground crew cheers as Lt. Comdr. Richard Evelyn Byrd and pilot Floyd Bennett roar down an icy track at Spitsbergen on May 9, 1926, pointing their Fokker trimotor toward the North Pole. During the Coolidge Administration aerial exploration came of age, spreading its wings even wider in 1929 when Byrd also conquered the South Pole by air.

First to fly the Atlantic alone, 25-year-old Charles A. Lindbergh thrilled the world in 1927. An unknown civilian aviator working for an airmail contractor, he flew from New York to Paris in his single-engine plane, *Spirit of St. Louis,* in 33½ hours. Guest of President Coolidge, he received a hero's welcome in Washington.

WIDE WORLD

"Admiral of the Ends of the Earth" receives the National Geographic Society's Hubbard Medal from President Coolidge on June 23, 1926, for his historic flight over the North Pole. On accepting the Society's highest honor for exploration, Byrd recalled the words spoken seven years earlier by Adm. Robert E. Peary: "Coming Polar explorers . . . are quite likely to use modern means which have sprung into existence within the last few years. According to my own personal impressions—aerial flights." Said the naval aviator, "How true his prophecy has turned out to be."

THIRTY-FIRST PRESIDENT 1929-1933

H ERBERT HOOVER was forced as President to cope with a severe worldwide depression. Unlike earlier depression Presidents, he used Government resources to help business recover, but his popularity had evaporated and he was defeated in 1932. In later years he was again hailed as an outstanding American leader.

Few men have lived such long, exciting lives. The son of a Quaker blacksmith, Herbert Hoover was born in West Branch, Iowa, on August 10, 1874. His father died when Herbert was six; his mother, two years later. He went to live with an uncle in Oregon, where he learned not only how to clear forest, but also how to type and keep books. He was one of the first students to enroll at Stanford University when it opened in 1891, and at 20, in the midst of a depression, he was graduated with a degree in geology.

After working as an ordinary miner in the Sierra Nevada, he took a job as typist with a firm of mining engineers. He quickly demonstrated his analytical and organizing talents, and at 23 took charge of some gold mines in the Australian desert. He developed one of the richest of all, the Sons of Gwalia mine.

In 1899 he became the chief mining expert for the Chinese Government. En route to China, he stopped in California to marry his Stanford sweetheart, Lou Henry. In June, 1900, the Boxer Rebellion caught the couple in Tientsin, and Hoover assumed responsibility for the civil administration and for husbanding food and water in the beleaguered foreign settlement.

By the early 1900's, Hoover had become famous in the mining industry. He developed great mines in Australia and Burma and rehabilitated others in Russia. When the chief accountant for a firm of British mining consultants, in which he was a junior partner, embezzled a million dollars, Hoover, in the absence of his senior partners, decided that the firm would make good the loss even though it was under no legal obligation. He personally assumed a substantial share of the loss, wiping out the greater part of his life's savings. The firm's reputation—as well as Hoover's personal standing—was greatly enhanced, and the incident became a legend in international business circles.

A week before Hoover celebrated his 40th birthday in London, Germany declared war on France, and the American Consul General asked his help in getting tourists home.

"I did not realize it at the moment," Hoover later

Brilliant mining engineer Herbert Clark Hoover had amassed a comfortable fortune when, at 40, he dedicated the rest of his long life to public service. In World War I he served without salary as U. S. Food Administrator and then, under Harding and Coolidge, as Secretary of Commerce. An astute professional man, he hated the waste of war; a Quaker and humanitarian, he detested the bloodshed and suffering it entailed. On accepting the Presidential nomination in 1928, he declared: "I think I may say that I have witnessed as much of the horror and suffering of war as any other American. From it I have derived a deep passion for peace."

Lou Henry Hoover spoke five languages and relaxed by reading sociology and economics. She filled the White House with books and art objects. Mrs. Hoover was a long-time member of the National Geographic Society; her name appeared among its 2,433 members as listed in the January, 1903, NATIONAL GEOGRAPHIC.

wrote, "but on Monday, August 3rd, my engineering career was over forever. I was on the slippery road of public life."

After helping 120,000 Americans return to the United States, Hoover took on a far more difficult task: to feed Belgium, which had been overrun by the German Army and faced starvation. Throughout the war his herculean program fed millions of Belgians and French behind the German lines.

After the United States entered the war, President Wilson appointed Hoover head of the Food Administration. Newspapers referred to its work as "Hooverizing." By voluntary methods, without rationing, Hoover succeeded in cutting home consumption of foods needed overseas and kept the Allies fed.

After the Armistice, Hoover had the responsibility of organizing shipments of food to starving millions in central Europe. In 1921

he extended the program to famine-stricken Soviet Russia.

"Twenty million people are starving," he replied to a critic. "Whatever their politics, they shall be fed!"

Shocked by both the radicalism and reaction he had seen in Europe, Hoover, as Secretary of Commerce in the Harding and Coolidge Administrations, advocated a middle path. He hailed the "rising vision of service" which led Americans to pursue community responsibilities rather than merely "the acquisition and preservation of private property...."

This was his own pattern of life; during his years in public service he refused to take even a token dollar a year for his own use. Conversely, he felt the Government should help business in practical ways, while putting as few restrictions on it as possible.

When Hoover received the Republican

American bounty for hungry Europe: During and after World War I, Hoover headed relief programs that spelled life for millions. While fighting still raged, he crossed the mine-infested English Channel and North Sea 40 times. Here, in 1920, he inspects a shipment of flour bound for war-ravaged children.

Grateful Polish youngsters hail him in Warsaw in 1946. As chairman of President Truman's Famine Emergency Committee, he surveyed food problems of 38 nations stricken by World War II.

Tuned in on a one-tube set, Secretary of Commerce Hoover personally checks on radio interference complaints in 1923.

nomination in 1928, no one seemed better qualified to state as he did in his acceptance address, "We in America today are nearer to the final triumph over poverty than ever before in the history of the land." Running against Governor Alfred E. Smith of New York, Hoover carried 40 of the 48 states, and his decisive victory seemed a guarantee of ever-rising living standards.

Yet less than a year later came the stock-market crash of 1929, and the Nation spiraled downward into depression. Hoover tried to use Government leadership to stimulate recovery through voluntary methods. He urged business not to cut payrolls, labor not to ask for higher wages, and farmers to practice crop control. Also he announced that, while keeping the budget balanced and currency sound, he would cut taxes and increase spending on public works, such as Hoover Dam, then being constructed on the Colorado River.

In 1931 repercussions from Europe deepened the crisis, even though the President arranged a one-year moratorium on reparations and war-debt payments. In December, 1931, Hoover asked Congress to enact an unprece-dented program: creation of a giant Federal loan agency (the Reconstruction Finance Corporation) to aid business; additional help for farmers facing mortage foreclosures; banking reform; a loan to states to aid in feeding unemployed; further expansion of public works; and drastic governmental economy.

The program had hard sledding with a hostile Congress dominated by Democrats and progressive Republicans. Slowly they passed part of the measures. Hoover, no man for political maneuvers, would not budge on his principles, and felt that demands that the Government go further presaged disaster.

"I was convinced that efficient, honest administration of the vast machine of the Federal government would appeal to all citizens," he wrote later. "I have since learned that efficient government does not interest the people so much as dramatics." Years earlier, when some of his backers showed him a press release describing his courage during the Boxer Rebellion, he tore the paper to shreds, saying, "You can't make a Teddy Roosevelt out of me."

While proposing his positive program to fight the depression, Hoover reiterated that

First President born west of the Mississippi, Hoover spent his infancy in this cottage in the Quaker hamlet of West Branch, Iowa. Today a national historic landmark, the site includes a blacksmith shop like that operated by Hoover's father, a Presidential library housing papers and mementos, and the graves of the President and his wife.

caring for the cold and hungry must be primarily a local and voluntary responsibility.

"If we start appropriations of this character," he asserted, "we have not only impaired something infinitely valuable in the life of the American people but have struck at the roots of self-government."

Hoover's opponents in Congress criticized him unfairly, making him the scapegoat for the depression, and he was badly defeated by Franklin D. Roosevelt in 1932. Subsequently he was a powerful critic of the New Deal, warning against tendencies toward statism.

In 1947 President Truman appointed Hoover to a commission, which elected him chairman, charged with reorganizing the executive branch. He was appointed chairman of a similar commission by President Eisenhower in 1953. Many economies resulted from both commissions' recommendations.

Hoover wrote many articles and books; he was working on a book when he died, at 90, in New York City, October 20, 1964. He lies beside his wife on a hillside at his Iowa birthplace. Nearby, the Herbert Hoover Library-Museum preserves his papers and mementos for study, and the two-room cottage in which he was born has been restored and opened to the public.

5 THE NUCLEAR AGE:

Fireball and cloud of a 1952 hydrogen test explosion in the Pacific symbolize the peril of atomic weapons. In the shadow of World War II, Franklin D. Roosevelt authorized the research that made

Its Problems and Promises

Franklin D. Roosevelt through Ronald Reagan

THE PRESIDENTS of the troubled decades that followed the Great Depression bore perhaps the heaviest responsibility in the history of the office: to guard the peace in a turbulent world while assuring the well-being of all the Nation's citizens. Much was demanded of these Chief Executives, from Franklin D. Roosevelt through Ronald Reagan, and each labored long and hard to meet his obligations.

Their primary task was to maintain stability and prosperity, acting with Congress to throw the weight of the Federal Government into the economic balance as needed. Franklin D. Roosevelt's first goal was to pull the Nation out of a disastrous depression and to halt plummeting deflation. Each of his successors worked to prevent recessions from turning into depressions, and, during decades of unprecedented prosperity, to restrain inflation.

With the outbreak of World War II, President Roosevelt assumed another major responsibility—to

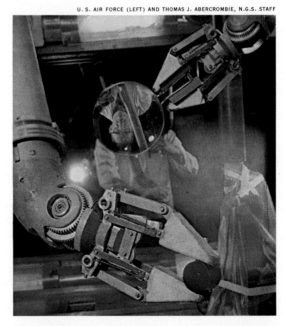

them possible. Every President since has worked tirelessly to prevent nuclear war.

Peaceful victories against sickness and hunger follow atomic research like this analysis of uranium.

191

foster collective security. Succeeding Presidents have marshaled the economic resources and armed strength of the United States in behalf of poor or threatened nations.

Maintenance of economic stability at home and peace abroad have been frustrating and often thankless tasks, demanding the full energies and resourcefulness of each of these Presidents. Each has contributed his own approach to these persistent problems.

Roosevelt, within a humanitarian framework, was frankly experimental. Harry S. Truman demonstrated an ability to make perilous decisions quickly and calmly. Dwight D. Eisenhower, the consolidator of the achievements of a score of years, stressed moderation. John F. Kennedy, bringing youth and style, focused on the demands of an urban age. Lyndon B. Johnson, contributing a consummate skill in obtaining legislative action, led the Nation toward a "Great Society."

Richard M. Nixon established new relationships with the Soviet Union and China.

Gerald R. Ford, coming to the office following a divisive scandal, sought to restore unity. Jimmy Carter bolstered social services at home and championed human rights abroad.

The complex problems that these modern Presidents have faced contrast sharply with the basic tasks that confronted George Washington: to establish a firm executive department for the fledgling Government and to obtain respect and security in a world dominated by unfriendly monarchies.

The present generation knows both promise and peril beyond the farthest vision of the Founding Fathers, Kennedy pointed out in his Inaugural Address: "The world is very different now. For man holds in his mortal hands the power to abolish all forms of human poverty and all forms of human life."

Nevertheless, Kennedy noted, the same beliefs for which Washington's generation had fought were still at issue throughout the world. And the fundamental principles of the Founding Fathers remain cogent to this day.

Johnson expressed it eloquently in his State of the Union Message in January, 1965:

"A President does not shape a new and personal vision of America. He collects it from the scattered hopes of the American past."

Assuming leadership after the rending experience of Watergate, President Ford assured the Nation: "Our Constitution works. Our great Republic is a government of laws and not of men. Here the people rule."

Like his predecessor, President Carter in his Inaugural Address hailed the paramount role of the people. "You have given me a great responsibility—to stay close to you, to be worthy of you, and to exemplify what you are," he said. "Let us create together a new national spirit of unity and trust."

As President Reagan took office, he reemphasized the principles that have made America great. "With the idealism and fair play which are the core of our system and our strength, we can have a strong, prosperous America at peace with itself and the world."

From the High Tide of War Rise Hopes for Peace and a New Frontier in Space

D-Day, June 6, 1944, saw the Allies storm Hitler's western wall at Omaha Beach (center) and four other Normandy beachheads. Lessons of history's costliest war convinced world statesmen of the need for a permanent peace-keeping organization. Efforts to establish and strengthen the United Nations (left) occupied the minds of America's Presidents at mid-20th century.

Successive administrations sought to move forward in the cause of freedom: rebuilding ravaged countries, aiding new nations emerging from the remnants of empire, and transforming the American economy to a postwar prosperity dedicated to eradicating poverty. The United States entered the era of manned space flight in 1961 with the suborbital ride of Astronaut Alan B. Shepard, Jr. In 1969, Neil A. Armstrong and Edwin E. Aldrin, Jr., became the first men to walk on the moon, and in 1981 the U. S. launched the space shuttle *Columbia* (right), the world's first reusable space vehicle.

193

Franklin D. Roosevelt (signature)

THIRTY-SECOND PRESIDENT 1933-1945

FRANKLIN D. ROOSEVELT sought a more abundant way of life for the American people, and for all humanity. He demonstrated his warm concern for mankind with a flair for brilliant improvisations; like a 19th-century Yankee inventor, he sought his great ends through trial-and-error experimentation. His love of innovation, his wit and jaunty optimism made him an exciting leader.

He became President at a time of national despair, at the depth of the Great Depression. First he helped the American people regain faith in themselves; then he led in the enactment of the most sweeping program of social legislation in the Nation's history.

In World War II, he assumed leadership for the United States in the struggle against totalitarianism and helped plan the United Nations to maintain the peace. He died in office shortly before final victory in 1945, having served longer than any other President.

Roosevelt, like his fifth cousin Theodore Roosevelt, came from a patrician New York family. He was born in 1882 on a pleasant estate overlooking the Hudson River at Hyde Park, New York. Both his parents and his headmaster, Endicott Peabody of Groton School, impressed on the young Roosevelt his responsibilities toward those less fortunate. Throughout his career this attitude shaped his thought and action.

At Harvard he became editor-in-chief of the *Crimson,* the student newspaper, then attended Columbia University Law School. On St. Patrick's Day, 1905, he wed his distant cousin, Anna Eleanor Roosevelt, a willowy, shy young woman, who was given in marriage by her uncle, the President.

Following the example of the first President Roosevelt, whom he enormously admired, Franklin D. Roosevelt decided to enter public service through politics. He had joined the Harvard Republican Club and in 1900 marched in a torchlight procession hailing the ticket of William McKinley and Theodore Roosevelt. But in 1910, in line with the tradition of his own branch of the Roosevelt family, he chose the Democratic Party. Campaigning flamboyantly in a red Maxwell automobile, he won election to the New York Senate. There he immediately began to capture headlines as a progressive reformer.

Crisis President: The Nation's gravest depression and greatest war burdened Franklin Delano Roosevelt during his 12 years and 40 days in office—the longest span served by any American Chief Executive. Roosevelt fought for social justice —a "new deal for the American people"—and for a lasting peace based on international cooperation.

"I have seen war. . . . I hate war." Roosevelt performed brilliantly as Assistant Secretary of the Navy during World War I, but he itched to get close to the fighting. Several times his inspections of U. S. bases took him within range of German artillery. Here he disembarks from a Navy seaplane at Pauillac, France, on August 14, 1918.

Painting by Frank O. Salisbury, White House Collection

Jaunty of manner, cigarette holder cocked upward, the smiling F.D.R. won the confidence of millions of Americans who elected him an unprecedented four times. Here, at Warm Springs, Georgia, Roosevelt drives a Ford for which he himself designed hand controls for clutch, brake, and throttle.

Undaunted by his handicap, Roosevelt refused to become an invalid. He sailed and swam, developing the powerful torso of an athlete. Here, in 1933, he steers *Amberjack II* on a cruise from Marion, Massachusetts, to Campobello Island, New Brunswick, his beloved Canadian summer home.

President Wilson appointed him Assistant Secretary of the Navy, a post once held by Theodore Roosevelt, and during World War I Franklin D. Roosevelt became known in Washington as a man who got things done. He was Democratic nominee for Vice President in 1920 and campaigned vigorously for the League of Nations. This won him a national reputation, and the Harding landslide did him no harm.

But in the summer of 1921, when he was 39, disaster struck. While vacationing at Campobello, after swimming in the icy Bay of Fundy, he was stricken with poliomyelitis. With indomitable courage, he fought to regain use of his legs, particularly through swimming.

"The water put me where I am," he remarked, "and the water has to bring me back." He found the water so beneficial at a resort in Georgia that he risked his none-too-ample inheritance to buy the property and set up the Georgia Warm Springs Foundation to treat polio sufferers. His Little White House there is a state memorial.

Despite the wishes of his mother, Sara Delano Roosevelt, that he give up politics, he continued to be active behind the scenes, and dramatically appeared on crutches before the 1924 Democratic Convention to nominate Al Smith as "the Happy Warrior." In 1928, when Smith received the Democratic nomination, he persuaded Roosevelt to strengthen the ticket in New York by running for governor. Asked whether Roosevelt was physically qualified to serve, Smith retorted, "A Governor does not have to be an acrobat."

During that campaign and after, Roosevelt made his way carefully with the aid of braces, a cane, and a strong arm to grasp, always with a broad smile on his face. While Smith lost the Presidency, Roosevelt won in New York by 25,000 votes. In Albany he proved a strong governor, remarkably the master of a Republican legislature.

He was elected President in November, 1932, defeating President Hoover. The depression grew steadily worse, and by the time he was inaugurated, on March 4, 1933, industrial production had sunk to almost half that of 1929; one worker in four was jobless.

To the disheartened Nation Roosevelt brought hope. He promised prompt, vigorous action and asserted in his Inaugural Address, "The only thing we have to fear is fear itself." His first moves were reassuring to businessmen—the proclamation of a national bank holiday; then a cautious reopening of banks that could prove their solvency, along

Replanting a charred hillside, Civilian Conservation Corps men help change the face of America. Three million jobless, including thousands of Indians and veterans, served in Roosevelt's peaceful army. They put out fires, protected wildlife, fought insect pests, and restored historic landmarks. Many former CCC youths served the Nation gallantly in World War II.

Social Security pioneer Miss Ida Fuller of Ludlow, Vermont, a retired legal secretary, received the first monthly benefit check under the New Deal law of August, 1935. That check, dated January 31, 1940, was for $22.54. Under the Medicare-Social Security law of 1965, she again got the first check. For her investment of about $22 in the original program, she received more than $20,000 before her death on January 27, 1975, at the age of 100.

197

with deep cuts in Government expenditures.

Next came the remarkable legislation of his first hundred days. He proposed, and Congress enacted, a sweeping program to bring recovery to business and agriculture and immediate relief to the unemployed and those in danger of losing farms and homes. Further, with the establishment of the Tennessee Valley Authority, he led the Federal Government into a precedent-setting venture in regional planning and development.

Like Theodore Roosevelt and Wilson, Franklin D. Roosevelt vigorously used all the powers of the Presidency. Like them, he wished the Government to function as an impartial arbiter among businessmen, farmers, workers, and consumers. But he went beyond them because of the drastic needs of the de-

pression years, and used the Government to provide strong aid to each group.

By 1935 the Nation was achieving some measure of recovery, but businessmen and bankers were turning against the "New Deal." They feared Roosevelt's experiments and concessions to labor, and were appalled that he had taken the Nation off the gold standard and allowed budget deficits.

Roosevelt's response to the attacks from the right was to push through Congress a new legislative program: Social Security, heavier income taxes, new controls over banks and public utilities, and an enormous work-relief program for the unemployed.

In 1936 he defeated Governor Alf Landon of Kansas, a Republican liberal, by a top-heavy margin, winning in every state but two.

Rebirth of a region: Tennessee Valley Authority, with its vast system of public and private dams, brought new life to a river basin involving seven states. Here Fontana Dam regulates the Little Tennessee River. A Government-owned corporation, TVA generates power and provides flood control, produces fertilizer, facilitates navigation, and conserves natural resources. During World War II, TVA power supplied the top-secret installations at Oak Ridge, Tennessee, that produced enriched uranium for the atomic bomb. Long considered one of the most successful of Roosevelt's New Deal agencies, TVA has inspired similar regional projects throughout the world.

Fireside chats brought Roosevelt's warm and vibrant voice into living rooms across the land. In calm, reassuring tones, F.D.R. explained his policies to the people. "His face would smile and light up as though he were actually sitting on the front porch or in the parlor with them," recalled his Secretary of Labor, Frances Perkins, first woman to serve in a Cabinet post.

Latter-day St. George: Cartoonist Jerry Doyle of the Philadelphia *Record* pictured Roosevelt fighting the dragons of fear and deflation during early New Deal days. F.D.R. wields the sword of confidence and the shield of the National Recovery Administration, an agency that managed Roosevelt's emergency program for revitalizing industry. But a Supreme Court decision in 1935 brought NRA to an end.

199

He was inaugurated on January 20, 1937—the first President sworn in on the new date provided by the Twentieth Amendment. In his Inaugural, he declared:

"I see a United States which can demonstrate that, under democratic methods of government, national wealth can be translated into a spreading volume of human comforts hitherto unknown, and the lowest standard of living can be raised far above the level of mere subsistence. But here is the challenge to our democracy.... I see one-third of a nation ill-housed, ill-clad, ill-nourished."

The Supreme Court had been invalidating key New Deal measures as unconstitutional, sometimes by a narrow 5-to-4 decision. Early in his second term, Roosevelt sought legislation to increase the size of the Court. Vehement protests were raised against "packing the Court," and in their midst the Court began to hand down decisions favorable to the New Deal, often by a one-vote margin. Roosevelt lost his Supreme Court battle, but a revolution in constitutional law took place. Thereafter the Government could legally engage in extensive regulation of the economy.

In his first Inaugural, Roosevelt had pledged the United States to the policy of the "good neighbor," and in relations with American republics to the South he transformed the Monroe Doctrine. From a unilateral American manifesto it became a mutual arrangement for concerted action against aggressors.

In Asia and Europe aggressor nations threatened a second world war, which was precipitated in 1939 by Hitler's invasion of Poland. Roosevelt tried through neutrality legislation to keep the United States out of war, yet strengthen nations under attack.

After France fell and Britain came under siege in the summer of 1940, Roosevelt began to send Great Britain all possible aid short of war. In September the United States gave the British 50 over-age destroyers, freshly

FRANKLIN D. ROOSEVELT LIBRARY

"He who plants must cultivate," the Roosevelts read the motto on their coat of arms. Roses in a field represent the family name. F.D.R. could claim relationship by blood or marriage to 11 former Presidents—Washington, both Adamses, Madison, Van Buren, both Harrisons, Taylor, Grant, Theodore Roosevelt, and Taft.

Portrait of a zestful lady: Wife, mother, writer, humanitarian, Anna Eleanor Roosevelt filled a multitude of roles. "She would rather light a candle than curse the darkness, and her glow has warmed the world," her friend Adlai E. Stevenson said upon her death in 1962. This magnificent and unusual portrait by Douglas Chandor—the only one for which she formally posed—hangs in the White House.

Stately Roosevelt home, a national historic site since 1946, overlooks the Hudson River at Hyde Park, New York. The original Victorian frame house in which the President was born evolved into this stucco and field-stone mansion through additions, many by F.D.R. himself. He and Mrs. Roosevelt lie buried in the rose garden. Presidential papers and mementos crowd the nearby Franklin D. Roosevelt Library. More than 300,000 people a year visit Hyde Park.

Soothing waters of Warm Springs buoyed Roosevelt's spirits. The President inspired and led the March of Dimes that financed polio's eventual defeat through the Salk and Sabin vaccines.

CULVER PICTURES

Christening a gallant ship: Mrs. Roosevelt helps launch the carrier *Yorktown* in 1943. With her stands Rear Adm. Elliott Buckmaster, captain of the vessel's namesake and predecessor when the Japanese sank her in the Battle of Midway the previous year.

The storied "Big E," the carrier *Enterprise* (below), goes down the ways at Newport News, Virginia, in 1936. A Navy booster since his days as Assistant Secretary of the Department, Roosevelt pushed a naval expansion program that built up America's defenses and provided work for thousands of unemployed.

WIDE WORLD

repaired and equipped, and received 99-year leases on eight bases in the Western Hemisphere. It was, Winston Churchill later wrote, "a decidedly unneutral act."

In the winter of 1940-41, when British ability to buy arms was nearly exhausted, Roosevelt devised "lend-lease." If a neighbor's house were afire, he explained, certainly one would lend him a fire hose to extinguish the blaze. Roosevelt also brought economic pressure on the Japanese to try to prevent their taking over Southeast Asia.

Aid to Allies precipitated a bitter debate between U. S. isolationists and interventionists. In the campaign of 1940, however, Roosevelt's opponent, Wendell Willkie, also favored aiding the Allies. F. D. R. won, with 449 electoral votes to Willkie's 82, and became the first President to serve a third term.

In January, 1941, though the United States was not yet directly involved in the conflict, Roosevelt proclaimed as war aims the Four Freedoms: freedom of speech and worship, and from want and fear. He met Churchill off Argentia, Newfoundland, in August, 1941, and they drew up the Atlantic Charter, which incorporated these aims.

Before the year was out, the Nation was precipitated into the war. Japanese airplanes broke the Sunday calm of December 7, 1941, striking Pearl Harbor with devastating effect. Congress declared war the next day. Three days later, Germany and Italy declared war on the United States.

As wartime Commander in Chief, Roosevelt delegated much of his responsibility for home-front war production and concentrated on worldwide strategy and diplomacy. The ultimate decisions were his: the invasion of North Africa in 1942, the appointment of Dwight D. Eisenhower rather than George C. Marshall to lead the Normandy D-Day assault. He told Marshall, "I could not sleep at night with you out of the country." But even as he fought the war, he planned for peace, giving much thought to a United Nations.

In 1944, defeating New York's Governor Thomas E. Dewey, Roosevelt won a fourth term. But, as the Allies poised on the brink of victory over the Nazis, his health deteriorated. On April 12, 1945, while posing for a portrait in the Little White House at Warm Springs, Georgia, he collapsed and died of a cerebral hemorrhage. The Nation was plunged into mourning. As a sailor in Times Square lamented, "You know it's tough when one of your buddies has to go, and President Roosevelt was our buddy."

President and future President share a jeep in Sicily in December, 1943. F. D. R. had just named Eisenhower to command the Allied invasion of France. Roosevelt was the first President to travel outside the U. S. in wartime.

"Unprovoked and dastardly," Roosevelt termed Japan's attack on Pearl Harbor, December 7, 1941—"a date which will live in infamy." Here *West Virginia* (foreground) and *Tennessee* blaze in the chaos of "Battleship Row."

THIRTY-THIRD PRESIDENT 1945-1953

HARRY S. TRUMAN, becoming President as World War II drew to a close, made some of the most crucial decisions in the Nation's history. He ordered the dropping of atomic bombs to hasten Japan's surrender. He broke the Soviet Union's postwar blockade of West Berlin with a titanic airlift. And he stemmed the Communist invasion of South Korea.

During his administration, the Nation grappled with problems of inflation and civil rights at home. Abroad, it initiated rehabilitation of war-torn areas, aid to underdeveloped countries, and new systems of collective security.

Truman was born in Lamar, Missouri, in 1884, and his birthplace there, at Truman Avenue and 11th Street, is now a state historic site. The son of a livestock dealer, he grew up in Independence, Missouri, and became a bank clerk. Then, needed on the family farm at Grandview, he spent 12 years, until he was 33, as a prosperous Missouri farmer, proud of his skill in planting a straight row of corn. He was the first President since Grant to have engaged in farming as an adult.

A member of the National Guard, he went to France during World War I, and fought on the western front in the field artillery. Returning home as a captain, he married his childhood sweetheart Elizabeth Virginia ("Bess") Wallace, and with an Army friend opened a haberdashery shop in Kansas City, Missouri. The shop failed in 1922, but Truman refused to go into bankruptcy and paid off the debts.

With the support of fellow veterans and the political machine of Tom Pendergast, boss of Kansas City, Truman was elected a "judge" (actually, an administrator) of Jackson County in 1922. Except for one defeat at the polls, when the Ku Klux Klan opposed him, he remained in office until 1934, building a notable reputation for honesty and efficiency.

He was elected Senator from Missouri in 1934, as a Democrat pledged to support Roosevelt, and was re-elected in 1940. During World War II he became famous as chairman of the Senate's Special Committee to

"He met the war, the peace and old insistent friends with the same magnified modesty but also with clear self-possession," biographer Jonathan Daniels wrote of Harry Truman. Suddenly thrust into the Presidency, the man from Missouri held unshakable faith in his country and his countrymen.

Rocky road traveled in his first year might have destroyed a less valiant and resolute Chief Executive than Truman. In a volume of his memoirs, aptly entitled *Year of Decisions,* he recounts his meeting with Eleanor Roosevelt after her husband's death. "Is there anything I can do for you?" Truman asked. "Is there anything *we* can do for *you?*" she responded. "For you are the one in trouble now."

Painting by Greta Kempton, White House Collection

1946 HERBLOCK © CARTOON, THE WASHINGTON POST

"SURE YOU HAVEN'T MISSED ANYTHING?"

"We fired our first barrage on the night of September 6 [1918]," Capt. Harry Truman remembered. He led Battery D of the 129th Field Artillery during the Meuse-Argonne offensive of World War I. "We were occupying an old French position which probably was fairly well known to the Germans, and as soon as we had finished the barrage they returned the compliment. My battery became panic-stricken, and all except five or six scattered like partridges. Finally I got them back together without losing any men, although we had six horses killed."

Twenty-seven years later the veteran "redleg," as an artilleryman is called, became Commander in Chief of a Nation at war, and his firsthand knowledge of warfare proved valuable. His Chief of Staff, Adm. William D. Leahy, said: "...he was amazingly well informed on military history from the campaigns of the ancients, such as Hannibal and Caesar, down to the great global conflict...."

Investigate the National Defense Program. Its work, Truman estimated, saved as much as 15 billion dollars.

In 1944, when the backers of Henry A. Wallace, James F. Byrnes, William O. Douglas, and Truman waged a vigorous contest for the Vice Presidential nomination, President Roosevelt settled it by choosing Truman. During his few weeks as Vice President, after Roosevelt's fourth-term victory, Truman scarcely saw the President and received no briefing from him on the development of the atomic bomb or the increasing difficulties with the Soviet Union.

Suddenly these and a host of other wartime problems became Truman's to solve when, on April 12, 1945, Mrs. Roosevelt told him that her husband was dead. Truman was President of the United States. "I felt like the moon, the stars, and all the planets had fallen on me," he told reporters the next day; "I've got the most terribly responsible job a man ever had."

Quickly he was briefed on the acute problems of both war strategy and peacemaking. V-E Day, end of the war in Europe, came less than a month later, but at the Potsdam Conference in the summer of 1945, he discovered firsthand how hard it was to make agreements with Stalin.

At Potsdam the Allies issued an ultimatum to the Japanese to surrender. Urged by his advisers in Washington, Truman decided that if the Japanese did not surrender, the United States would drop the newly developed atomic weapons on Japan. Two bombs were dropped. Japanese surrender quickly followed, and World War II came to an end. The new machinery hopefully fabricated to preserve the peace, the United Nations, already existed. President Truman had witnessed the signing of the charter at San Francisco in June.

Thus far, the new Chief Executive had followed almost directly the lines laid down by his predecessor. But by the fall of 1945 he was developing his own policies, and presented to Congress a 21-point program, later named the Fair Deal. It covered expansion of Social Security, full-employment measures, a permanent Fair Employment Practices Act to protect minority rights, public housing and slum clearance, and Government aid to scientific research. In additional messages he recommended Federal aid to education and health insurance.

The Fair Deal, Truman himself wrote, "symbolizes for me my assumption of the office of President in my own right."

"**It is a mighty leap** from the vice presidency to the presidency when one is forced to make it without warning," Truman declared. In the White House on April 12, 1945, Chief Justice Harlan Fiske Stone swears him in as the 33rd President. Witnesses are (from left): Secretary of Labor Frances Perkins, Secretary of War Henry L. Stimson, Secretary of Commerce Henry A. Wallace, War Production Board Chairman J. A. Krug, Secretary of the Navy James Forrestal, Secretary of Agriculture Claude R. Wickard, Deputy Chairman of War Manpower Commission Frank McNamee (behind Wickard), Attorney General Francis Biddle, Secretary of the Treasury Henry Morgenthau, Jr., Secretary of State Edward R. Stettinius (almost hidden by Truman), Mrs. Truman, Secretary of the Interior Harold L. Ickes, Margaret Truman, Speaker of the House Sam Rayburn, War Mobilization Director Frederick M. Vinson, and House Minority Leader Joseph W. Martin.

Congress enacted only a few of the measures the President recommended. A limited full-employment program provided for a Council of Economic Advisers; the Atomic Energy Commission was established; and a considerable reorganization of Government agencies included unification of Army, Navy, and Air Force under a Secretary of Defense.

The Truman Administration's efforts to check inflation had hard sledding, since business opposed price controls and labor chafed under wage ceilings. By the fall of 1946 few controls remained, and Truman removed most of those after Republicans won decisive victories in the Congressional elections.

The new 80th Congress also made its weight felt in labor policy, overriding a Presidential veto of the Taft-Hartley Labor-Management Relations Act, which placed restrictions on union activities. This law prohibited the "closed shop," in which a worker cannot be hired unless he belongs to a union, and allowed states to go still further by enacting "right-to-work" laws.

Truman delighted and sometimes dismayed the public with his peppery forthrightness. It helped him reach his great decisions and was invaluable in interpreting them to the Nation. But he created a national sensation, which he long relished, when he sent a blistering note to a music critic who had written a harsh review in a Washington newspaper of his daughter Margaret's singing.

His simple directness was a vital asset during the 1948 campaign. For 35 days he toured the country by train, traveling 31,700 miles,

and making as many as 16 whistle-stop speeches a day. He had told Senator Alben Barkley, the nominee for Vice President, "I'm going to fight hard, and I'm going to give 'em hell!" In his plain, extemporaneous style, he did. And he won the crowds with his open affection for his wife and daughter. "How would you like to meet my family?" he would ask after his talk. Then he would introduce "the boss"—Mrs. Truman—and "my baby," who was also "the boss's boss," Margaret.

According to the polls, the President seemed to have little chance in the 1948 election. But directing his attack more against the Republican 80th Congress than against his opponent, New York Governor Thomas E. Dewey, Truman emerged the winner. He gathered the votes of many workingmen who resented the Taft-Hartley Act, of farmers disappointed by lawmakers' failure to provide crop storage facilities, and of others who felt they had suffered from Congressional actions. Moreover, the Democrats regained control of both the Senate and the House of Representatives.

In foreign relations, President Truman provided his most effective leadership. When the Soviet Union pressured Turkey and, through guerrillas, threatened to take over Greece, the President, in March, 1947, asked Congress to aid the two countries.

In his message he enunciated the doctrine that took his name: ". . . it must be the policy of the United States to support free peoples who are resisting attempted subjugation by armed minorities or by outside pressures."

Military aid was not enough; economic productivity had to be restored to counter the Communist threat. In June, 1947, Secretary of State George C. Marshall proposed a program of combined aid and self-help that came to be known as the Marshall Plan. Within three years, through the expenditure of 12 billion dollars, the United States helped lift Western Europe's economy above prewar levels and diminish the strength of its Communist parties.

In a historic meeting, Allied leaders at Potsdam, Germany, draft an ultimatum to Japan in July, 1945, and debate postwar problems. President Truman sits at upper right, British Prime Minister Winston Churchill at lower center. Marshal Josef Stalin (leaning back) wanted to "act in concert about the surrender of Japan," although Russia had not yet declared war on the Asian nation.

Act of surrender: Aboard the U.S.S. *Missouri* in Tokyo Bay, Gen. Douglas MacArthur receives the Japanese surrender on September 2, 1945. Maj. Gen. Yohijiro Umezo signs for Japan. In a line beside Fleet Admiral Chester W. Nimitz (left) stand senior military and naval officers of the Allied powers. "My choice of the *Missouri* was an obvious one," Truman recalled. "She was one of the newest and most powerful battleships in our fleet; she had been named after my own state; my daughter Margaret had christened her...."

In his Inaugural Address, on January 20, 1949, President Truman proposed that the United States extend its aid to the "more than half the people of the world . . . living in conditions approaching misery." He listed a number of ways to help them, including the now renowned "Point Four" of his address: to provide them with technical assistance and investment capital so that they could expand their economies.

Out of his proposal came the Point Four program, which grew in time into the Nation's multibillion-dollar outlays for foreign aid. To Truman, elimination of poverty seemed one of the most promising as well as humane ways to check the growth of Communism.

Direct military moves by the Communists also had to be met. As the Western powers laid plans for self-government in West Germany, the Soviet Union imposed a blockade of Berlin in June, 1948. As Truman put it, the "main question was: How could we remain in Berlin without risking all-out war?" He

answered it with his famous airlift and a new military grand alliance for the protection of Western nations, the North Atlantic Treaty Organization, established in 1949.

A new and more dangerous threat from the Soviet Union appeared in the atomic realm. Since 1946 Truman had been recommending to the United Nations the adoption of a thoroughgoing system of international supervision of atomic energy, including on-the-spot inspection. The United States offered to place its stockpile of atomic bombs under international control when the system was put into effect. The Soviet Union steadfastly blocked the American proposals. Then, in the fall of 1949, President Truman announced: "We have evidence that within recent weeks an atomic explosion occurred in the U.S.S.R."

Truman's response to the Soviet test was to order rapid development of "super" atomic weapons, and on November 1, 1952, in Eniwetok Atoll, the first full-scale hydrogen explosion was set off, leaving an underwater crater

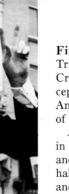

First White House television tour: Truman escorts commentator Walter Cronkite through the Diplomatic Reception Room in 1952. Portrait shows Angelica Van Buren, daughter-in-law of the eighth President.

A committee appointed by Truman in 1948 inspected the White House and found it "standing up purely from habit." Renovation cost $5,800,000 and took three and a half years. Meanwhile the Trumans lived in Blair House, normally used for state guests.

British lion, Winston Churchill, and Truman motor through Jefferson City, Missouri, in March, 1946, en route to Westminster College at Fulton, where Churchill alerted the free world to Communist dangers: "... an iron curtain has descended across the [European] Continent."

"**That's one for the books,**" a joyous Harry Truman said in St. Louis, Missouri, as he held aloft an early and erroneous headline in the Chicago *Tribune* of November 3, 1948. In a stunning upset, Democrat Truman defeated Republican Thomas E. Dewey by two million votes.

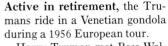

Active in retirement, the Trumans ride in a Venetian gondola during a 1956 European tour.

Harry Truman met Bess Wallace in Sunday school. "She had golden curls and ... the most beautiful blue eyes," he wrote. They attended school together from fifth grade through high school, and married in 1919.

Mrs. Truman enjoyed being a Senator's wife, Truman later wrote, "and had fallen in love with Washington." But as First Lady she was "not especially interested ... in the formalities and pomp" that "surround the family of a President."

She died on October 18, 1982.

a mile in diameter where a coral island had been.

Looking back on this "awesome" new force, Truman wrote: "It will always remain my prayer that . . . there will never again be any need to invoke the terrible destructive powers that lie hidden in the elements."

During these same years Communism was spreading rapidly in Asia, and by the end of 1949 had overrun the Chinese mainland. Suddenly, in June, 1950, the Communist government of North Korea launched a full-scale attack on South Korea. President Truman, conferring promptly with his diplomatic and military advisers, ordered American units into battle as the United Nations Security Council—with Russia boycotting its sessions—called all U.N. members to defend South Korea. The U.N. organized a force of other nations to fight beside the Americans and South Koreans under a unified command.

A long, discouraging struggle followed, as U.N. troops, predominantly American, were at first forced back, then drove almost to the Chinese border, only to be pushed back again, this time by hordes of Chinese. After counterattacks, the U.N. held a line above the old boundary of South Korea.

Truman insisted on a war of containment; he would not risk its enlargement into a major conflict with China, and perhaps Russia. When Gen. Douglas MacArthur, commander of U.N. forces in Korea, issued statements contrary to this policy, the President dismissed the "old soldier."

In 1953 Truman retired to Independence, Missouri, and continued to make lively comments on national and world affairs. He published three volumes of memoirs and took keen interest in the Harry S. Truman Library and Museum. But his real monuments are the Fair Deal and the collective security systems against Communism. He died December 26, 1972, after a stubborn fight for life.

Birth of the United Nations: Secretary of State Stettinius signs the charter in San Francisco on June 26, 1945. Truman, witnessing the event, said of the U.N., "If we fail to use it, we shall betray all those who have died in order that we might meet here in freedom and safety to create it." Five years later, Communist North Korea invaded South Korea. Truman announced U. S. intervention; the U.N. called for a defense force. And guns boomed in Korea for three long years (below).

ROBERT MOSIER

213

DWIGHT D. EISENHOWER brought to the Presidency not only his prestige as the victorious commanding general in Europe in World War II, but also a warmth of popular affection and respect.

He sought during his two terms to maintain peace and prosperity for the American people. He obtained an armistice in Korea and worked incessantly to ease the cold war between Communist countries and the United States and its allies. At home he pursued the moderate policies of "modern Republicanism," and as he left office he could say, "America is today the strongest, the most influential, and most productive nation in the world."

Born in Denison, Texas, in 1890, Eisenhower grew up in Abilene, Kansas, the third of seven sons of a creamery mechanic. Today the Eisenhower Presidential Library and Eisenhower Museum stand near his boyhood Abilene home.

In high school young "Ike" (a nickname he acquired as a child) excelled in football and baseball. At West Point he was a lithe, dynamic halfback until a knee injury ended his playing days. Stationed in Texas as a second lieutenant, he met Mamie Geneva Doud, whom he married in 1916.

During World War I he failed to obtain assignment in France but rose to the temporary rank of lieutenant colonel. Through long years in the peacetime army he especially excelled in staff assignments, serving under Generals John J. Pershing, Douglas MacArthur, and Walter Krueger.

Soon after Pearl Harbor, Gen. George C. Marshall, in the light of Eisenhower's knowledge of the Philippines, brought him to Washington to plan moves in the Pacific. Eisenhower showed such great organizational ability and dealt so tactfully with other branches of the armed services that Marshall assigned him to command American forces in the European Theater of Operations.

Arriving in England in June, 1942, he was shortly named commander of the Allied forces for the November invasion of North Africa. On D-Day, June 6, 1944, he was Supreme Commander of the troops invading France. He directed the operations of millions of Allied

UNITED STATES ARMY

After leading Allied armies to victory in World War II, national hero Dwight David Eisenhower was sought as Presidential standard-bearer by both Republicans and Democrats. But it was the Republicans who convinced him that he should seek public office in 1952. With shouts of "We like Ike" echoing across the land, Eisenhower swept his party to its first national victory in 24 years. Peace, progress, and prosperity were his keynote for eight years.

"Full victory—nothing else." The Supreme Commander of the Allied Expeditionary Force exhorts men of the 101st Airborne Division near Newbury, England, on the eve of the Normandy invasion.

Painting by J. Anthony Wills, White House Collection

215

WIDE WORLD (ABOVE) AND CARL MYDANS, LIFE

Ike pledged to go to Korea if elected in 1952. Here the President-elect visits the front in December of that year; six months later an armistice was signed.

At the summit: The Big Four meet in Geneva in July of 1955. Eisenhower (upper center), with John Foster Dulles on his right, faces Britain's Prime Minister Sir Anthony Eden and Foreign Secretary Harold Macmillan. Nikita Khrushchev (far left) and Nikolai Bulganin of the Soviet Union sit opposite Premier Edgar Faure of France. The Russians rejected Ike's "Open Skies" proposal—aerial inspection and exchange of blueprints of military installations—but this first postwar summit raised hopes for relaxation of tensions.

Tireless diplomat John Foster Dulles, Eisenhower's first Secretary of State, traveled the world in a quest for peace. Here he consults his President at a villa near Geneva.

troops with a skillful mixture of firmness and diplomacy that won him loyalty and acclaim. He often left headquarters, Gen. Omar Bradley noted, to "talk with his men" in the field. His rapid promotion reached a climax in late 1944 with the fifth star of a General of the Army, a rank Congress made permanent in 1946.

At war's end, Eisenhower confided to friends that he had tasted enough of glory and would like to retire and become president of a small college, perhaps doing some farming on the side. Instead he became president of Columbia University in New York City. Then he took leave from that post to assume supreme command over the new NATO forces being assembled in 1951 for the common defense of the United States and its European allies.

To his headquarters near Paris came emissaries from the Republican Party to urge him to run for President. In 1948 he had refused similar overtures from public figures of both parties, but in 1952 he consented to run to ensure continued American leadership in international affairs.

The electorate that year was troubled by rising taxes and prices, by charges of a "mess in Washington," and especially by the drawn-out Korean war. The voters turned to General Eisenhower as a leader they thought could bring them security. "I like Ike" was an irresistible slogan; he won a sweeping victory over Governor Adlai E. Stevenson of Illinois.

In his first Inaugural Address, President Eisenhower declared: "Americans, indeed, all free men, remember that in the final choice a soldier's pack is not so heavy a burden as a prisoner's chains." Negotiating from military strength, he tried to reduce the tensions of the cold war.

In the summer of 1953, the signing of a final armistice brought an armed peace along the border of South Korea. Announcing the end of the fighting, Eisenhower warned, "We may not now relax our guard...."

The death of Stalin in the spring of 1953 also brought some shifts in relations with the Soviet Union. The new Russian leaders consented to a peace treaty neutralizing Austria. Meanwhile both the Soviet Union and the United States were developing hydrogen bombs—the Americans testing a device so powerful that it could have destroyed all New York City.

With the threat of such destructive force hanging over the world, President Eisenhower met the leaders of the British, French, and Soviet Governments at Geneva in July, 1955. At one of the sessions the President, putting down his glasses, unexpectedly proposed to the Soviets that they and the United States immediately exchange complete blueprints of their military establishments. He further suggested that each "provide within our countries facilities for aerial photography to the other country."

He explained, "I have been searching my heart and mind for something that I could say here that could convince everyone of the great sincerity of the United States in approaching this problem of disarmament." At first the Soviet conferees greeted the proposal with silence, but they were so cordial throughout the meetings that a relaxation of tensions took place.

Suddenly, in September, 1955, President Eisenhower suffered a moderately severe heart attack while vacationing in Denver. As he lay in the hospital slowly recovering, tens of thousands of sympathetic letters and telegrams came in. "It really does something for you," the President told Mrs. Eisenhower, "to know that people all over the world are praying for you."

As a birthday joke, White House correspondents gave him gaudy red pajamas with five gold stars embroidered on each collar tab;

when he began to improve, he good-humoredly wore them. He received Cabinet officers and more and more resumed his duties as President. After nearly seven weeks he left the hospital and flew back to Washington.

"Misfortune, and particularly the misfortune of illness," he said in a brief speech, "brings to all of us an understanding of how good people are." A panel of doctors in February, 1956, reported that the President's injured heart muscle had healed. The way was clear for him to run for a second term,

WAYNE MILLER, MAGNUM (BELOW); GILBERT M. GROSVENOR

Eisenhower's distinctive wave greets citizens of Anchorage, Alaska. "Ike is nifty, started out with 48; ended up with 50," rhymed a slogan in recognition of Alaska's becoming a state on January 3, 1959, followed by Hawaii eight months later.

Record Presidential traveler Eisenhower, his daughter-in-law Mrs. John Eisenhower, and the Prime Minister of India, the late Jawaharlal Nehru, pause beside the reflecting pool of the Taj Mahal. In the cause of world peace, Eisenhower visited 27 lands. His longest tour was reported in "When the President Goes Abroad," by Gilbert M. Grosvenor, GEOGRAPHIC, May, 1960.

and in November, 1956, he again defeated Adlai Stevenson by a wide margin.

In domestic policy, modern Republicanism, as the President interpreted it, came to mean a middle-of-the-road course. He continued most New Deal and Fair Deal programs, but in a conservative way, with emphasis on balancing the budget.

In 1954 Eisenhower obtained from Congress a tax-reform bill, almost a thousand pages long, aimed at stimulating business growth. In public-power development the President emphasized decentralization; he favored cooperation between the Federal Government and local government or private enterprise over wholly Federal projects. For the Hell's Canyon project on the Snake River, he therefore preferred the construction of three power dams by a private utility rather than one large multipurpose dam by the Federal Government.

Similarly, he proposed limited programs of school construction and public health insurance, with the Federal Government helping underwrite local enterprise. He asked Congress to increase Federal research on air pollution, and to give the states greater assistance in their programs to control pollution of lakes and rivers. He sometimes called this approach "dynamic conservatism."

Among Eisenhower's major achievements as President was his speeding of a large-scale highway program to build 41,000 miles of new interstate roads. Virtually the entire system—with the Federal Government paying 90 percent of the cost out of gasoline and other highway-user taxes—was in operation before 1980, offering motorists multilane, limited-access roads with never a stop light.

As Eisenhower himself proudly described it, this was "not only the most gigantic federal undertaking in road-building" in American history but also "the biggest peacetime construction project of any description ever undertaken by the United States or any other country."

During the Eisenhower Administration, Social Security and unemployment insurance were extended to millions more people. The 1959 labor-management act required union and business officials to file reports of transactions that affected the welfare of union members and the general public. The St. Lawrence Seaway was dedicated. And Alaska and Hawaii attained statehood.

As desegregation of schools began, in keeping with the 1954 Supreme Court decision, President Eisenhower sent troops into Little Rock, Arkansas, to assure compliance with the orders of a Federal court.

Eisenhower also ordered the complete desegregation of the Armed Forces. In 1957 he signed the first civil rights legislation to pass Congress in 82 years, a bill that gave the Federal Government new powers to protect the right to vote. Another civil rights act became law in May, 1960.

"There must be no second class citizens in this country," the President wrote.

In his last State of the Union Message, while granting that problems of unemployment and recessions remained unsolved, Eisenhower noted the unprecedented economic progress during his two terms. With almost no new inflation, the productivity of the Nation had risen nearly 25 percent, the

"Magnificent symbol" of Canadian-United States ties—thus Ike hailed the St. Lawrence Seaway as he and Queen Elizabeth II dedicated the joint project at Montreal in 1959. Biggest ditchdigging job since the Panama Canal, the system of locks, channels, and dams opened the Great Lakes to ocean shipping. Starting with Woodrow Wilson, every President had favored such a project.

Stairsteps to North America's middle, Snell Lock and six others lift vessels 224 feet in the 189 miles of seaway. Snell helps ships pass Moses-Saunders Powerdam, which harnesses Great Lakes drainage and generates electricity for the neighboring nations.

Concrete ribbons lace the states with expressways and fulfill a cherished dream. The Interstate Highway System, a state-Federal venture enacted in 1944, grew slowly at first. Eisenhower urged Congress to increase Federal participation to 90 percent; it did so in 1956. By 1980, millions of drivers traveled daily over a network extended by law in 1968 to a maximum of 42,500 miles.

real wages of factory workers 20 percent, and average family income 15 percent.

Above all, President Eisenhower concentrated on keeping the peace in a world threatened with thermonuclear destruction. His Atoms for Peace program, announced in 1953, offered the United Nations loans of American uranium for peaceful use by "have-not" countries. The United States, he promised, would "devote its entire heart and mind to find the way by which the miraculous inventiveness of man shall not be dedicated to his death, but consecrated to his life."

Throughout his eight years in office, he tried to reach an accord with the Soviet Union to end atomic tests and limit nuclear armaments.

In the fall of 1957 the hopes raised at the Geneva summit conference vanished. The Soviet Union, on October 4, launched the first earth satellite, giving rise to fears that it might now deliver thermonuclear warheads anywhere in the world.

The President responded to "sputnik diplomacy" by increasing American armaments and foreign aid, speeding an American satellite program, and then renewing his efforts to negotiate with the Soviet Union.

He even invited Premier Khrushchev to visit the United States, but, though the Premier came, new crises drove the two nations further apart: the shooting down of an American U-2 reconnaissance plane over the Soviet Union, and the breaking of diplomatic relations with Communist Cuba. The Soviets still refused to agree to a secure atomic test-ban treaty, and the best that could be achieved was a temporary abstinence from testing.

To maintain security as well as to assist suffering peoples, Eisenhower year after year requested large appropriations for the foreign-aid program. He himself in his final months of office visited many nations around the globe. To cheering multitudes wherever he went, he repeatedly proclaimed the American desire for peace.

Before he left office in January, 1961, for his Gettysburg farm, he urged the necessity of maintaining military strength, but cautioned that vast, long-continued military expenditures could breed potential dangers to our way of life.

The retiring President pointed out that the "conjunction of an immense military establishment and a large arms industry is new in the American experience.... We must never let the weight of this combination endanger our liberties or democratic processes. We should take nothing for granted."

Speaking as "one who has witnessed the horror and the lingering sadness of war," he concluded with a prayer for peace "in the goodness of time." Both themes remained timely and urgent when he died, after long illness, on March 28, 1969.

Distinguished world traveler, Britain's Prince Philip receives the National Geographic Society's Special Gold Medal from President Eisenhower in 1958. Earlier, Society President Melville Bell Grosvenor, standing behind the Chief Executive, read the inscription: "To His Royal Highness, the Prince Philip, Duke of Edinburgh, whose questing spirit has taken him to the far corners of the globe and brought to millions a better understanding of our planet and its peoples." Dr. Gilbert H. Grosvenor, Dr. Hugh L. Dryden, and Dr. John Oliver La Gorce of the Society's Board of Trustees watch the presentation at the White House.

Four years before, Eisenhower had become the eighth President to present medals on behalf of the Society when he awarded the Hubbard Medal to Sir Edmund Hillary, Sir John Hunt, and Tenzing Norkey of the British Mount Everest Expedition for the first conquest of earth's highest mountain.

NATIONAL GEOGRAPHIC PHOTOGRAPHER BATES LITTLEHALES

"**I've found my career** — and its name is Ike," said Mamie Doud Eisenhower early in her married life. Her experience as the wife of an Army officer and university president made easy the transition to First Lady. Mrs. Eisenhower's great interest in the historical traditions of the White House inspired donors to complete the Presidential china collection. Other contributions include a settee and chairs for the Lincoln Room, and Federal-style furnishings for the Diplomatic Reception Room.

Her love for children prompted the First Lady to reinstate the custom of Easter-egg rolling on the White House lawn, a ceremony discontinued for 12 years during and after World War II.

Mrs. Eisenhower died on November 1, 1979.

Proud grandfather and his son Maj. John Eisenhower watch young David take two of his sisters on a pony ride at the President's Gettysburg farm. The elder Eisenhowers purchased the rolling Pennsylvania acreage in 1950, and the remodeled farmhouse became the first home of their own since their marriage in 1916.

PAINTING BY THOMAS E. STEPHENS, WHITE HOUSE COLLECTION

Fast friends, the President and Winston Churchill tour Ike's farm in a golf cart. Sir Winston visited the Eisenhowers in both Washington and Gettysburg during his trip to the United States in 1959. The two leaders first met in wartime Washington in 1942. Mutual trials and responsibilities strengthened their ties.

UNITED PRESS INTERNATIONAL (LEFT) AND WIDE WORLD

223

THIRTY-FIFTH PRESIDENT 1961-1963

JOHN F. KENNEDY, the first President born in the 20th century, called on the American people in his Inaugural Address to enlist in "a struggle against the common enemies of man: tyranny, poverty, disease and war itself." The struggle would not be finished in a hundred days or a thousand, he predicted: "But let us begin."

Kennedy did begin, urging the "New Frontier" program upon Congress and resisting the Communist threats even into the shadow of nuclear war. To the leadership of the Nation he brought realism, efficiency, verve—and the promise of increasing greatness.

Abruptly, in November, 1963, when he was scarcely past his first thousand days in office, he died by an assassin's bullet. Kennedy was the youngest man elected President; he was the youngest to die. Yet in his brief tenure he had firmly embarked the Nation on a forward course; his successor could pay no higher tribute than to proclaim, "Let us continue."

The second of nine children, Kennedy was born in Brookline, Massachusetts, a suburb of Boston, on May 29, 1917. He was proud that his forebears came from Ireland, rising swiftly in America to wealth and political prominence. His maternal grandfather was Mayor of Boston; his father, Ambassador to Great Britain.

After graduation *cum laude* from Harvard, Kennedy entered the Navy in World War II. As a lieutenant (j.g.), he commanded a PT boat in the Solomon Islands. Shortly after midnight on August 2, 1943, a Japanese destroyer sliced through it. Kennedy's back, already weak from a football injury, was badly hurt, but after 15 hours in the water he led the survivors to a small island. He spent the rest of his naval service in hospitals and as an instructor.

Early in 1946 Kennedy fought his first political campaign, in a Democratic primary for a Congressional district in the Boston area. The 28-year-old candidate stumped energetically among the working people and received

225

Weight of office bows John F. Kennedy during a moment of decision. Youngest elected President, he stirred the Nation and the world. With his strong sense of purpose, his tough yet supple mind, he projected an image of confidence that promised progress. But an assassin's bullet ended his life on November 22, 1963. Of this thoughtful pose, the artist said: "I wanted to recall his anguish, his humanity, his intelligence, his courage."

Elegant and eloquent, Jacqueline Kennedy enriched the White House with art treasures and conducted a tour of the Executive Mansion on nationwide television. Traveling abroad with her husband, whom she called an "idealist without illusions," she charmed dignitaries with her command of languages. Here, in 1961, she holds Caroline, age 4, and John, Jr., 1.

Painting by Aaron Shikler, White House Collection

MARK SHAW

Awaiting action in the Pacific during World War II, Lieutenant Kennedy relaxes in his torpedo boat, PT 109. When a Japanese destroyer cut the craft in half, Kennedy saved his crew and won the Navy and Marine Corps Medal. Asked how he became a hero, he replied: "It was easy—they sank my boat."

nearly twice as many votes as his nearest opponent. He won easily in November.

During his six years in the House, Congressman Kennedy labored for the betterment of his constituents, voting for slum clearance and low-cost housing bills, and opposing the Taft-Hartley bill to restrict labor unions. At a Washington dinner party, he met beautiful Jacqueline Lee Bouvier, whom he married on September 12, 1953.

By this time, Kennedy had advanced from House to Senate, defeating Republican Senator Henry Cabot Lodge in the 1952 elections. As Senator, Kennedy made good his campaign slogan to "do *more* for Massachusetts." But increasingly he took a national view; he voted for reciprocal trade legislation and the St. Lawrence Seaway, even though they were not popular in Massachusetts.

Kennedy's old back injuries had become increasingly painful, and in October, 1954, he underwent a critical operation. While convalescing, he wrote *Profiles in Courage,* sketches of eight Senators who had risked their careers for their convictions. The book won a Pulitzer Prize for biography.

In 1956 Senator Kennedy came close to receiving the Democratic nomination for Vice President; in 1960 he went forthrightly in quest of the Presidential nomination. He fought intensely in several primaries and won, and at the Democratic Convention was nominated on the first ballot. He offered to share the ticket with his most powerful rival, Senate Majority Leader Lyndon B. Johnson.

"We stand today on the edge of a New Frontier," Kennedy proclaimed in his acceptance speech. "Beyond that frontier are uncharted areas of science and space, unsolved problems of peace and war, unconquered pockets of ignorance and prejudice, unanswered questions of poverty and surplus."

Millions watched his vigorous television debates with the Republican nominee, Vice President Richard M. Nixon. Kennedy won the election by 303 to 219 electoral votes, but his margin in the almost 69,000,000 popular votes was a hairline 118,574. He was the first Roman Catholic to be elected President. The only other Catholic nominated by a major party had been Democrat Alfred E. Smith, badly defeated in 1928.

On a tide of youth, Kennedy sweeps the nomination for President at the 1960 Democratic Convention in Los Angeles. "The torch has been passed to a new generation of Americans," he said at his Inaugural.

226

In his Inaugural Address, Kennedy, aged 43, said "a new generation of Americans" had taken leadership. To all Americans he said: "Ask not what your country can do for you—ask what you can do for your country."

His vision of America extended beyond the Nation's material needs to the quality of American life and culture. Perhaps no President has ever so recognized the central place of the arts in a vital society.

Kennedy sent message after message to Congress to outline the New Frontier program. He called for legislation to speed economic growth, cut unemployment, rehabilitate depressed areas, reform the tax structure, modernize cities, husband natural resources, improve the lot of farmers, aid education, and provide medical care for old people.

For the next two years, he faced a conservative Congress. Nevertheless, he obtained much new legislation, including a reciprocal trade act, aid to higher education, and measures to pull the Nation out of the economic setback of 1960-61. In 1963, he fought hard for new civil rights legislation and for a cut in taxes to stimulate the economy. Both bills became law after his death.

Under Kennedy, the United States made strides in space. In May, 1961, shortly after Astronaut Alan B. Shepard, Jr., had completed the first American suborbital flight, the President asked Congress to undertake Project Apollo, to land a man on the moon by 1970 and return him safely.

First Presidential candidates to debate on television, Kennedy and Republican nominee Richard M. Nixon argue issues in a New York studio in October, 1960. This and three other verbal clashes, which reached four out of five voters, recalled the Lincoln-Douglas debates of 1858 in impact and had a decisive effect at the polls.

"Ich bin ein Berliner—I am a Berliner." Kennedy practiced the phrase so he could speak it to West Berliners during his European tour in 1963. He termed it "the proudest boast" in the world of freedom. With Mayor Willy Brandt (center) and Chancellor Konrad Adenauer, he sets out to inspect the wall that has divided East and West Berlin since August, 1961. Crowds cheer (below) as Kennedy rides past the war-scarred spire of the Kaiser Wilhelm Memorial Church.

First Roman Catholic President calls on Pope Paul VI in Rome (opposite). In October, 1965, Kennedy's successor, Lyndon B. Johnson, met the Pontiff in New York—first visit of a Pope to the Western Hemisphere.

In foreign affairs, Kennedy asserted energetic, imaginative, and effective leadership—though his administration began with a fiasco. He permitted a force of anti-Castro Cubans, armed and trained by the United States before his Inauguration, to land on the coast of Cuba in April, 1961, in a disastrous attempt to overthrow the dictator.

In the aftermath of this setback, Kennedy pressed his Alliance for Progress program to eliminate the poverty that might lead to further Castro-style revolutions. This was "a vast new ten-year plan for the Americas, a plan to transform the 1960's into an historic decade of democratic progress." The United States offered loans and grants to assist our hemispheric neighbors in their development.

Another Kennedy program was establishment of the Peace Corps, which has trained thousands of idealistic Americans—mostly young people—and sent them to work in underdeveloped countries all over the world.

In June, 1961, Kennedy went to Vienna to talk with Soviet Premier Khrushchev, particularly in regard to Soviet pressure on Berlin. But Khrushchev seemed to be set on driving the Western allies out of that city; he fixed an end-of-the-year deadline for settlement of the Berlin issue, and in July announced a one-third increase in the Soviet military budget. Kennedy reacted firmly, requesting Congress to authorize strengthening of American forces. Meanwhile, he insisted, negotiations should go on, "in formal or informal meetings. We do not want military considerations to dominate the thinking of either East or West."

In August, Communist East Germany erected a wall of barbed wire and concrete blocks between East and West Berlin, and the Soviet Union announced a series of nuclear

tests that doubled the fallout from all previous tests. Reluctantly Kennedy resumed small-scale American tests. The tension over Berlin eased, only to be succeeded by the Cuban crisis.

In October, 1962, Kennedy received photographic proof of Soviet missile bases in Cuba. With intermediate-range missiles installed, Khrushchev could have commanded an arc covering the contiguous forty-eight states and parts of Canada.

Acting deliberately and coolly, President Kennedy, in a memorable telecast, announced a naval quarantine on all offensive weapons bound for Cuba. "I call upon Chairman Khrushchev to halt and eliminate this clandestine, reckless, and provocative threat to world peace," the President declared. "He has an opportunity now to move the world back from the abyss of destruction."

A week of tension followed. Kennedy personally directed the quarantine fleet, forbidding interceptions far at sea in order to give Soviet ships laden with missiles more time to stop and turn around. Finally Khrushchev removed the missiles.

After this confrontation, Kennedy repeatedly emphasized the necessity of great powers working together to preserve the human race. He obtained an agreement with Russia banning nuclear tests in the atmosphere, in space, and under water—the first arms-control treaty since the cold war began.

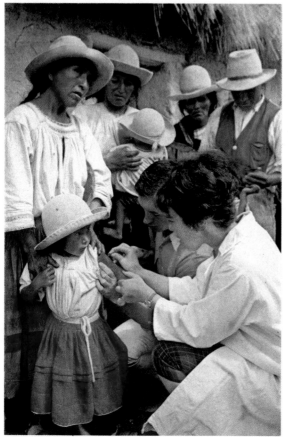

War on human misery: Rita Helmkamp and Edward Dennison, Peace Corps Volunteers in Bolivia, vaccinate a youngster against smallpox.

President Kennedy launched the Corps in March, 1961, and saw its members number more than 7,000, serving in 47 countries. Forsaking many luxuries, this goodwill army aids self-help efforts of other nations. In Africa they work to strengthen health services; in the Philippines, to improve fishery and livestock practices; in Latin America, to foster better and more abundant food crops.

Showdown on the high seas: In October, 1962, Americans learned that Russia was building missile bases in Cuba. "This...clandestine decision to station strategic weapons for the first time outside of Soviet soil...cannot be accepted by this country," Kennedy declared on television (right).

In Florida the largest invasion force since World War II massed to meet the Red threat 90 miles away. Simultaneously, the U. S. Navy established a quarantine around Cuba to block Soviet shipments. But the crisis ended when Russia met Kennedy's terms and ordered withdrawal of the missiles. The destroyer *Barry* (foreground) checks a Soviet freighter removing rockets from the island. A Navy observer plane flies overhead.

231

For Dr Melville Bell Grosvenor — with our deepest appreciation and good wishes alwa

6-28-62

Jacqueline Kennedy
[signature]

NATIONAL GEOGRAPHIC PHOTOGRAPHER THOMAS NEBBIA; UNITED PRESS INTERNATIONAL (BELOW, LEFT)

"And here's one for you too, Mr. President." The Chief Executive smiled approvingly as Dr. Grosvenor reversed protocol by presenting the first leather-bound souvenir copy of the White House guidebook to Mrs. Kennedy as its guiding spirit. The First Lady had invited the National Geographic Society, as a public service, to produce the guide (right) for the nonprofit White House Historical Association, headed by David E. Finley (center); proceeds from the book provide funds for refurnishing the mansion. The Society's President later received this autographed picture.

Patrons of the arts, the Kennedys entertain novelist Pearl Buck and poet Robert Frost at the White House. For the Inauguration, Frost recited his poem "The Gift Outright," a J.F.K. favorite.

232

Before Kennedy could build further on these auspicious beginnings, he was murdered. On November 22, 1963, while riding with his wife through the streets of Dallas, Texas, hailed by happy crowds, the President was fatally shot. The Nation mourned his death with an outpouring of grief comparable to that which marked the death of Abraham Lincoln. High officers of state from more than a hundred other countries came to Washington for the funeral, as their people shared America's sorrow.

President Kennedy is buried at Arlington National Cemetery, in a grave marked by an eternal flame. Hundreds of sites and memorials around the world have been dedicated to his memory. Among the most famous are John F. Kennedy Space Center at Cape Canaveral, Florida; Mount Kennedy, a peak in the Canadian Yukon; three acres of ground and a memorial at historic Runnymede, England; the John Fitzgerald Kennedy School of Government at Harvard University; and the John F. Kennedy Center for the Performing Arts in Washington, D. C.

Kennedy exemplified intelligence, vitality, charm, and what he had referred to as "that most admirable of human virtues—courage." President Johnson, two days after the funeral, voiced the feeling of the Nation: "No words are sad enough to express our sense of loss. No words are strong enough to express our determination to continue the forward thrust of America that he began."

Signing the nuclear-test-ban treaty in October, 1963, the President seals a pact outlawing atomic explosions in the atmosphere, space, and under water by the U. S., United Kingdom, and Soviet Union. Vice President Lyndon B. Johnson (right) and other dignitaries cluster in the Treaty Room of the White House. Restored to its Victorian elegance, the chamber had not beheld such a ceremony since the signing in 1898 of the protocol that ended hostilities in the Spanish-American War.

CECIL W. STOUGHTON

LYNDON B. JOHNSON rallied the American Nation toward a "Great Society" at home, and through the vicissitudes of the Viet Nam War toward peace with security in international affairs.

In his first years in office, he obtained passage of one of the most sweeping legislative programs in American history. When controversy over the war in Viet Nam became acute, he withdrew as a candidate for re-election to a second full term to devote his full efforts, unimpeded by politics, to the quest for peace.

Johnson was born on August 27, 1908, in the grasslands of central Texas, not far from Johnson City, which his family had helped settle. His grandfather had fought in the Confederate Army and served as a member of the Texas Legislature; his father, who also served in the legislature, was a firm opponent of the Ku Klux Klan.

Young Johnson felt the pinch of rural poverty in the 1920's. "I know that as a farm boy I did not feel secure," he once reminisced, "and when I was 14 years old I decided I was not going to be the victim of a system which would allow the price of a commodity like cotton to drop from 40 cents to 6 cents and destroy the homes of people like my own family."

While working his way through Southwest Texas State Teachers College, he took a year off to teach Mexican-American children at Cotulla, Texas. A classmate remembers him as "a beanpole who was 6 foot 3, as tall as he is now, but who then weighed only 135 pounds. Lyndon was full of nervous energy . . . always doing two or three things at a time."

After graduation, his inner drive for public service steered him into politics. In 1931 he went to Washington as secretary to a Texas Congressman, Richard M. Kleberg.

On a visit to Austin in September, 1934, he met Claudia "Lady Bird" Taylor, who has said she was taken aback at first, "then I realized he was handsome and charming and terribly bright." They were married in an Episcopal ceremony that November.

The Johnsons had two daughters, Lynda and Luci, both of whom were married while their father was President.

Johnson became the Texas director of the National Youth Administration in 1935, and within two years developed what was regarded in Washington as a model among state youth programs. In 1937 he campaigned for

With a "Great Society" as his goal, Lyndon Baines Johnson won the 1964 election by an unprecedented popular majority of 61 percent. Entering the White House with greater congressional experience than any predecessor, the dynamic Texan obtained passage of such landmarks in domestic legislation as Medicare, three civil rights acts, aid to education, and programs to combat poverty and crime.

Despite the beginning of major social reforms, urban unrest and controversy over the war in Viet Nam troubled the Nation. In March, 1968, Mr. Johnson announced that he would not seek re-election, but would devote the remaining months of his Presidency to the quest for peace.

Choosing programs in her husband's administration "that made my heart sing most," Mrs. Johnson gave them her fullest support. Among the most energetic of First Ladies, "Lady Bird" visited Head Start projects for pre-school children and anti-poverty and educational training centers. She campaigned to beautify the Nation's Capital and all America.

Paintings by Elizabeth Shoumatoff, White House Collection

"I do solemnly swear...." Only two hours earlier a sniper struck down President John F. Kennedy as he rode through cheering throngs in downtown Dallas, Texas. Now Vice President Johnson takes the oath of office, his right hand raised in pledge, his left hand on a small leather-bound Bible. Thus, in the midst of chaos, the orderly transfer of power takes place. The Nation was shocked by the fourth Presidential assassination in its history, but it was not paralyzed.

At 12:30 p.m. on November 22, 1963, Mr. and Mrs. Johnson rode two cars behind President and Mrs. Kennedy in a motorcade through the Texas metropolis. At the first crack of the rifle, a Secret Service agent threw himself across the Vice President in a protective move. The Johnsons' car sped to the hospital where the mortally wounded Kennedy had been taken. Alert to the possibility of a widespread plot against the Government, Mr. Johnson hurried under guard to the Presidential plane at the Dallas airport for the flight to Washington. After Mrs. Kennedy boarded, Federal District Judge Sarah T. Hughes swore in the 36th President of the United States, becoming the first woman to administer the oath of office. Beside the new President at the sorrowful oath-taking stand Mrs. Johnson and Mrs. Kennedy, who still wears the pink suit chosen for what had promised to be a festive occasion.

Arriving in Washington that evening, President Johnson made a brief statement, concluding: "I will do my best. That is all I can do. I ask for your help—and God's."

Across the land, the people mourned. Addressing Congress five days later, President Johnson paid tribute to his predecessor and recalled Kennedy's dreams for the Nation. He urged, "All my fellow Americans, let us continue."

the House of Representatives on a New Deal platform and defeated his nearest opponent two to one. In the House he became an effective lieutenant of Majority Leader Sam Rayburn and a protégé of President Roosevelt.

Immediately after Pearl Harbor he volunteered for active military service. As a Navy lieutenant commander, he won a Silver Star before he and other Congressmen were recalled to Washington.

In 1948, after five and a half terms in the House, Johnson won the Democratic primary contest for Senator by a margin of 87 votes. Once nominated, however, he easily defeated his Republican opponent.

The young Senator was elected Democratic Minority Whip after only three years' service and, in 1953, Minority Leader at the age of 44—the youngest in Senate history. When the Democrats gained control of the Senate in 1954, Johnson became Majority Leader and a commanding figure in Congress.

He suffered a severe heart attack in July, 1955, but made a complete recovery. As a Democratic Majority Leader in a Republican administration, he won a reputation for the statesmanlike way in which he supported or opposed White House measures on their basic merits. He refused to engage in partisanship as he guided through the Senate vital measures of national security and civil rights.

When Johnson failed to obtain the Democratic nomination for the Presidency in 1960, he accepted Kennedy's offer of the Vice Presidential nomination. On November 22, 1963, when President Kennedy was assassinated in Dallas, Texas, Vice President Lyndon Johnson was sworn in as the 36th President of the United States.

When he took the Chief Executive's oath Johnson knew the policies and emergency plans of the Government in detail. He saw that in such a "very abrupt and sudden transition" of leadership, confusion at home and abroad might create dangers; swiftly and surely, he took action to avert them.

As President he tried to exemplify the view he had expressed in 1958 that it was unacceptable in the American Nation for a question to be settled by a partisan majority overriding a minority.

"I do not believe," he said, "we have arrived at an answer until we have found the national answer, the answer all reasonable men can agree upon." To Congress in January, 1964, in his State of the Union Message, he recommended what he believed to be some of the national answers:

236

Making friends for the United States, the genial Texan visited 27 countries as Vice President. The National Geographic Society recognized his extensive travels on June 8, 1962, by presenting him with its Jane M. Smith Award, a citation praising his "efforts to bring the peoples of the world closer together." He made a trip to Scandinavia in 1963, the first time such a high-ranking U. S. official had toured that area. Here, with Lady Bird and Lynda, he inspects a Lapp's reindeer in Finland. Vice President Johnson described his journey in the February, 1964, NATIONAL GEOGRAPHIC.

One of the most active Vice Presidents in history, Johnson was chairman of the National Aeronautics and Space Council, the National Advisory Council of the Peace Corps, and the President's Committee on Equal Employment Opportunity.

"Come now, and let us reason together." In the spirit of his favorite Biblical verse—Isaiah 1:18—Senate Majority Leader Johnson confers with colleagues in 1960: Senators Mike Mansfield (center) of Montana, Joseph S. Clark (left) of Pennsylvania, and William Proxmire of Wisconsin. Working 12 to 16 hours a day, Johnson piloted through the Senate the first civil rights act in 82 years. He impressed even opponents as "one of the ablest political craftsmen of our time."

VOLKMAR WENTZEL, N.G.S. STAFF (ABOVE); GEORGE THAMES, NEW YORK TIMES

"Let this session of Congress be known as the session which did more for civil rights than the last hundred sessions combined; as the session which enacted the most far-reaching tax cut of our time; as the session which declared all-out war on human poverty and unemployment in these United States.... All this and more can and must be done."

Congress did accept these answers. The Civil Rights Act of 1964 strengthened earlier legislation, opened large categories of public accommodations to Negroes, and enlarged their opportunities. Congress also enacted tax-reduction and antipoverty measures.

Johnson envisaged going still further, toward the goal of what he called a Great Society. In accepting the Democratic nomination for the Presidency in August, 1964, he declared: "This nation, this generation, in this hour has man's first chance to build a great society, a place where the meaning of man's life matches the marvels of man's labor."

In the 1964 election, Johnson won against Republican Senator Barry Goldwater by one of the biggest popular margins in American history—more than 15,000,000 votes.

To the 89th Congress, meeting in January, 1965, he outlined his objectives: aid to education, an attack on disease, urban renewal, beautification of America and elimination of air and river pollution, development of depressed regions, control and prevention of crime and delinquency, removal of every obstacle to the right to vote, honor and support to art and thought, and a vigorous campaign against waste and inefficiency. Congress, at times augmenting or amending, rapidly enacted the legislation he recommended to make a beginning on each of these programs.

Congress gave the President bipartisan support when, in response to the frustrations of Negroes seeking to register to vote in some areas of the South, he proposed a bill to strike down restrictions to voting.

"To deny a man his hopes because of his color or race, his religion or the place of his birth," Johnson declared, "is not only to do injustice, it is to deny America and to dishonor the dead who gave their lives for freedom."

On August 6, the President signed the strong Voting Rights Act of 1965.

A week earlier, he had flown to Independence, Missouri, and signed the Medicare-Social Security measure in the presence of former President Truman, first Chief Executive to propose health insurance as part of the Social Security program.

In the presence of Mayor Robert F. Wagner of New York, son of the leading New Deal proponent of public housing, the President signed a housing bill going far beyond any of its predecessors.

Johnson enlisted the support of many Republicans as well as most Democrats. He was unusually successful in convincing businessmen that the Government wished to aid rather than hinder them.

Under Johnson the country scored spectacular advances in space. It so effectively cut the Russian lead that only 11 weeks after a Soviet cosmonaut floated outside his space vehicle, Astronaut Edward H. White II took a "walk" in space.

In December, 1965, Astronauts Frank Borman and James A. Lovell, Jr., kept Gemini 7 in orbit for a record-breaking 14 days and for the first rendezvous in space. Then, in December, 1968, Borman, Lovell, and William A. Anders, crew of Apollo 8, became the first men in history to fly beyond the gravitational pull of earth and to enter lunar orbit, paving the way for man's epic landing on the moon.

In relations with other nations, the President faced perplexing problems. When reports of a revolution in the Dominican Republic reached the White House in the spring of 1965, he acted quickly. He landed troops to protect American lives in a situation that appeared to be developing sinister dimensions.

"The American nations," he later declared, "cannot, must not and will not permit the establishment of another Communist government in the Western Hemisphere." He turned to the Organization of American States, which within a few days negotiated a cease-fire, dispatched an Inter-American Peace Force, and began to work toward a peaceable settlement. Ultimately, through a free election, a democratic government was restored.

In South Viet Nam, Johnson faced far more serious difficulties which in time sharply divided the American people. The United States had long sought to stem the tide of Communism in Southeast Asia. Under the Geneva

"**The best instrument** yet devised to promote the peace of the world." Thus President Johnson described the United Nations when he renewed his country's support of the international body in an address to the General Assembly on December 17, 1963. He once defined a peaceful world as a place "where differences are solved without destruction, and common effort is directed at common problems."

"A triumph for freedom as huge as any victory won on any battlefield," the President calls the 1965 Voting Rights Act, which struck down practices denying minorities the vote. His words echo around statues of Lincoln in the Capitol Rotunda. He signed the bill in the President's Room, where, in 1861, Lincoln had signed a bill that freed any slave serving the Confederate Army or Navy.

Strike against Viet Cong: In South Viet Nam, helicopters land paratroops seeking out Communist guerrillas. Mr. Johnson sent more U. S. troops there, saying in 1966: "To yield to force...would whet the appetite of aggression."

Waging war on poverty, Mr. Johnson inspected the economically distressed Appalachian region in April, 1964. "I know what poverty means to people," he once said. "I have been unemployed. I have stood in an employment office, waiting for an assignment...." Here he visits a jobless sawmill worker.

Talks in Paris, a step toward peace: "Many days of hard discussions lie before us," W. Averell Harriman warned the North Vietnamese delegation at the opening session of negotiations, May 13, 1968. The United States delegation (left), then headed by Harriman and Cyrus R. Vance, faced the North Vietnamese, led by Xuan Thuy and Col. Ha Van Lau. The talks later included representatives of South Viet Nam and the National Liberation Front. In October President Johnson halted the bombing of North Viet Nam, believing that proceedings had "entered a new and a very much more hopeful phase."

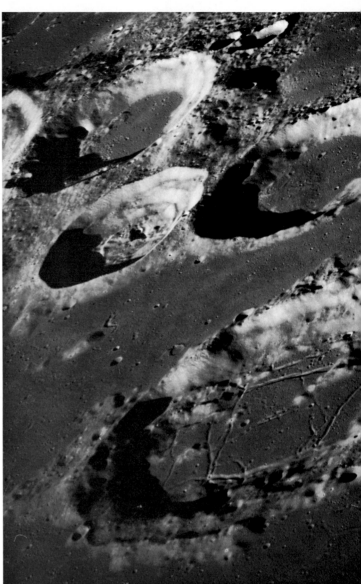

Agreement of 1954, all the Indochina states had won their independence and all—including North Viet Nam—had accepted neutralization.

This agreement was flouted almost immediately. Communist guerrillas known as the Viet Cong, supported from the North, increasingly threatened to take over South Viet Nam. The Eisenhower Administration sent aid and advisers, and Kennedy, stepping up the commitment, dispatched 3,200 military advisers and technicians in 1961. During the Johnson Administration the growth of Viet Cong forces and the active intervention of North Vietnamese troops in South Viet Nam led to still sterner countermeasures.

By early 1968, American forces had approached a half-million men, and more tonnage of bombs had been dropped on North Viet Nam than upon Europe in World War II. Casualties also had increased. Despite President Johnson's reiterated statement of his goal—"to bring an end to aggression

Flight of Apollo 8: On December 21, 1968, three American astronauts began an epic Christmas journey from Cape Kennedy (far left) to the moon. Spacecraft commander Col. Frank Borman, Capt. James A. Lovell, and Maj. William A. Anders traveled 230,000 miles in three days before entering an orbit only 70 miles from the forbidding lunar surface (center).

When Sputnik I astounded the world in 1957, Lyndon Johnson, then Senate Majority Leader, became the chief congressional advocate of the American space program. He secured passage of the 1958 Space Act and served as the first chairman of the National Aeronautics and Space Council. Below, in a White House ceremony, he presents NASA's Distinguished Service Medal to Borman, as co-recipients Anders (left) and Lovell applaud.

NATIONAL GEOGRAPHIC PHOTOGRAPHER BRUCE DALE (BELOW) AND NASA

and a peaceful settlement"—the North Vietnamese would not agree to attend a peace conference. Escalation of the war had not brought the sought-for end, and was leading to increasingly sharp criticism within the United States.

Then, on March 31, 1968, Johnson in a dramatic television broadcast announced that he was ordering a halt to the bombing of North Viet Nam in the hope that this could lead to a beginning of peace negotiations.

He went on to declare: "What we won when all of our people united just must not be lost in suspicion and distrust and selfishness and politics among any of our people.... With American sons in the fields far away, with America's future under challenge right here at home, with our hopes and the world's hopes for peace in the balance every day, I do not believe that I should devote an hour or a day of my time to any personal partisan causes. ... I shall not seek, and I will not accept, the nomination of my party for another term as your President."

Thus the President eased much of the harsh controversy at home; his announcement of the bombing halt led North Viet Nam to take a tentative step toward negotiations. Preliminary talks, raising world hopes for peace, were under way in Paris when he left office. Negotiations continued during the next four years. Johnson barely missed seeing them succeed; he died at his Texas ranch on January 22, 1973, the day before the peace agreement was signed.

Richard Nixon (signature)

THIRTY-SEVENTH PRESIDENT 1969-1974

RECONCILIATION was the first goal set by President Richard M. Nixon. The Nation was painfully divided, with turbulence in the cities and war overseas. During his Presidency, Nixon succeeded in ending American fighting in Viet Nam and improving relations with the U.S.S.R. and the People's Republic of China. But the Watergate scandal brought fresh divisions to the country and led ultimately to his resignation.

To the world, the President declared, "I shall consecrate my Office, my energies, and all the wisdom I can summon to the cause of peace among nations."

To his fellow Americans he asserted:

"No man can be fully free while his neighbor is not. To go forward at all is to go forward together.

"This means black and white together, as one nation, not two. The laws have caught up with our conscience. What remains is to give life to what is in the law: to insure at last that as all are born equal in dignity before God, all are born equal in dignity before man."

Nixon's election in 1968 climaxed a career unusual both for his early success and for his comeback after being defeated for President in 1960.

Born in Yorba Linda, California, in 1913, he was brought up in nearby Whittier, where his parents ran a grocery store and worshiped at the Friends' Meeting. His father, of Scots-Irish descent, numbering among his ancestors the Revolutionary War hero "Mad Anthony"

Wayne, had adopted the Quaker faith of his Indiana-born wife. It was an upbringing notable for its frugality and industry.

When Nixon was a teen-ager, his parents turned over to him the vegetable section of the grocery store, and let him save the profits to finance his college education. He rose at four in the morning and drove to Los Angeles to purchase produce. He began habitually to work a sixteen-hour day, and has continued to do so through much of his adult life. He performed even small tasks with thoroughness. His mother remembered that he made the best mashed potatoes of any of her sons: "He never left any lumps."

Nixon made a brilliant record at Whittier College, where he was a debater and student-

UNITED PRESS INTERNATIONAL

"Forward together," Richard M. Nixon's theme during his 1968 campaign and at the outset of his first administration, called the American people to unity and to new hopes. In the cause of peace, he addressed himself equally to the peoples of the world. Nixon had won the highest office after service in the House of Representatives and the Senate, and two terms as Vice President—the second youngest in the Nation's history.

Quaker household of Yorba Linda, California, about 1917: Francis A. and Hannah Milhous Nixon, with Harold (left), Donald, and Richard, who wears the haircut and costume made popular in that day by comic-strip hero Buster Brown.

Painting by Alexander Clayton, White House Collection

245

Congressman Nixon examines the "pumpkin papers," microfilms of secret government documents that figured as proof of espionage in the investigation of Alger Hiss. This case, a sensation in 1948-49, made Nixon famous as an enemy of subversion and a spokesman for anti-Communism.

Vice President Nixon, on a goodwill visit, and Soviet Premier Khrushchev wage an impromptu "kitchen debate" on the nature of free government, at the American exhibition in Moscow in 1959.

During the third major illness of President Eisenhower, Nixon holds his first formal news conference in the White House, November 27, 1957, to explain duties he will assume temporarily. Eisenhower later sent him a letter outlining circumstances of "any disability of mine" in which Nixon should serve as "acting President."

body president, and at Duke University Law School. After entering law practice in Whittier, in 1940 he married Patricia Ryan, a high-school teacher. They have two daughters, Tricia (Mrs. Edward Finch Cox) and Julie (Mrs. David Eisenhower).

After the Japanese attack on Pearl Harbor, Nixon served six months in Washington as a lawyer for the Office of Price Administration, an experience which left him permanently interested in improving the efficiency of the bureaucracy. Then he obtained a commission in the Navy. He fought in the South Pacific, receiving two battle stars and two commendations, and rising to the rank of lieutenant commander before completing his tour of duty in January, 1946.

Immediately upon leaving the service, he ran for Congress in his California district as a Republican, and was elected. In Washington, he quickly gained a reputation as a Congressman concerned with the security of the Nation both abroad and at home.

When, as a member of the Herter Committee, he visited Western European nations in the fall of 1947, he was so shocked by their state of imminent economic collapse that he returned to fight for passage of the Marshall Plan. This program, enacted with bipartisan support, helped bring a remarkable recovery.

Within the United States, Nixon adopted a notably conservative position. He helped draft the Taft-Hartley Act, which among other provisions required union officials to

file affidavits that they were not Communists, and the Mundt-Nixon bill requiring the registration of Communist and Communist-front organizations. As a member of the House Un-American Activities Committee he persisted in questioning Alger Hiss, who at first seemed a most unlikely person to be suspected of supplying classified State Department documents to a Communist courier before the war. Ultimately Hiss was convicted of perjury.

As President, reminded by a reporter of his earlier views, Nixon pointed out that times had changed; two decades had elapsed. He had come to regard as outmoded the Taft-Hartley Act method of stopping strikes that threaten a national emergency. When a reporter asked him, in the light of the Hiss case, to comment on the right-wing attack

upon one of his appointees, he replied, "What I am looking to now is his capability to handle the problems of the future and not events that occurred over twenty years ago. There is no question about his loyalty to this country."

After a hard-fought campaign in 1950, Nixon won election to the Senate by a wide margin. As a Senator, he was renowned as a forceful speaker, appearing at innumerable Republican functions throughout the country to build party unity and strength. This reputation helped win him the Vice Presidential nomination in 1952, when he was only 39 and had celebrated his first political victory only six years earlier.

During his eight years as Vice President, Nixon turned a traditionally inconsequential office into one of considerable stature. He was

Learning in New York of his victory, he celebrates with Mrs. Nixon, his daughters Tricia (at his right) and Julie, with her fiancé David Eisenhower. Julie made the gift he displays, a crewel-work rendering of the Great Seal of the United States.

Campaign cheers, music, and hand-lettered signs greet the front-runner on August 5, 1968, as he arrives at Miami's Hilton Plaza for the Republican National Convention. Unsuccessful in his bid for the Presidency in 1960 and for the California governorship in 1962, he won his party's nomination for a second time and chose Governor Spiro T. Agnew of Maryland as his running mate. "I don't promise," Mr. Nixon said in his acceptance speech, "that we can eradicate poverty and end discrimination and eliminate all danger of wars in . . . four, or even eight years. But I do promise action." Calling for "complete reappraisal of America's policies in every section of the world," he defeated the Democratic nominee, Hubert H. Humphrey, and third-party candidate George C. Wallace of Alabama in the November election.

President-elect receives the oath of office from Chief Justice Earl Warren on January 20, 1969, in the presence of President Johnson and Mrs. Nixon. In his Inaugural Address, the new Chief Executive spoke to a Nation "rich in goods but ragged in spirit." Now, he said, "because our strengths are so great, we can afford to appraise our weaknesses with candor and to approach them with hope."

249

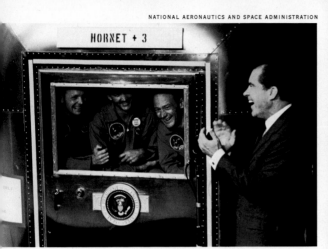

HORNET + 3

"Gee, you look great!" exclaims President Nixon as he greets the crew of Apollo 11, quarantined aboard the carrier U.S.S. *Hornet.* Astronauts Neil A. Armstrong, Michael Collins, and Edwin E. Aldrin, Jr., had splashed down from their historic July, 1969, trip to the moon only minutes earlier. At right, troops of the 1st Battalion, Ninth Marine Regiment, board a transport at Da Nang soon after President Nixon announced plans in June, 1969, for a phased withdrawal of ground combat forces from South Viet Nam. Reflecting a nationwide mood of unrest, dissenters (below) wave placards around the statue of Daniel Webster during a 1970 demonstration in Boston following the military operation in Cambodia.

LEE LOCKWOOD, BLACK STAR

the most indefatigable campaigner in every election, and undertook significant duties in the Eisenhower Administration. Three times he filled in with discretion and effectiveness while the President was recuperating from illnesses. The settlement of the 116-day steel strike of 1959 was among his achievements. He was a strong and successful advocate of the U. S. space program.

As Vice President, Nixon was repeatedly Eisenhower's personal emissary abroad, visiting 55 countries, studying firsthand the international problems involving the United States.

Nixon was nominated by acclamation at the Republican convention of 1960 and campaigned vigorously, but lost the election to John F. Kennedy by a margin of less than 120,000 votes. When he ran for Governor of California in 1962, again he lost.

His political career apparently at an end, Nixon moved to New York City in 1963 to join a law firm. He continued, nevertheless, to be a hardworking Republican campaigner, and retained his great popularity with party

officials and workers. Even as late as 1966, he said that "as a practical political realist," he did not expect to be a nominee for President again.

Two years later, however, he did decide to seek the Presidency. He emerged the victor in all the state primaries he entered, and easily won the nomination. His running mate was Governor Spiro T. Agnew of Maryland.

Nixon defeated the Democratic candidate, Vice President Hubert H. Humphrey, and a third-party candidate, George C. Wallace of Alabama, receiving approximately 43.5 percent of the popular vote.

Soon after taking office President Nixon began proposing sweeping reforms to Congress. He requested changes in the Electoral College, selective service, the postal service, the tax system, and poverty and welfare programs. Congress enacted some changes, including sharing Federal tax revenues with state and local governments. It considered other of the Nixon proposals.

President Nixon succeeded in attaining one of his goals, to appoint to the Supreme Court men of a more conservative legal philosophy. He promoted a distinguished Federal judge to be Chief Justice of the United States, Warren E. Burger, noted for his emphasis upon law and order. Later he appointed three other conservatives to the Supreme Court.

In August, 1971, Nixon undertook bold measures to counter the continuing inflation resulting from the Viet Nam War. He obtained controls on wages and prices within the United States, and to stop the drain of the dollar to other nations, reduced its value in relation to foreign currencies. Congress later increased the price of gold.

President Nixon's most difficult task was to try to bring American involvement in the drawn-out Viet Nam conflict to a conclusion. He undertook to bring troops home as rapidly as he felt that the South Vietnamese could assume their own defense.

To facilitate this, in the spring of 1970 he authorized American troops to sweep across the South Vietnamese border to destroy

251

"I began by telling the President that there was a cancer growing on the Presidency," testifies former White House Counsel John W. Dean III. Appearing in June, 1973, before a Senate committee chaired by Senator Sam Ervin, Dean accused the President and his top-level advisers of covering up their knowledge of a break-in at the Democratic National Committee's offices in Washington. Dean blamed the President's "insatiable appetite for political intelligence" for the events that came to be called "Watergate."

sanctuaries of North Vietnamese armies in Cambodia. Into 1972, Americans continued to train South Vietnamese troops, while other Americans returned home. The maximum troop level had been 543,400 in April, 1969. By July 1, 1972, pullouts reduced troop strength in Viet Nam to fewer than 49,000.

Still, neither negotiations in Paris nor President Nixon's secret offers to the North Vietnamese (which he made public in 1972) could secure peace. Demonstrations in cities and on college campuses, which had reached a peak during the Cambodian invasion, abated; but deep national concern continued.

President Nixon undertook to reduce tensions with the Russians and the Communist Chinese, yet maintain adequate defenses. He

obtained authorization from Congress to begin construction of a new anti-missile system for national defense. But he also gave support to negotiations with Russia to limit strategic arms. These negotiations began in Vienna in April, 1970. Unilaterally he announced that the United States would destroy its stockpiles of germ-warfare weapons and would use chemical weapons only for defense.

In spectacular fashion, President Nixon in February, 1972, broke through twenty years of barriers to seek a new relationship between the United States and the People's Republic of China. He visited Peking to confer for many hours with Premier Chou En-lai and call upon Chairman Mao Tse-tung.

The visit—in Nixon's words, "the week

that changed the world"—did not bring formal recognition and establishment of embassies, but did symbolize the intention of both nations to work toward peaceful solutions to the numerous points of dispute between them. Interchanges followed, culminating in 1973 with the establishment of Chinese and American liaison offices at each other's capitals.

Nixon achieved a further easing of tensions and a number of tangible agreements when he visited Moscow in May, 1972, for a summit conference with leaders of the Soviet Union. Lengthy negotiations preceded the meeting.

"This was a working summit," the President reported to Congress upon his return. The two nations agreed to cooperate in concrete ways to promote trade, to improve the environment, and to advance medicine, public health, and scientific knowledge.

Probably the most important achievement of the conversations was a treaty to limit strategic nuclear weapons.

The President continued to seek means to improve relations with other nations and to reduce world tension. In June, 1973, he was host to General Secretary Leonid I. Brezhnev of the Soviet Union in a second summit meeting. Again they signed a number of accords.

In 1972 Nixon and Agnew defeated Democrats George M. McGovern and Sargent Shriver by one of the widest margins in American history. Nixon won every electoral vote except those of Massachusetts and the District of Columbia.

In his second Inaugural Address, President Nixon hailed the impending close of the Viet Nam War and urged, "Let us again learn to debate our differences with civility and decency." Three days later, on January 23, 1973, he announced the signing of accords with North Viet Nam, and the achievement of "peace with honor."

Within a few months, the Nixon Administration was embroiled in the so-called Watergate scandal, stemming from a break-in at the offices of the Democratic National Committee during the 1972 campaign. The break-in was traced to officials of the Committee to Re-elect the President. A number of Administration officials resigned; some—including John Mitchell, former Attorney General; H. R. Haldeman, former White House Chief of Staff; and John D. Ehrlichman, former Chief Domestic Affairs Adviser—were later convicted of offenses connected with efforts to cover up the affair. Nixon denied any personal involvement, but the courts forced him to yield tape recordings

In a Federal courtroom presided over by Judge John J. Sirica (above), participants in the Watergate cover-up trial listen to conversations secretly taped by the President. Of the defendants (from left center): John D. Ehrlichman, H. R. Haldeman, Robert C. Mardian, Kenneth Parkinson, and John Mitchell, the jury found all but Parkinson guilty.

Faced with almost certain impeachment for his role in the Watergate cover-up, President Nixon appears on television on August 8, 1974, to announce that he will resign—the only Chief Executive ever to do so.

which indicated that he had, in fact, tried to divert the investigation.

As a result of unrelated scandals in Maryland, Vice President Spiro T. Agnew resigned in 1973. Nixon nominated, and Congress approved, House Minority Leader Gerald R. Ford as Vice President.

Faced with what seemed almost certain impeachment, Nixon announced on August 8, 1974, that he would resign the next day to begin "that process of healing which is so desperately needed in America."

Gerald R. Ford

THIRTY-EIGHTH PRESIDENT 1974-1977

WHEN GERALD R. FORD took the oath of office on August 9, 1974, he declared, "I assume the Presidency under extraordinary circumstances never before experienced by Americans. This is an hour of history that troubles our minds and hurts our hearts."

It was indeed an unprecedented time. In 1973, he had been the first Vice President to take office under the terms of the Twenty-fifth Amendment, and, in the aftermath of the Watergate scandal, was succeeding the first President ever to resign. He cheered Americans by asserting, "Our long national nightmare is over. Our Constitution works. Our great Republic is a government of laws and not of men. Here the people rule."

Almost insuperable tasks remained. In addition to seeking solutions to an array of critical problems he had inherited, Ford was faced with the task of restoring confidence in the Presidency. The Nation was suffering from inflation, a depressed economy, and an energy crisis. The possibility of renewed conflict in the Middle East threatened to make these problems more acute. Ford offered no quick solutions, but he did bring a reputation for integrity and openness which had made him popular in Congress.

Ford came to the Presidency after 25 years of service in the House of Representatives; since 1965 he had been House Minority Leader. On the eve of assuming the Presidency he remarked, "I don't think I have a single enemy in the Congress. . . . Tomorrow I can start out working with Democrats and with Republicans in the House as well as in the Senate, to work on the problems . . . which we have at home."

Ford was born in Omaha, Nebraska, in 1913. He began life as Leslie King, Jr., but his parents were divorced when he was two. His mother took him to Grand Rapids, Michigan. There she met and married Gerald R. Ford, who adopted the small boy and gave him his name. The senior Ford, a businessman, was a prime influence in the life of his adopted son, bringing him up to be truthful and hardworking.

Young Ford attended the University of

Future President of the United States, Leslie King, Jr., rests in the arms of his mother, Mrs. Dorothy King, a few months after his birth in 1913. His parents were later divorced, and Mrs. King married Gerald R. Ford, a businessman of Grand Rapids, Michigan. He adopted young Leslie and gave the boy his name.

"I assume the Presidency under extraordinary circumstances," said Gerald Ford. The first Vice President chosen under the terms of the Twenty-fifth Amendment, in the wake of Spiro Agnew's resignation, Ford also became the first Chief Executive to succeed a President who had resigned. In his Inaugural Address he reassured Americans that their Constitution worked: "Our great Republic is a government of laws and not of men. Here the people rule." But one of his early actions— a full pardon of Richard Nixon—jeopardized his popularity.

Painting by Everett Raymond Kinstler, White House Collection

While Betty Ford holds a family Bible, Chief Justice Warren Burger administers the oath of office to Gerald Ford on August 9, 1974. The new President promised an administration of openness and candor. He also acted quickly to fill the Vice Presidency, nominating Nelson Rockefeller of New York. Rockefeller took office on December 19 after confirmation by Congress.

Seeking to slow the nuclear arms race, President Ford and Soviet Party Chief Leonid Brezhnev meet near Vladivostok, Siberia, late in 1974. They agreed to a limit of about 2,400 missile launchers—such as bombers and submarines—for each country, and to 1,320 multiple-warhead missiles. "A breakthrough," Secretary of State Henry Kissinger called the talks.

of civil rights measures. He once declared, "The Great Society of Lyndon Johnson has become a runaway locomotive with a wild-eyed engineer at the throttle."

His honesty, industriousness, and warmth brought him prominence among Republicans in the House of Representatives. Democratic President Lyndon Johnson appointed Ford to the Warren Commission to investigate the assassination of President Kennedy. Subsequently Ford collaborated on a book, *Portrait of the Assassin,* on the investigation. In 1965, he won the House Minority Leadership, promising that every House Republican would be "a first-team player." Always loyal to his party, Ford extended that loyalty to President Nixon after the 1968 election.

Both Republicans and Democrats in Congress supported President Nixon's nomination of Ford to replace Spiro Agnew as Vice President. They applauded vigorously when Ford was sworn in on December 6, 1973, and asserted, "I am a Ford, not a Lincoln." During his eight months as Vice President, Ford was not successful in his desired role as "a ready conciliator and communicator between the White House and Capitol Hill." That was an impossible undertaking as the Watergate crisis intensified. Rather, as Ford traveled and spoke extensively, he became a fresh national voice around whom the Republican leadership rallied. In May, 1974, a team began planning, without his knowledge, for the possibility of his succeeding Nixon, but it was not until August 7, 1974, that he learned he was likely to become President.

Ford assumed office only two days later, and in unpretentious fashion set out to restore confidence in the Presidency. Appearing on August 12, 1974, before a joint session of Congress, he pledged cooperation, a pledge that he renewed from time to time. In foreign affairs, he promised continuity and gave indication of it by retaining Henry Kissinger as Secretary of State. Concerning domestic matters, he candidly stated, "My instinctive judgment is that the state of the Union is excellent. But the state of our economy is not so good." These were the themes with which he began his administration.

In an effort to close the book on earlier controversies and out of compassion, Ford granted a full pardon to Richard Nixon, even though it jeopardized his own popularity. Subsequently Ford appeared voluntarily before a Congressional subcommittee to assure its members that there had been no deal of any kind regarding the Nixon pardon and

"A normal American family," First Lady Betty Ford says of her husband and children. Here she gathers them around her in the Oval Office on Inauguration Day. Daughter Susan, a student at Holton-Arms School in Maryland, stands at the President's left. At Susan's left stand her eldest brother, Michael—a theology student in Massachusetts— and his wife, Gayle. Youngest brother Steven, beside his mother, was working as a cowhand on a Utah ranch; Jack was majoring in forestry at Utah State University.

that he had acted "out of my concern to serve the best interests of my country." Attempting to end bitterness over Viet Nam, the President announced a program of leniency for draft evaders and deserters.

Slowly, Ford built his own administration. He nominated Nelson Rockefeller of New York to be Vice President; after lengthy hearings Rockefeller was confirmed by the Democratic Congress and in December, 1974, took office. One by one, Ford replaced a number of Nixon appointees in the Cabinet and on the White House staff.

During his first months in office he broadened the range of political viewpoints and backgrounds represented in his Cabinet. He appointed a black lawyer, William T. Coleman, as Secretary of Transportation, and a

woman, Carla A. Hills, as Secretary of Housing and Urban Development.

For the most part, the President gave his Cabinet officers more freedom to advance their viewpoints than had his predecessor. The most remarkable transformation in the White House was one of spirit. Ford's staff operated less through strict chain of command and enjoyed more access to the President.

Ford carried this openness into his entire conduct of the administration, even though it meant extending his working day to almost double the normal eight hours. Unusual energy and physical fitness were required to maintain such a schedule; Ford's energy was like that of Theodore Roosevelt. He arose before six in the morning and exercised hard for 20 minutes; when he could find the time,

259

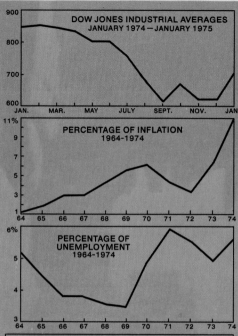

DOW JONES INDUSTRIAL AVERAGES
JANUARY 1974 – JANUARY 1975

PERCENTAGE OF INFLATION
1964-1974

**PERCENTAGE OF
UNEMPLOYMENT**
1964-1974

Economic woes—a curious mixture of recession and inflation—faced the new President soon after he took office. Bad news came in three areas: the stock market, the cost of living, and the level of unemployment.

In 1974 cautious investors watched as the monthly Dow Jones Industrial averages headed down from a high of 860.53 in February to a low of 607.87 in September. In early 1975 the average remained 150 points lower than in January of the year before.

Of even more concern to consumers: the increasing level of inflation. In 1974 the Consumer Price Index rose 11 percent compared to a 1.3 percent increase in 1964.

November and December unemployment rates of 6.6 percent and 7.2 percent helped to boost the 1974 year's average to 5.6 percent. The number of unemployed continued to mount in the early months of 1975.

Economic problems in 1974 came from other sources as well. Interest rates first went down, then turned upward: Prime rates on bank loans hit 12 percent in July.

The Nation's balance of trade showed a 1.3-billion-dollar surplus in 1973. Largely because of increases in the price of oil, this became a 3.1-billion-dollar deficit in 1974.

President Ford and Congress disagreed about how to solve the Nation's growing economic problems.

he would swim 14 laps, or ski, or play golf.

With this same vigor, Ford consulted each day with scores of people, either in person or by telephone, worked through stacks of policy papers, and sat in numerous meetings. In the fall of 1974, he brought a number of distinguished economists to the White House and listened to their differing advice on dealing with the Nation's problems. It was typical of his range of inquiry. In his first message, he promised members of the House and Senate that his door would be open to them.

As the President struggled to combat the country's economic malaise, he consulted with Congressional leaders, insistently but pleasantly seeking their support. In addition, he took his program directly to the people, seeking public support through televised press conferences and personal appearances in various parts of the country. He thrived on a regimen which left him only six or seven hours a night for sleep.

Ford was deliberate in proposing solutions to economic problems. For some months he emphasized budget cutting and financial restrictions to curb inflation. He proposed a 31-point program; Congress did not act upon it, and overrode his veto of three bills.

By early 1975, the Nation's economic problems had deepened into the worst recession since the 1930's. Ford summed up the three gravest difficulties as "recession, inflation, and energy dependence." Each aggravated the others in complicated ways.

Huge price increases imposed by the oil-exporting nations were compounding an energy crisis. Ford wanted to raise the duties on foreign oil to promote American self-sufficiency, and did so by proclamation. The new Congress, even more heavily Democratic than the last, favored other measures and passed a bill that the President vetoed. Not until December did a compromise energy bill become law.

Ford hoped to end the recession by proposing tax cuts and by accepting unparalleled peacetime deficits in the federal budget. Meanwhile, he tried to control inflation by a moratorium on new spending programs. His was a program of delicate balance between controls and stimulants.

Congress wanted large expenditures to spur the economy and fight unemployment. When it passed bills that involved more spending than he thought prudent, the President vetoed them.

In 1976 he asserted: "Fifty-five times I vetoed extravagant and unwise legislation.

Forty-four times I made those vetoes stick. Those vetoes have saved American taxpayers billions and billions of dollars."

In his final State of the Union message, in 1977, he declared, "We have successfully cut inflation by more than half." He noted that four million more people were employed than in the spring of 1975, but lamented that "there are still too many Americans unemployed." More than seven million were vainly seeking work.

In global strategy also, President Ford made significant gains and met with frustrations. He studied two matters with special care before undertaking negotiations: preventing war in the Middle East, and curbing an arms race with the U.S.S.R.

Under his direction, Secretary Kissinger persuaded the Israelis and the Egyptians to sign a peace agreement concerning the Sinai territory in the fall of 1975. Ford called this development "an historic first step that promises an eventual just settlement for the whole Middle East."

The President conferred in person with Soviet leader Leonid Brezhnev near Vladivostok, Siberia, late in 1974. They agreed to

Uneasy peace in the Middle East spawns an energy shortage in the U. S. In the Persian Gulf tankers take on crude oil. To protest American aid to Israel, the Arab nations used their enormous reserves to apply political and economic pressure: By January, 1975, the price of their oil had increased 400 percent in 15 months. An embargo by the Arabs had caused near panic and some hardship in the U. S. A roadside sign reminds motorists of the embargo of 1973-74, when long lines of cars inched toward gas pumps.

LEROY WOODSON, JR.

Campaigning for the Presidency, Ford debates with Democratic nominee Jimmy Carter at Williamsburg, Virginia, on October 22, 1976. Two other televised debates preceded this; in the first, an audio failure vexed both candidates.

Bicentennial guest, Queen Elizabeth II waltzes with President Ford at the White House on the evening of July 7; Prince Philip and Mrs. Ford dance at right; in the background are the Vice President and Mrs. Rockefeller.

new limits on nuclear weapons; and Ford announced, "We have averted an arms race of unbelievable cost."

In diplomacy, Kissinger characterized the President as "tough, steady, and totally unflappable."

When Ford signed an agreement at the Helsinki summit of 1975, some critics charged that this gave the Soviet Union its long-sought recognition of Eastern European boundaries. The administration answered that although the Helsinki accords are not legally binding, any signatory nation has made a moral commitment to human rights. At the conference, Ford had told the leaders from Eastern Europe: "We will spare no effort to ease tensions . . . between us, but it is important that you recognize the deep devotion of the American people and their government to human rights and fundamental freedoms."

In the spring of 1975 Ford proved himself a President acting within constitutional bounds even when he disagreed sharply with Congress on foreign policy. He requested funds for military aid to Cambodia and South Viet Nam, tottering under Communist assaults. Congress refused; and while the two countries were collapsing, Ford abided by the 1973 law that banned military or paramilitary intervention there.

Similarly, in 1976, he abided by the Congressional decision to refuse further aid to warring factions in Angola.

In many primaries and at the Republican convention in 1976, Ford defeated a formidable conservative opponent, former Governor Ronald Reagan of California. The President chose as his running mate Senator Robert Dole of Kansas.

According to public opinion polls, Ford began his campaign as an underdog nominee; his Democratic opponent, former Governor Jimmy Carter of Georgia, enjoyed a margin as wide as 33 percent. The candidates campaigned energetically, and Ford closed much of the gap. He lost in the popular vote by only 2.1 percent.

After the election Ford cooperated with his successor in almost unprecedented fashion, assuring a smooth transition. For his part, President Carter on Inauguration Day made these his first words after taking the oath of office: "For myself and for our Nation, I want to thank my predecessor for all he has done to heal our land." A grateful people concurred, and the Fords left Washington with the best wishes of their fellow citizens.

DAVID HUME KENNERLY/CPS (ABOVE AND BELOW)

Term of office ended, Mr. and Mrs. Ford smile and wave as they board a Marine Corps helicopter on the snowy grounds of the Capitol immediately after the new President's inauguration on January 20, 1977. Mrs. Rockefeller (at right) and her husband rode with the Fords to nearby Andrews Air Force Base. From there, a Presidential jet took the Fords to California; they have chosen Palm Springs for a home in retirement.

A last nostalgic look: From the helicopter, Ford gazes at the Capitol, where he served for a quarter of a century. At his request, the pilot circled the Capitol and then flew over the heart of the city for a farewell view of the White House. After two and a half years as President, Ford left Washington with the esteem of a grateful Nation.

JIMMY CARTER aspired to make government "competent and compassionate," responsive to the American people and their aspirations. Assuming an office that had recently been criticized as "imperial," he undertook to restore simplicity.

Carter hailed the traditional American credo as he took office on January 20, 1977, the first new President in the third century of independence. Then, in his Inaugural Address, he declared:

"We have learned that 'more' is not necessarily 'better,' that even our great Nation has its recognized limits, and that we can neither answer all questions nor solve all problems. . . . So together, in a spirit of individual sacrifice for the common good, we must simply do our best."

His own career, from his boyhood on a Georgia farm through the governorship of his state, had been marked by determination to excel. Writing his autobiography at the outset of his campaign for the Presidency, he entitled it *Why Not The Best?* In the White House he continued to insist upon high standards, for himself and the Nation.

Jimmy Carter—who has rarely used his full name, James Earl Carter, Jr.—was born in 1924 near Plains, a small Georgia town. His was the seventh generation of Carters to grow up tilling the soil. The first of his American ancestors, Thomas Carter, had come to Virginia as an indentured servant in 1637. His mother, Lillian Gordy Carter, was the daughter of a postmaster who was a friend of the southern populist leader Tom Watson.

Peanut farming, talk of politics, and devotion to the Baptist faith were significant in Carter's upbringing. "In general, the early years of my life on the farm were full and enjoyable, isolated but not lonely," he has written. "We always had enough to eat, no economic hardship, but no money to waste. We felt close to nature, close to the members of our family, and close to God."

As a small boy, he learned to work hard, doing chores in the fields and farmyard. When he was five, he began selling boiled peanuts on the streets of Plains. Still, he had time to enjoy a Tom Sawyer type of existence with boys from neighboring farms, who with few exceptions were black:

"We hunted, fished, explored, worked, and slept together. We ground sugar cane, plowed mules, pruned watermelons, dug and bedded sweet potatoes, mopped cotton, stacked peanuts, cut stovewood, pumped water . . . and hauled cotton to the gin together. . . .

COLUMBUS LEDGER-ENQUIRER

Jimmy Carter assumed office on a wave of goodwill. The smiling man from Georgia would need solid popular support to deal with the problems that confronted him: worldwide inflation, unemployment and an energy crisis at home. Carter promised an administration that would govern with competence and compassion.

Honeymoon-bound, Jimmy and Rosalynn Carter drive off from Plains, Georgia, on their wedding day, July 7, 1946. Carter wears his newly earned U. S. Navy ensign's stripes. The Carters had four children, John William, James Earl III, Donnel Jeffrey, and Amy Lynn.

Painting by Herbert E. Abrams, White House Collection

"We ran, swam, rode horses, drove wagons and floated on rafts together. We misbehaved together and shared the same punishments. We built and lived in the same tree houses and played cards and ate at the same table.

"But we never went to the same church or school. Our social life and our church life were strictly separate. . . . There was a scrupulous compliance with these unwritten and unspoken rules. I never heard them questioned. *Not then*."

Even before the first grade, Jimmy Carter wanted to go to the U. S. Naval Academy at Annapolis. After high school he attended a junior college for a year, Georgia Tech for a year, then entered the Academy as a sophomore. He was graduated in 1946, fifty-ninth in a class of 820.

That July, Carter married Rosalynn Smith, who also had grown up in Plains. They have three sons, John William (Jack), James Earl III (Chip), Donnel Jeffrey (Jeff), and a daughter, Amy Lynn.

For seven years, Carter served in the Navy. Capt. Hyman Rickover accepted him in the nuclear submarine program, and he became expert in reactor technology. Rickover, with his phenomenal industry and exacting

demands on subordinates, made a profound impression on Carter. Nevertheless, Carter decided after his father died in 1953 to resign his commission and return to Plains.

"I had only one life to live," he has explained, "and I wanted to live it as a civilian, with a potentially fuller opportunity for varied public service."

Gradually, with the aid of Rosalynn, he built and expanded a thriving family business, raising seed peanuts, wholesaling peanuts, and selling fertilizer.

Soon he was a leader in civic and church enterprises, and was using his influence against segregation. In the Navy, he had gained a new perspective on racial matters, and in Plains he stood out against the community. Alone among local businessmen he refused to join the White Citizens' Council. When his church's congregation voted to keep blacks out of worship services, six voted to admit them: Jimmy, Rosalynn, Jack, Chip, "Miss Lillian," and one neighbor.

"It is disconcerting," Carter reflected years later, "to remember with what mistaken notions many of us clung for a long time to the rigid structure of segregation without realizing for a while what a blessing it

Three-year-old Amy gets a lift from her father and press secretary Jody Powell as the Carters move into the Governor's Mansion in Atlanta early in January, 1971.

Whistlestop tour traced part of Truman's 1948 campaign route, from New York City to Pittsburgh. Carter salutes enthusiastic followers at Overbrook, Pennsylvania. Candidates for state office joined him here; Governor Milton J. Shapp—not running for re-election in 1976—wears a railroad engineer's cap.

Poster displayed in Plains urges black voter registration. A drive for registration in 13 key states gave Carter the margin of victory in a notably close election. On November 2, 1976, some 92 percent of blacks voted for Carter and his running mate, Senator Walter F. Mondale of Minnesota.

DENNIS BRACK, BLACK STAR (ABOVE); JODI COBB (BELOW AND LOWER LEFT)

Hands that pick cotton...
now can pick our public officials

Register And Vote!
Sumter County Improvement Assn.
Phone - 929-3215 or 924-5598

Post-election visitors stand outside Plains Baptist Church, too crowded to seat them. Long opposed to segregation, Carter sought to open the church's services to worshipers regardless of race. The congregation adopted this policy on November 14, 1976.

would be when we passed on to a new and free relationship."

A chance to enter politics came in 1962, when the Georgia Senate was reapportioned. Winning a seat, Carter mastered the key issues within the state and prepared himself for his next step—running for governor.

He demonstrated his tenacity in the two campaigns it took him to win the governorship. When he ran in 1966, so few voters knew him that some newspapers labeled him "Jimmy Who?" By 1970 Carter had developed an effective amateur organization—and he was elected.

Among the new young southern governors, Carter attracted attention by emphasizing efficiency in government, ecology, and the erasing of racial barriers. In his inaugural remarks he declared, "the time for racial discrimination is over," and none of his actions was more symbolic than the hanging of a portrait of Martin Luther King, Jr., in the state capitol. Struggles with the legislature marked an administration that Carter himself has called "highly-controversial, aggressive, and combative." He undertook the overhaul of mental-health and criminal-justice programs, and sought to preserve natural and historical resources. By the end of the single four-year term a Georgia governor could serve then, he had established a record on which to run for the Presidency.

In December, 1974, Carter announced his candidacy and began a two-year campaign. It

Setting the pace for an administration that pledged to stay close to the people, Carter and his family walked down Washington's Pennsylvania Avenue on Inauguration Day.

Camp David Summit: Egyptian President Anwar Sadat and Israeli Prime Minister Menachem Begin meet with Carter in 1978 to seek a settlement of long-standing disputes. The talks produced a framework for peace—and a triumph for Carter. The breakthrough, attributed to his leadership, raised his sagging popularity in the polls. The pact that was later signed raised hopes for a lasting Middle East settlement.

seemed futile at the start—there were so many other candidates much better known. He prepared himself systematically: reading widely, traveling abroad, and serving on the Trilateral Commission, a study group with 200 members from the U. S., Canada, Western Europe, and Japan.

At first he attracted relatively little public attention. Sometimes he felt lonely as he traveled, endlessly shaking hands, smiling, introducing himself: "Hi, I'm Jimmy Carter and I'm running for President." He promised repeatedly that he would never lie or misrepresent a matter—"I'll try not to disappoint you." Gradually he won support, beginning in the Iowa caucuses and the New Hampshire primary. At the Democratic Convention he was nominated on the first ballot, and chose Senator Walter F. Mondale of Minnesota as his running mate.

Carter campaigned hard, debating with President Ford three times on television. He won a close election with 50.1 percent of the popular vote, by 297 electoral votes to 241 for Ford. As a candidate the South could call its own, he carried all the states of the former Confederacy except Virginia—and his decisive margin came from black voters.

At his Inauguration, President Carter declared that the ceremony marked "a new dedication within our Government, and a new spirit among us all." He promptly demonstrated his determination to keep in touch with the people. Breaking precedent, he and his wife walked down Pennsylvania Avenue in the Inaugural Parade. Many times during his term he visited different towns, staying in the homes of local citizens and appearing before local audiences to answer questions.

Carter's popularity grew as for several

Runaway property taxes in California spark a "taxpayer's revolt" in 1978. Voters passed Proposition 13, an initiative that rolled back property taxes in the state by 57 percent. Midway through Carter's term, inflation became the most urgent domestic issue.

months he built his administration and planned his programs. The Cabinet he announced was well received. It included experts from earlier administrations, business and legal figures, and two women, one of them black. Many of the White House staff and personal advisers were Georgians who had served him in the past. Near the end of his administration he spoke with pride of the fact that he had made judicial appointments of "more blacks, more women, more Hispanics in three and a half years than all of the other previous Presidents in 200 years."

Mrs. Carter continued to be one of the most influential of her husband's advisers. She acted as his personal representative on a trip to Latin America, and unlike any of her predecessors as First Lady, she attended Cabinet meetings. So far as they could, the Carters brought their Georgia life-style unembellished to the Capital. They attended a Baptist church in Washington, and the President taught a men's Bible class. They enrolled their daughter, Amy, in an integrated public school. They both marshaled their energies to put in long, often grueling, days at work.

Yet admiration for Carter's personal style and way of life did not kindle widespread support for his programs. With less controversy than had been expected, he immediately pardoned more than 10,000 Viet Nam War draft evaders. But when he halted construction on major water projects, pending an evaluation of their ecological and economic soundness, Congressmen and citizens in the areas affected protested vigorously. Carter proposed numerous measures to Congress—to stimulate the economy and yet combat inflation, to revise the tax system, and especially to conserve energy resources. Although many of his bills were passed into law, they often met opposition and little quick action.

Early in the administration, Carter's Budget Director, Bert Lance, came under fire for matters in his banking career in Georgia. Carter defended him for weeks but ultimately accepted his resignation. (Lance was later exonerated in court.) "We knew Washington would be a tough town," lamented Hamilton Jordan, one of Carter's assistants, "but it is tougher than we expected."

Capitol Hill proved especially tough. In the

aftermath of the Viet Nam War, legislators were less susceptible to party discipline and White House pressure, more responsive to local and particular interests.

The comprehensive energy program that the President proposed soon after taking office illustrated his legislative difficulties. Although Carter asserted that the country's energy independence required his program's success, Congress acted slowly. It did authorize a Department of Energy, but only in 1978 did it act on deregulation to encourage conservation and exploration for new oil and gas supplies. An accompanying tax to recover "windfall profits" from the oil industry was not passed until 1980. Both were short of what Carter had wanted.

The President had even greater difficulties with the problem of inflation. He set voluntary ceilings (with some government force behind them) on increases in prices, wages, and salaries. The Federal Reserve Board cooperated by setting high interest rates and tightening the money supply, despite the danger of recession and rising unemployment. In addition, Carter put more and more emphasis on a lean Federal budget. Nevertheless, in the last two years of his administration double-digit inflation persisted, fueled in part by sharp increases in world oil prices.

In foreign policy, Carter gained some long-sought objectives. Like Presidents Johnson, Nixon, and Ford, he hoped to defuse resentment of the U. S. in Panama by negotiating treaties relinquishing control of the Panama Canal by the year 2000 and guaranteeing the canal's permanent neutrality. After much lobbying, in 1978 he persuaded the Senate to ratify the treaties—by a narrow margin.

Carter's greatest personal achievement came in September, 1978, when he undertook the apparently impossible task of negotiating at Camp David with Prime Minister Menachem Begin of Israel and President Anwar Sadat of Egypt, working toward a treaty of peace between the two countries. Time after time his firm, knowledgeable, and resourceful efforts kept the discussions from breaking down. Finally Begin and Sadat professed agreement, and the peace treaty was signed. This cheered the Nation, and sent Carter's popularity and prestige soaring.

In a dramatic speech on December 15, 1978, Carter announced the U. S. would establish full diplomatic relations with the People's Republic of China on January 1, 1979, as a measure to contribute to world peace.

By the end of his term, Carter could point

JAMES ANDANSON, SYGMA

In 1978 the dollar slipped to its lowest exchange rate against foreign currencies (above) within the decade. The President ordered varied countermeasures, but complex factors fostered a continuing decline, intensifying the problems Carter would have to confront before the 1980 election.

Panama Canal shipping moves as before—but the U. S. relinquishes control: a major foreign-policy achievement for Carter. After a tough fight in the Senate, he won ratification of two treaties with Panama. One gave that country complete jurisdiction over the waterway by the year 2000; the other guaranteed the canal's permanent neutrality.

JOHN LOPINOT, BLACK STAR

to several achievements in domestic affairs. He had established a national energy policy and stimulated domestic oil production. He had sought to improve and protect the environment: With the signing of the landmark Alaskan Lands Bill, he expanded the national park system by 43.5 million acres and extended Federal protection to an additional 60.5 million acres. He has pointed out, "This involves more public land than any single action that the Government has ever taken."

Carter promoted government efficiency through Civil Service reform. He proceeded with deregulation of the airline, railroad,

Anti-U. S. demonstrators in Iran carry an effigy of President Carter in June, 1979, five months after the fall of the shah. Five months later, some 500 militants seized the U. S. Embassy in Tehran and held 52 Americans captive for more than a year.

trucking, communications, and banking industries to increase competition and lower rates. He vetoed several projects that he considered wasteful and inflationary. To increase educational and social services, he created the Department of Education and bolstered the Social Security system.

In foreign affairs, the President encountered increasing difficulties. Détente with the Soviet Union became seriously strained. Carter championed the human rights of dissidents throughout the world. Some nations took offense. There were vehement Soviet protests, and warnings that arms-limitation talks might be affected. Carter calmly held that the Soviet Union would accept arms arrangements it considered to its advantage, and negotiators did agree upon a new Strategic Arms Limitation Treaty (SALT II). Shortly thereafter Soviet troops invaded Afghanistan. Carter expressed the Nation's outrage by asking the Senate to defer further consideration of the treaty. He also stopped new grain

sales to the Soviet Union and persuaded the United States Olympic Committee not to send a team to the 1980 games in Moscow.

Even more acute problems with Iran upset the American public and contributed to a sharp decline in Carter's popularity. Unrest in Iran led to the overthrow of the government of Shah Mohammad Reza Pahlavi and shut off the production of oil for export. After Carter permitted the gravely ill shah to enter the United States for medical treatment, Iranian students, with the encouragement of their national leaders, seized the U. S. embassy staff in Tehran as hostages.

The hostage crisis dominated the news during the last 14 months of Carter's administration. The consequences of Iran's holding Americans captive, together with continuing inflation at home, contributed to Carter's defeat in 1980. Even then, he continued the difficult negotiations over the hostages. Iran finally released the 52 Americans the same day Carter left office.

FROM "HERBLOCK ON ALL FRONTS" (NEW AMERICAN LIBRARY, 1980)

MICHEL PHILIPPOT, SYGMA

RICK SMOLAN, CONTACT PRESS IMAGES

Soviet troops move into Kabul, Afghanistan (left), following an invasion begun in 1979 to put down Muslim revolutionaries. In response to the Soviet action, the U. S. led several nations in boycotting the 1980 Moscow Olympics. Cartoonists ridiculed the Soviet attitude that the Olympics should proceed despite the invasion (top). Above, anti-draft demonstrators protest President Carter's plan to reinstate draft registration, a move intended to demonstrate determination "to deter further aggression beyond Afghanistan."

273

Ronald Reagan

FORTIETH PRESIDENT 1981-

THROUGH AN INNOVATIVE conservative program, Ronald Reagan sought to restore "the great confident roar of American progress and growth and optimism." Taking office at a time when the Nation was beset by persistent internal and external problems, he undertook to renew the country's economic well-being, strengthen its security, and move it toward a larger vision of the future. "We are too great a nation to limit ourselves to small dreams," he said as he took office on January 20, 1981. "We are not, as some would have us believe, doomed to an inevitable decline."

Upon assuming office, Reagan undertook to reverse the grim national mood that had prevailed during previous months, the feeling that the living standard at home and the prestige of the United States abroad were declining. In accepting the Republican nomination for President, Reagan had emphasized the causes of that mood. "Never before in our history have Americans been called upon to face three grave threats to our very existence, any one of which could destroy us," he asserted. "We face a disintegrating economy, a weakened defense, and an energy policy based on the sharing of scarcity."

Throughout his campaign, Reagan stressed the program that he planned to implement immediately as President. He was determined to reverse trends of the previous half-century by reducing the role of the Federal Government in the economy. He meant to achieve this through the lowering of taxes and the reduction of spending and regulation. These changes, he believed, would curb inflation, stimulate economic growth, and increase employment. Speaking about foreign policy and national security, he pledged to keep the Nation from war by improving the quality of the armed forces. His credo was, "Peace is *made* by the fact of strength—economic, military, and strategic."

From his upbringing, Ronald Wilson Reagan acquired many of the qualities and beliefs that distinguish him as a public leader. He was born in Tampico, Illinois, on February 6,

THE WHITE HOUSE, COURTESY OF THE REAGAN FAMILY

Promise of change swept Ronald Reagan into office. Capitalizing on Americans' dissatisfaction with continuing inflation and on the widespread perception of diminished national prestige, Reagan used his political skills, his calm, assured manner, and his devotion to old-fashioned virtues to win voter support. During the campaign, Reagan proposed to reduce taxes, to limit Government involvement in the business of its citizens, and to strengthen the armed forces. His lopsided election victory helped him gain enough Congressional support to enact tax-trimming and budget-cutting measures. These legislative successes came within his first seven months in office, shortly after he had recovered from a bullet wound suffered during an attempted assassination in March, 1981.

Family portrait: John Edward and Nelle Wilson Reagan stand with their younger son, Ronald Wilson (nicknamed "Dutch"), and his older brother, John Neil, in a photograph taken about 1913 in Illinois. Reagan said of his childhood days that "Ours was a family that loved each other up to the point where the independence of each member began."

THE WHITE HOUSE, MICHAEL EVANS

"Where's the rest of me?" asks Reagan in the film *King's Row* (above), in which he portrayed a man who had lost his legs. The line became the title of Reagan's autobiography and a symbol of his expanding interests: as a sportsman—he worked as a lifeguard in his hometown of Dixon, Illinois (top), and competed on the swimming and football teams at Eureka College—as a radio announcer, as an actor, as a union leader, and finally as a politician.

1911, to Nelle Wilson and John Edward Reagan. Reagan learned tolerance from his Irish Catholic father, a first-generation American. His father, Reagan has recounted with pride, vigorously opposed discrimination against blacks and Jews. His mother was of Scots-English descent, and a Protestant. Known for her charitable works and dramatic readings, she instilled in her son an impetus toward leadership in public causes. She also gave him his first acquaintance with acting.

Reagan went to high school in Dixon, Illinois, and later worked his way through nearby Eureka College. For seven summers during high school and college he was a lifeguard at Dixon's Rock River swimming beach. At Eureka he played guard on the football team and was on the swimming team. Once, when the football squad worked out in his hometown, no hotel would take in the team's two black players, so Reagan brought them home to stay with his family.

Throughout college, Reagan was one of the leading players in dramatic productions. Looking back on those years, Reagan has commented, "I loved three things: drama, politics, and sports, and I'm not sure they always come in that order." Each in time was to become his career.

Sports broadcasting, combining as it did Reagan's interest in athletics and show business, became his first vocation after completing college in 1932. Reagan soon became the sports announcer of a Des Moines radio station, where one of his tasks was to transform brief telegraph bulletins about sports events into vivid play-by-play descriptions. He presented these descriptions on the air as if he were actually watching the events.

Describing football this way was easy, for Reagan had played the game for eight years. But he had to learn to do the same for baseball, since the mainstay of the sports broadcasts was the home games of the Chicago Cubs and Chicago White Sox. "Before too long," Reagan has said, "I was spinning out games for all the world as if I were not four hundred miles from the ball park." Once, when the telegraph connection was broken for six minutes, Reagan calmly filled in by describing the hitting of one imaginary foul ball after another. The quick wit before a microphone and relaxed skill under pressure he displayed were to serve him well in the future.

In the spring of 1937 Reagan began a career in motion pictures. While reporting on the Chicago Cubs' spring training at Catalina Island, he took a screen test in Hollywood and won a contract with Warner Brothers. At once he became a leading man, making eight pictures during his first year and becoming a polished actor. Film star Pat O'Brien was particularly helpful to Reagan in his efforts to learn acting. Reagan later played one of his most famous roles, Notre Dame football player George Gipp, in a film which starred O'Brien as coach Knute Rockne. After Reagan became President, he received an honorary degree from Notre Dame and publicly paid tribute to O'Brien, who also received a degree at the ceremony. In a span of twenty years, Reagan appeared in some fifty movies.

While in Hollywood, Reagan married and began rearing a family. He has two children, Maureen and Michael, from his first marriage, to actress Jane Wyman. In 1952 he married actress Nancy Davis; their children are Patricia Ann and Ronald Prescott.

Early in his film career, Reagan rose to leadership in the Screen Actors Guild. As a novice contract player in 1938, he was appointed to the guild's board and began seeking better working conditions and pay for actors. After the war Reagan was elected

"There is nothing more beautiful than California in the spring," wrote Reagan in his autobiography. Here as governor of California he indulges in one of his favorite pastimes. During two terms as governor, Reagan pushed through reforms on taxes, welfare, and aid to education, turning the state's budget deficit into a 550-million-dollar surplus.

MICHAEL EVANS, SYGMA

president of the guild and served six terms. Through his many years of service, Reagan became skilled in the give and take of contract negotiations. He is proud that he is the only President of the United States who has also been the head of a union.

During World War II, Reagan served in the Army, both with the cavalry and the air forces. In the 1930's he had become a reserve officer in the cavalry. Shortly after the war began he was called to active duty. Within a year, he was serving with an Army Air Forces motion picture unit in Hollywood, where he helped train combat camera crews and produce training films.

Following the war, Reagan came to question his earlier advocacy of liberal causes. He had become a leader of the American Veterans Committee, one of several veterans' organizations that sprang up after the war. His talent as a public speaker soon made him "an easy mark for speechmaking on the rubber-chicken and glass-tinkling circuits."

But at one of the organization's meetings,

On the stump in Houston, Texas, Presidential candidate Reagan campaigns with his wife, the former Nancy Davis. Earlier, at the Republican Convention, he had selected a Texan, George Bush, as his running mate. Opposite: Departing from tradition, Reagan took the Presidential oath of office on the West Front of the U. S. Capitol, overlooking the Washington Monument. He and Mrs. Reagan wave moments after the ceremony.

THE WHITE HOUSE, BILL FITZ-PATRICK

After the inauguration, the Reagan family gathers in the Red Room of the White House. Flanking the President and Mrs. Reagan, from left to right: Geoffrey and Anne Davis, Mrs. Reagan's nephew and niece; Dennis Revell and his then fiancée, Maureen Reagan, now Mrs. Revell; the President's son Michael and his wife, Colleen, with their son, Cameron; Neil Reagan, the President's brother, and his wife, Bess; Richard Davis, Mrs. Reagan's brother, and his wife, Patricia; Patti Davis, the Reagans' daughter; and the Reagans' son, Ronald P. Reagan, with his wife, Doria.

GIANFRANCO GORGONI, CONTACT PRESS IMAGES (OPPOSITE)

Reagan added to his stock denunciation of Fascism an attack upon Communism, and he was startled by the silence of the audience. Reagan concluded that the members of the group had Communist sympathies, and as a result he gradually began to change his "whole view on the American dangers." He energetically resisted Communist influence in the film industry and in the American Veterans Committee, from which he later resigned.

During this period, Reagan also became concerned with the excesses of governmental bureaucracy. He remembered the frustrations of his father as a Works Progress Administration official in the 1930's, and he recalled his own troubles trying to get rid of an inefficient secretary while in the Army.

By the 1950's Reagan was articulating a full conservative ideology, warning against

Canadian Prime Minister Pierre Elliott Trudeau and President Reagan listen to the U. S. national anthem during Reagan's first foreign visit as President. Through the trip to Ottawa in March, 1981, Reagan hoped to forge closer ties with our North American neighbor.

both "the swiftly rising tide of collectivism that threatens to inundate what remains of our free economy," and "the problems of centralizing power in Washington, with subsequent loss of freedom at the local level."

During the eight years that he worked as the host of a television show, he toured the Nation for his sponsor and became an acclaimed spokesman for conservatism. In thousands of appearances he set forth his views in a nonpartisan way. These matters, he felt, were vital to both parties.

In 1964 Reagan finally plunged into Republican politics. He became involved with California Citizens for Goldwater. Late in the Presidential campaign he gave a rousing speech on national television that brought in millions of dollars in contributions. This was a turning point in Reagan's career. The speech was so effective that it led a group of California Republican leaders to persuade Reagan to run for governor in 1966.

Styling himself a "citizen politician," Reagan campaigned on the issues he had dramatized in a homey way on the banquet circuit. His stand for fewer taxes, reduced spending,

and less government regulation impressed California voters. They elected him by nearly a million votes and re-elected him in 1970.

During his two terms as governor of California, Reagan took pride in the efficiency and fiscal prudence of his administration. In six of his eight years as governor he had to make concessions during hard bargaining with Democratic majorities in the legislature, and although he did not obtain as much positive legislation to reduce government controls as he would have liked, he did veto a number of bills that would have increased social programs and expenditures. He pared the higher-education budget by 27 percent, and saved, he estimated, two billion dollars by tightening the state welfare program.

Although California's budget doubled during his administration, Reagan kept the number of state employees from growing. And the tax measures he sponsored produced a surplus in the state treasury. When he came into office the state had a deficit of nearly 200 million dollars and was spending a million dollars a day more than it received in taxes; by the time that he left office, Reagan had built a surplus of about 550 million dollars.

Throughout his years as governor, Reagan continued to take the view that he was "just a citizen temporarily in public service." Early in his administration he remarked: "For a lot of years I was going around the country talking about Government usurpation of our lives, and now I've got the opportunity to put into practice the things I've been talking about. That's what I like about this job."

Reagan was elected to the Presidency in 1980, on his second try. After completing his second term as governor of California, he had embarked upon a heavy schedule as a national speaker and radio commentator. He campaigned energetically for the 1976 Republican nomination for President, losing narrowly to Gerald Ford. Four years later he overwhelmed his Republican opponents in the primaries and won the nomination. His closest challenger, former Texas congressman and ambassador to the United Nations George H. Bush, became Reagan's running mate. A Nation pinched by inflation and

MARK POKEMPNER, BLACK STAR

Increased defense spending, called for during Reagan's campaign, aimed at expanding the Nation's arsenal, including more of the F-16 fighters under construction at left. However, controversy over defense issues such as the neutron bomb and the MX missile deployment system vexed the administration. Reagan's defense budget also spawned protests from citizens who felt the Federal Government should spend less on defense, more on social programs. The rally above took place in May, 1981, on the campus of the University of Notre Dame.

HERMAN KOKOJAN, BLACK STAR

troubled by the Soviet invasion of Afghanistan and the year-long imprisonment of Americans in Iran swept the Republican ticket into office. Reagan won 489 electoral votes to 49 for Jimmy Carter. It was the first time in 48 years that an elected incumbent President had failed to win re-election.

In the weeks after the election, Reagan planned his administration with unprecedented care, organizing a transition team that numbered about a thousand members. The cabinet he chose represented a wide range of viewpoints within the Republican Party and among those who had supported him in the campaign. His cabinet contained both a woman and a black. Overall, Reagan's appointees represented his own firm conservative views. Their concept of the role of Government was in decided contrast to that of those they succeeded.

Breaking tradition with previous inaugural ceremonies, Reagan took the oath of office on the west rather than the east side of the Capitol, looking down at an expanse of faces stretching toward the Washington Monument. Reagan came into office at age 69, the oldest man ever elected President, but the energy and firmness with which he undertook his duties belied his age. He at once set about putting into action what he had promised in his acceptance address: "The time is *now,* my fellow Americans, to recapture our destiny, to take it into our own hands."

In a history-making move, Reagan named Sandra Day O'Connor, a distinguished Arizona state appeals court judge, to the U. S. Supreme Court early in his administration. The widely acclaimed nomination of the first woman ever chosen for the high court won Senate approval by a 99 to 0 vote.

Within a few days he sent to Congress recommendations for extensive budget cuts trimming almost every domestic program, but maintaining "our responsibility to all who need our benevolence." The cuts would sharply shift the course of Government since the years of the New Deal and of the Great Society. The one major area exempted from these cuts was defense. Reagan proposed a large increase in military appropriations.

Accompanying Reagan's proposed reductions in expenditures were to be substantial reductions in taxes, both for individuals and for businesses. "The taxing power of Government must be used to provide revenues for legitimate Government purposes," Reagan asserted. "It must not be used to regulate the economy or bring about social change. We've tried that and surely must be able to see it doesn't work."

Reagan noted that despite the extent of his proposed reductions, the cuts would do no more than reduce the rate of increase in Government spending and taxation. To further reduce the impact of Government upon free enterprise, Reagan's administrators issued

Marchers temper the administration's euphoria over early legislative successes. On Solidarity Day, September 19, 1981, some 240,000 Americans gathered to voice concern about the President's sweeping cuts in New Deal and Great Society programs.

executive orders lessening Federal regulation.

The President hailed his economic plan as a "new beginning"—a plan "for economic recovery, a program that will balance the budget, put us well on the road to our ultimate objective of eliminating inflation entirely, increasing productivity and creating millions of new jobs." To Congress he laid down a challenge: "The people are watching and waiting. They don't demand miracles, but they do expect us to act. Let us act together."

While Congress was considering his measures, Reagan was struck in the chest by a bullet during an assassination attempt on his 70th day in office. The President's cheerful courage—he joked as he walked into the hospital although he was in acute pain—and the resilience he demonstrated in his rapid recovery added to his stature and popularity.

Not long after returning to his White House duties, Reagan was cheered by Congressional approval of his proposed budget cuts. Shortly thereafter, with the President lobbying effec-

tively on behalf of of his program, both houses of Congress approved the administration's proposed tax cuts as well. Reagan's early months in office were further highlighted by his announcement of the historic appointment of a woman to the Supreme Court.

After setting forth his domestic program, Reagan addressed himself to foreign policy and defense questions. The Government, he said, had neglected defense while it had engaged in social experimentation. "Our margin of safety in an increasingly hostile world was allowed to diminish," he told the cadets at the West Point commencement in 1981.

The President then hailed the new mood of confidence he perceived in the Nation. "The era of self-doubt is over. We've stopped looking at our warts and rediscovered how much there is to love in this blessed land. . . . Let friend and foe alike be made aware of the spirit that is sweeping across our land, because it means we will meet our responsibilities to the free world."

INDEX

Composition for *Our Country's Presidents* by National Geographic's Photographic Services, Carl M. Shrader, Director, Lawrence F. Ludwig, Assistant Director. Printed and bound by Holladay-Tyler Printing Corp., Rockville, Md. Color separations by Lanman Progressive Co., Washington, D. C., and Sterling Regal, Inc., Carlstadt, N.J.